PUBLIC ENTREPRENEURS

PUBLIC ENTREPRENEURS

AGENTS FOR CHANGE
IN AMERICAN GOVERNMENT

Mark Schneider
and Paul Teske
with Michael Mintrom

PRINCETON UNIVERSITY PRESS   PRINCETON, NEW JERSEY

Library of Congress Cataloging-in-Publication Data
Schneider, Mark, 1946–
Public entrepreneurs : agents for change in American
government / Mark Schneider and Paul Teske with Michael Mintrom.
p. cm.
Includes bibliographical references and index.
ISBN 0-691-03725-6
1. Entrepreneurship—United States.
2. Government business enterprises—United States.
3. Local government—United States.
I. Teske, Paul Eric. II. Mintrom, Michael, 1963–. III. Title.
HB615.S353 1995
306.2—dc20 94-21311 CIP

This book has been composed in Baskerville

Contents

List of Figures

List of Tables

Acknowledgments

WE RECOGNIZE many intellectual debts we incurred in the writing of this book. First, Bryan Jones, Clarence Stone, and Gary Miller all read earlier versions of this manuscript and provided helpful comments. Elinor Ostrom, as always, was an intellectual catalyst to many of the arguments presented here. Bob Stein provided many valuable insights, especially in the analysis of city managers, and he strongly urged us to be bolder in the development of our theory. Vincent Ostrom, Gerry Wright, and Roger Parks also provided valuable comments in the early stages of the development of many of the arguments in the book. The research upon which this book is based was supported by a grant from the National Science Foundation (grant numbers: SES8508473 and SES9024116).

Part One

A THEORY OF THE
PUBLIC ENTREPRENEUR

IN THIS PART, we argue that change occurs in all political and economic systems and we develop components of our theory of entrepreneurs as agents of change in the public sector. While most social scientific theories focus on change as occurring in incremental fashion, change can be sudden, producing radical shifts in the status quo. In complex human social systems, radical changes can be produced by actors within the system. That is, actors can perceive opportunities for major change and create the incentives and forces to affect such change. In political systems, radical change is often associated with the emergence of new leaders, the development of new political movements, and the introduction of new policies. Old ideas and established coalitions that appeared entrenched are washed away more quickly than seemed possible.

We view leaders associated with radical change as the public sector equivalent of private sector entrepreneurs—individuals who create dynamic change in markets. In this book, we specifically focus on identifying entrepreneurs as agents of change in what we call the local market for public goods. Entrepreneurs propel change by being alert to opportunities for "profits" (broadly defined) that emerge in the institutionally defined environment of local government in the United States.

While many social science disciplines have analyzed entrepreneurial behavior, entrepreneurs have been considered most important in economic markets. Yet economics as a discipline has not focused much energy on developing theories or empirical data about entrepreneurs. In chapter 1, we introduce our argument. In chapter 2 we illustrate how neoclassical economics, especially the model of perfect competition, limits the role of entrepreneurship in the theory of the market. We relax the strict assumptions of the neoclassical model and show how the range of strategic options available to actors in real economic situations increases, producing opportunities for alert entrepreneurs.

In chapter 3, we develop our definition of the entrepreneur. We begin by comparing the tasks facing public and private sector entrepreneurs and try to develop a definition that identifies the function of the entrepreneur regardless of the arena in which he or she is operating. We argue that despite obvious differences in the locus of their activities and the nature of their goals, to a considerable degree all entrepreneurs must perform particular functions and, in order to do this, they share certain characteristics.

We begin by arguing that *all* entrepreneurs must perform three functions. First and foremost, entrepreneurs discover unfulfilled needs and select appropriate prescriptions for how those needs may be met—that is, they must be alert to opportunities. Second, as they seize these opportunities, entrepreneurs bear the reputational, emotional, and, frequently, the financial risk involved in pursuing a course of action with uncertain consequences. Finally, entrepreneurs must assemble and coordinate teams or networks of individuals and organizations that have the talents and/or resources necessary to undertake change.

CHAPTER 1.

Public Entrepreneurs as Agents of Change

POLITICAL and economic systems are continually changing. Most social science theories view change as occurring in incremental or evolutionary fashion, and these theories usually model adaptations as responses to environmental forces. But change can be sudden, producing radical shifts in the status quo. In many natural systems, radical change is often the result of exogenous events—a volcano erupts, a large meteor hits the earth, or a virus mutates and hitches a ride into a new population. Exogenous events can also create radical changes in social and political systems. But of even greater interest to us is a basic fact evident in many complex social systems: radical change is often produced by actors within these systems and strong forces for change are released as these actors perceive opportunities and create the incentives and forces to challenge existing political, social, and economic conditions.

In political systems, radical change is often associated with the emergence of new leaders, the development of new political movements, and the introduction of new policies. Ideas and coalitions that appeared firmly entrenched and impervious to change are washed away more quickly than seemed possible. New issues emerge and come to dominate political discourse. Policy innovations sweep through capitals and communities across the country, transforming established practices and procedures.

We argue that leaders who advocate political innovations can play the public sector equivalent of private sector entrepreneurs—they perceive opportunities for political and policy change, they advocate innovative ideas, and they transform political arenas (or "markets"). In this book, we study public entrepreneurs as agents of change in what we call the "local market for public goods."

We recognize that there are many forces besides the actions of entrepreneurs that propel change in economic and political markets and that there are many different theories of change. But there are two underlying dimensions that cut across these theories. Some theories postulate that change is caused by random forces that are not easily amenable to social scientific study. The "garbage can model" is perhaps the best known statement of the idea of change that is essentially random (Cohen, March, and Olsen 1972). Other social scientists argue that change results from more structured processes. For example, the growing literature on agenda setting seeks to develop a systematic analysis of the forces propelling change (e.g., Cobb and Elder 1983; Milward and Laird 1990; Baumgartner and Jones 1993). Similarly, game theory seeks to identify the underlying structure of interactions between individuals. Game theorists have developed approaches, such as cooperative and noncooperative games, and concepts, such as structure-induced equilibria, to analyze how change comes about in complex systems (Shepsle 1979; Shepsle and Weingast 1981).

The second dimension of theories of change is concerned with whether the forces for change are exogenous or endogenous to the system under study. Economic models often point to technological factors, demographic transitions, and changes in relative prices as critical forces of change—that is, they tend to emphasize exogenous factors. Political models of change tend to mix both endogenous and exogenous factors, merging together the effects of public opinion, interest groups, and actors within policy communities. Our focus on public entrepreneurs takes an endogenous, structured view of change; that is, we argue that entrepreneurs are "embedded" in the system they are trying to change and we strongly believe that entrepreneurial activity can be systematically modeled.

WHO AND WHAT ARE ENTREPRENEURS?

Many academic disciplines are concerned with how entrepreneurs emerge and how they foster change. Economics, business administration, public administration, political science, sociology, and psychology have all contributed to the study of entrepreneurship. As a field of intellectual analysis, however, the study of entrepreneurs is dominated by case studies and biographies. Truly rigorous theories of entrepreneurship are few and the study of entrepreneurship is not cumulative. In our reading of the existing studies of entrepreneurship, we found wide disagreement over the definition of entrepreneurs, the degree of risk absorbed by entrepreneurs, the impact of entrepreneurs, and the appropriate approaches to the study of entrepreneurial activity. Indeed, we even found that many analysts argue that the systematic study of entrepreneurs is impossible—that by their very nature, entrepreneurs are rare and that the emergence of entrepreneurs cannot be subject to rigorous, systematic study. For example, according to James Q. Wilson, studies of innovative leadership show that the personalities and actions of individual executives are critical to explaining innovative bureaucratic change.

Given this, Wilson (1989: 227) argues that: "It is not easy to build a useful social science theory out of 'chance appearances.'" We disagree.

Rather than accepting the notion that entrepreneurship is beyond systematic study, we respond to an intellectual challenge put forward by Israel Kirzner, a leading student of entrepreneurship. Kirzner argued that we need "to know about the institutional settings that are most conducive to opportunity discovery"—such discovery being the defining characteristic of entrepreneurs (1979: 8). It is this task that motivates our work. We demonstrate that there are identifiable conditions that systematically affect the likelihood that public entrepreneurs will emerge and that entrepreneurial policies will be pursued.

In this book, we draw on a wide range of studies of entrepreneurship and we root our work in a broader systematic intellectual framework than is usually found in the study of entrepreneurship. As will become evident in the pages that follow, we draw on a variety of disciplines and approaches in our study. And we empirically test components of our theory using data from a large number of communities.

Our focus is on entrepreneurs in the public sector. While we found concepts from economics to be particularly useful in organizing our thoughts and generating hypotheses about the emergence and the role of entrepreneurs, economics simply does not provide a sufficiently strong theoretical base for our work. In turn, we integrate insights from economic theory with the growing contribution that political scientists have made to the study of entrepreneurship and leadership in politics.

While economists have spent decades studying entrepreneurs, they have not developed an accepted theory of the emergence of entrepreneurs or of their impact on markets. More incomplete still is an understanding of entrepreneurial behavior in politics. Many political scientists have recognized the importance of entrepreneurs in the development of innovative public policies. Recent work on agenda-setting (Kingdon 1984; Riker 1982), on the origin of policies (Milward and Laird 1990), on policy innovation and diffusion (Walker 1969; Gray 1973; Polsby 1984; Berry and Berry 1992), and on the politics of ideas (Wilson 1980; Derthick and Quirk 1985) all provide evidence of opportunities for entrepreneurial actors. But little or no agreement exists on the characteristics of entrepreneurship, except that entrepreneurship is important and that it is often critical.

The importance of political entrepreneurs in organizing efforts to solve collective problems has been recognized for some time (Salisbury 1969; Frohlich, Oppenheimer, and Young 1971; Olson 1965; Moe 1980). Following this tradition, recently developed formal models of political systems confirm an important role for entrepreneurs. Using a radically different style of argument, case studies of individuals or particular policies have presented even more evidence on the emergence and functions of entrepreneurial leadership. While case studies and formal modeling efforts contribute to our understanding of entrepreneurial behavior, they have not constituted a theory of public entrepreneurship.

One reason for the absence of successful theories of entrepreneurship is that many social scientific theories perform best in explaining the status quo in politics and in markets or in illustrating minor perturbations in the status quo. But theories of change are much less successful and the explanation, much less the prediction, of change remains elusive. According to Lavoie (1991: 35), "change usually appears in economist's models only as deterministic tendencies toward a fixed equilibrium, like the movements of a clockwork mechanism, not as a truly creative process." While Lavoie was concerned specifically with the discipline of economics, similar statements can be made about the many models of political change that simply extrapolate the present into the future.

We believe that models of change that focus on nonincremental change must be developed. We further believe that entrepreneurs must be recognized as crucial figures in the process of change in public and private markets and within formal hierarchical organizations. Entrepreneurs see opportunities that others do not and they seek personal gain by taking action to seize the opportunities created in an uncertain environment. In the process of taking such risks, entrepreneurs help radically transform economic and political systems. While North argues that "incremental change comes from the perceptions of the entrepreneurs in political and economic organizations that they could do better by altering the existing institutional framework at some margin" (1990: 7), we believe that entrepreneurs often alter political situations in more than marginal or incremental ways.

Because successful entrepreneurs often achieve dramatic change, many studies portray them as exceptional individuals, somehow operating with a set of decision rules that are different from those held by other participants in political or economic markets. In contrast, we believe that entrepreneurs actually respond to rational benefit/cost calculations in choosing their actions: that is, they are motivated by a desire for "profits" or personal gain. While in economics these expected benefits usually revolve around monetary profits, an expanded notion of benefits that includes psychological and policy rewards is necessary in the study of public sector entrepreneurs.

Entrepreneurship is risky by definition, and not all entrepreneurs profit by their actions. Failed entrepreneurs are common and even successful entrepreneurs face continual challenges to their ideas and to their profits. In the long run, the individual entrepreneur cannot expect to win every time. Successful entrepreneurs may be flattered by the competition offered by newcomers who imitate their successes. However, over time competition erodes the entrepreneur's profits by turning the entrepreneur's unique insights into routine products or commodities: "Competition means that entrepreneurs are unlikely to earn consistently superior returns. Although constantly changing market conditions suggest that there are likely to be profit opportunities, the constant striving for profit greatly reduces the chances of economic successes. Clearly entrepreneurial profit-seeking activity is a game worth winning, although in retrospect it frequently is a game not worth playing" (Pasour 1989: 104).

While entrepreneurial profits may be ephemeral for the individual actor, economic and social systems benefit from entrepreneurial activities. Schumpeter, among others, argued that the "creative destruction" resulting from entrepreneurial activity is a mainspring of capitalism. Thus, despite the success or failure of individual entrepreneurs, their actions generate considerable benefits for society as a whole. Following Schumpeter, a core component of our argument is that the "market" for public entrepreneurship not only produces opportunities and rewards for individual entrepreneurs, this market also produces benefits for society.

DEFINING THE ENTREPRENEUR

We begin here by briefly defining what we mean by the "entrepreneur." We then discuss the specific political arena within which we study public entrepreneurship.

Ultimately, any modern definition of the entrepreneur must trace back to the work of Joseph Schumpeter, who argued that the function of the entrepreneur is innovation—the novel recombination of existing factors of production or the introduction of a new production function (Schumpeter 1939: 102). Going beyond Schumpeter's specific concern for new combinations of the factors of production, scholars have gradually expanded the idea of entrepreneurship to include a concept of the market much broader than the world of production functions, a concept that encompasses innovation in the world of ideas (in political science, see, e.g., Kingdon 1984; Polsby 1984; Walker 1981; or Roberts 1991).

The concept of entrepreneurship has been most actively and consistently pursued in the work of the Austrian School of Economics. We build our definition of the entrepreneur most directly on the work of

Israel Kirzner, an economist of the Austrian School who has actively studied entrepreneurship for the last twenty years. According to Kirzner (1985), the most common focal point in the recent economic literature on entrepreneurship is the emphasis on the "discovery" of market opportunities by "alert" individuals. From this perspective, entrepreneurs engage in the act of "creative discovery"—they try to take advantage of newly *discovered* or newly *created* possibilities in order to earn entrepreneurial profits (Casson 1982; Ricketts 1987). In their drive for profits, private entrepreneurs discover, create, and exploit new opportunities through arbitrage, speculation, or innovation.[1] But while entrepreneurs play an important role in explaining how markets function, traditional economic theory has surprisingly little to say about them. We begin our analysis by addressing this intellectual problem.

In this first part of the book, we show how neoclassical economic theory, especially the model of perfect competition and the resulting emphasis on equilibrium, severely limits the role of entrepreneurs, making them virtually irrelevant to the functioning of competitive markets. Some economists have recognized this, and using exceptionally lyrical language (at least for economists) have bemoaned the fact. For example, Pasour argues that if "markets are in equilibrium, economic activity is perfectly coordinated and there is no scope for profit seeking activity. In this situation, a blindfolded monkey *can* handle the entrepreneurial function, for it has no duties" (1989: 96). Baumol makes the same point using a more literary metaphor: "Look for [the entrepreneur] in the index of some of the most noted of recent writings on value theory, in neoclassical or activity analysis models of the firm. The references are scanty and more often they are totally absent. The theoretical firm is entrepreneurless—the Prince of Denmark has been expunged from the discussion on Hamlet" (1968: 66).

While elegant and rigorous models of markets have been developed in the neoclassical approach, we show that once the stringent assumptions of neoclassical economics are relaxed and their highly abstract model of the market made to more closely resemble the "real world," the range of strategic options available to actors in the market dramatically increases, and the opportunities for entrepreneurs correspondingly increase.

In addition to the central feature of alertness to opportunity, we also define entrepreneurs by two other factors: their willingness to take risky action in the pursuit of the opportunities they see, and their ability to coordinate the actions of other people to fulfill their goals. Later, we discuss the three dimensions of this definition more fully, and we examine in more detail the specific techniques and mechanisms successful entrepreneurs utilize in politics.

ENTREPRENEURS IN LOCAL GOVERNMENT

We believe that there are entrepreneurs in the public sector who actively seek opportunities for dynamic changes in policy or politics. While such entrepreneurs are found at all levels of the relatively open American political system, our research focuses on entrepreneurial behavior at the local level. In particular, we test our theories empirically in the context of American suburban governments—the environment in which most Americans now live. Our data base includes suburbs in major metropolitan areas, ranging from relatively small municipalities of 2,500 people to suburban cities with populations in excess of 200,000 people. We believe that these communities are small enough for entrepreneurial individuals to make an important difference.

While suburbs are still often pictured as devoid of the problems facing large central cities, the reality is that they too face increasingly complex "urban" issues. In the past fifteen years, among other fundamental changes to suburbia, the effects of growth on suburban environments have become evident and politically contentious, migration has changed the racial and demographic composition of suburbs, fiscal challenges have emerged as intergovernmental aid has been cut, property tax revolts have strained the flow of revenues, and crime and drugs have moved into suburban areas. In some communities, entrepreneurs stepped forward as these new kinds of problems transformed the relatively more quiescent suburban politics that existed prior to the late 1970s.

The entrepreneurs we identify are not heroic, larger-than-life figures. Many are ordinary citizens who entered the vortex of local politics because of a single issue about which they cared, often with a passion. We show that such political activity is surprisingly common in American local governments. We also show that sometimes entrepreneurial individuals find that their skills allow them to move beyond a single issue and they can become an important political force for change in the very structure of local politics.

We argue that the local governments we examine operate in a quasi-competitive environment that we call "the local market for public goods" (Schneider 1989). In this market, given the importance of local taxes for financing services, each community has strong incentives to attract and retain desirable and mobile residents and businesses who contribute the most in tax dollars (Peterson 1981; Schneider 1989).

Businesses and households often change location. While most of the factors driving locational choices are exogenous to local politics, for example technological changes in manufacturing techniques or change in household marital status, other factors, such as the local tax rate, are directly affected by local policy choices. Thus, public entrepreneurs are not only engaged in struggles for change within their community, but they both are affected by and affect the competitive climate of their metropolitan area. Some entrepreneurial innovations allow communities to improve their own prospects at the expense of their neighbors. In turn, neighboring communities may imitate and adapt successful innovations to their own political context. Historically, reforms have repeatedly swept across American communities (e.g., Knott and Miller 1987). We believe that entrepreneurs play a major role in the diffusion of these waves of innovation.

We examine entrepreneurial behavior in the context of institutional and environmental changes. Hirschman's (1970) classic work *Exit, Voice, and Loyalty* lays out the basic forms of response to organizational change. These responses are well known to political analysts, especially "voice," which refers to citizens contacting public officials or acting as individuals or groups in expressing dissatisfaction (e.g., Sharp 1986). The exit option is central to Charles Tiebout's model of local government (Tiebout 1956; extended by Ostrom, Tiebout, and Warren 1961), which established one of the strongest research traditions in the study of local governments and which continues to underlie many modern theories of local government competition (see, e.g., Peterson 1981; Schneider 1989). In addition to exit and voice, in chapter 10, we add *entry* as a critical component of the competitive process.

In this competitive climate, we believe that entrepreneurs inject innovation into the practices of their own local governments, which can then diffuse throughout the entire system of local government. Paralleling economic models of entrepreneurship, such as those developed by Schumpeter, the local public sector entrepreneur engages in the "creative destruction" of old policies and political paradigms. Because of the force of competition, successful innovations, especially those that increase efficiency in the production of local services and improve governmental responsiveness to the demands of citizens, will elicit a positive response in the local market for public goods. Thus, while public entrepreneurs seek to maximize their own profits, they produce benefits that others garner. And, just like economic entrepreneurs, public entrepreneurs provide important pecuniary externalities to other actors in the system.

HOW MANY ENTREPRENEURS ARE THERE?

Unlike case studies that emphasize the importance of one or, at most, a few heroic individual entrepreneurs, we show that entrepreneurship is surprisingly common in local government. We believe that the concept of entrepreneurship as the "domain" of a small number of dynamic and forceful individuals is a result of the biographic approach common to the study of entrepreneurship and driven by a fixation on a "great man" or "great woman" approach to change. Clearly, a small number of public entrepreneurs have truly transformed important policies and institutions and radically reshaped policy domains. The actions of such "larger-than-life" entrepreneurs as Lyndon Johnson, Robert Moses, Admiral Hyman Rickover, and others have been well documented in careful case studies. There can be no doubt of the transformations of politics driven by these individuals.

We recognize the importance of the "dynamic few." But we base our approach on a different conception of entrepreneurial behavior. We believe that there is a broad distribution of leadership talents and skills and that change can be propelled by actors other than the small number of highly visible entrepreneurs about whom biographies are written. While we do not know the exact shape of the distribution of leadership talents, if we assume that these skills are normally distributed across the large number of political actors in governments across the United States, then clearly the biographical approach to entrepreneurship focuses on the extreme "tail" of that distribution. That is, books are written about individuals who are several standard deviations above the mean in leadership skills. In contrast, we define entrepreneurs as individuals who certainly are above the mean in leadership but may not be in the extreme 1 or 2 percent of the distribution that the biographical approach emphasizes. Our entrepreneurs are dynamic, but they are more than just a few.

But even if our approach to entrepreneurship is different than the biographical approach, our study of local government entrepreneurship is still fundamentally important for the study of the dynamic few who rise to national prominence and become the subject of biographies. Many nationally recognized "heroic" entrepreneurs began their careers in some aspect of local government. And many entrepreneurs seeking to become nationally recognized run aground on the shoals of local politics. We believe that activity in local government can act as a "screening mechanism" to determine where an entrepreneur falls in the distribution of talent and leadership. That is, even the most dynamic and successful entrepreneur had to pass many tests on the way to national prominence, and service in local government poses one of the most common domains in which leaders are tested.

While we expand the range of action we consider entrepreneurial, we do not take the extreme view that all important actions in a market setting are entrepreneurial (cf. Mises 1962). Instead, we define entrepreneurial activities as those that propel dynamic political change. We therefore begin by focusing on two classes of public sector actors: *political entrepreneurs*, such as mayors and city council members who operate in the world of electoral politics; and *managerial* entrepreneurs, such as city managers or high-level managers of public bureaucracies who control the resources of established agencies. In addition, we recognize that in the porous system of local government, the actions of individual citizens and businesses can affect public entrepreneurship. Thus, in later chapters we explore the role of mobile citizens and local businesses in propelling change and in creating a climate supportive of entrepreneurship.

OUR METHODOLOGY

While none of the social sciences has produced a fully formed theory of entrepreneurship, we found the economic approach the most fruitful avenue to follow. As we argued above and as we illustrate in detail in the next chapter, much of mainstream economics has underestimated and underanalyzed the role of entrepreneurs. But some offshoots of traditional theory, especially those stimulated by the Austrian School, bring the role of the entrepreneur into central focus. As we examine the emergence and behavior of public sector entrepreneurs, we adapt an economic approach to politics informed by these offshoots. We also draw on the literature on entrepreneurship found in sociology, psychology, and other social sciences, integrating these observations into our political economic approach.

Fundamental to our study is the argument that entrepreneurs engage in rational benefit/cost analyses when deciding to pursue opportunities. As we argued above, there is a population of potential entrepreneurs distributed across local governments. The size of the local population with entrepreneurial skills and ambitions is a function of the characteristics of the community, such as its income and education level (Ronen 1983; Ricketts 1987) and the economic composition of the region and the city itself (see chapter 9).[2] Potential entrepreneurs have energies and talents they could invest in alternate spheres of activity. The rate at which they are attracted to the local *public sector* (as compared to some other domain) is a function of the costs they face in entering the public arena and the benefits they garner if they succeed as public entrepreneurs.

We argue that the level of these costs and benefits is embodied in measurable facets of local government. For example, we show in later chapters that, among other considerations, costs are a function of the collective action problems entrepreneurs face and the ease with which these problems can be solved. Similarly, we show that benefits to entrepreneurship are a function of the slack resources that exist in a community.

An economic approach raises the question of the type of gains public sector entrepreneurs seek. Unlike many economic entrepreneurs, public entrepreneurs usually are not seeking large increases in personal wealth, which, though possible in politics, are not common in local politics (at least not within the confines of legal activities).[3] Public entrepreneurs have utility functions that must include the desire for power, prestige, and popularity, the desire to influence policy, and other factors in addition to any monetary income derived from their political activities. These benefits may be a function, among other things, of the budgetary slack of the local community, which affects the entrepreneur's ability to reallocate resources to achieve the policy goals held by the entrepreneur.

Since we conceive of public entrepreneurship taking place in a quasi-competitive local market, we utilize a basic microeconomic model of supply and demand for entrepreneurship. Thus, we analyze the impact of supply-side factors such as individual entrepreneurial characteristics, the local entrepreneurial business climate, and opportunity costs relative to expected entrepreneurial gains in political institutions. On the demand side, we consider factors related to the actions of citizen/voters and the effects of local fiscal and economic situations.

It is clear that the local market for public goods, while embodying many competitive forces, does not meet the requirements of a perfectly competitive model. For example, each community has a partial spatial monopoly over the public goods and services delivered to its residents. In many parts of the country, market entry by new communities is limited. Local governments also cannot easily adjust their service/tax mix because they are constrained by intergovernmental mandates (see Schneider 1989). Thus, the local market for public goods is an imperfect market, and, as we show in the next chapter, in any imperfect market, the range and impact of entrepreneurial strategies on the functioning of the market increases.

Political scientists have long been interested in understanding the motivations, actions, and impacts of public sector entrepreneurs. But most have not employed a market model and have taken the stand (either implicitly or explicitly) that markets and politics are different. However, recent work in political science studying strategic behavior, especially in formal and game theoretic models, and most evident in Riker's (1986) work on heresthetics and Baumgartner and Jones's (1993) work on punctuated equilibrium, has provided a theoretical foundation upon which to build a theory of public sector entrepreneurs and how they can propel change from a status quo that seems to be in equilibrium.

Interestingly, these approaches, especially Riker's, harken back to the fundamental critiques of static market models in economics evident in the work of Schumpeter, Kirzner, and other Austrian economists. We integrate these approaches into a political economic theory, and we also incorporate elements of strategic behavior drawn from applied theories of private market competition.

Beyond developing a more rigorous theory of public entrepreneurship, we develop elements of our theory in a manner that can be tested empirically. Specifically, we believe that the emergence of entrepreneurs can be analyzed probabilistically as a function of specific political, fiscal, economic, and demographic factors that influence the supply and demand for entrepreneurs. However, we recognize that not all aspects of the theory are immediately testable with the data available; particularly we are not yet able to test the long-term dynamic impact of entrepreneurship on local government systems. Thus, this book lays down a challenge for further empirical work on dynamic change in political systems.

THE LAYOUT OF THE BOOK

We explore the central issues in a theory of public sector entrepreneurship in the rest of this first part of the book. No one has yet developed a comprehensive theory of public entrepreneurs and tested it empirically. We move in that direction.

We turn first to the development of ideas about entrepreneurship in economic markets and then show how these ideas can be applied to the world of politics and, particularly, to the study of the local market for public goods. Chapter 2 develops the rationale for entrepreneurial behavior in markets by relaxing the highly restrictive assumptions of the neoclassical model of microeconomic markets. In particular, we show that when information is costly, when products are not homogeneous, when sellers are few, and when transaction costs are not zero, opportunities for entrepreneurship emerge in the neoclassical market model. Entrepreneurs exploit these opportunities.

In chapters 3 and 4, we more carefully develop a definition of the entrepreneur and illustrate the specific mechanisms that political entrepreneurs employ to achieve their goals. We explore the dimensions of the collective action problem, which is usually a more difficult barrier for political entrepreneurs than it is for private sector entrepreneurs. We also illustrate how a market for political entrepreneurs operates, identifying specific components of the supply and demand sides of that market.

Part 2 of the book is devoted to empirical analysis of entrepreneurs in local governments across the country. In chapter 5, we introduce our empirical evidence, which is based on a survey of over 1,000 communities around the nation coupled with extensive objective data gathered from census reports and from state and local studies of local fiscal conditions. We use this evidence to show how measurable aspects of the costs and benefits of entrepreneurship across local governments affect the probable emergence of entrepreneurs across communities. We also provide more detail about the backgrounds of our entrepreneurs, and present some case histories to illustrate examples of political entrepreneurship.

Chapters 6 and 7 show how ongoing struggles over growth in local government are addressed by entrepreneurial politicians. Using a property rights approach, we show how traditional progrowth activities, more innovative progrowth programs, and antigrowth activities have had cycles of innovation related to citizen demand—cycles propelled and structured by the opportunistic behavior of public entrepreneurs.

In chapter 8, we examine managerial entrepreneurs who are full-time career employees of local government. Since most of the managerial entrepreneurs in our sample are city managers, we analyze the factors that affect the emergence of entrepreneurial city managers and contrast the factors that drive this alternative source of entrepreneurship with those affecting the emergence of political entrepreneurs. We also provide detailed analysis of the strategies and goals of these bureaucratically based actors.

In part 3, we examine broader issues that influence the supply and demand sides of the market for political entrepreneurs. Chapter 9 explores the milieux of the entrepreneurial market in more detail. Some areas of the United States are sources of a disproportionate number of innovative ideas. We explore the importance of entrepreneurial milieux empirically, by focusing on business sectors characterized by substantial employment in the high technology and finance, insurance, and real estate (FIRE) services sectors. We argue that public sector entrepreneurs are embedded in networks of economic actors that can support and encourage entrepreneurship.

In chapter 10, we move from entrepreneurs within government to those in the citizenry at-large. We look at individual movers and established residents who have high levels of information about local government. As careful and informed shoppers in the local market for public goods, we show how such individuals can act as entrepreneurs whose entry decisions and subsequent use of political voice provide benefits to all citizens in a region. Certainly there are more of these citizen/consumer entrepreneurs than there are entrepreneurs in formal government and political positions. Austrian economists have debated the issue of the number of entrepreneurs ("the few or the many") that are found in markets and who propel change. We explore this issue and argue that ultimately the set of informed citizens (the relatively many) help form coalitions supporting political entrepreneurs (the relatively few) in their efforts to propel policy change.

In chapter 11 we conclude our work. We argue that the emergence of public entrepreneurship is more predictable than others have argued. We reiterate our fundamental belief that public entrepreneurs respond to rational benefit/cost calculations that are a function of specifiable institutional and political conditions embodied in the structure of local government. While we do not have enough longitudinal data to establish statistically that these entrepreneurs have made a marked difference in tax rates or patterns of growth, our case studies suggest that many local entrepreneurs are making dynamic changes in the politics and policies of their communities, changes which seem likely to have a significant and measurable impact on the future development of their cities.

CHAPTER 2.

Bringing Back the Entrepreneur: Neoclassical Economic Models and the Role of the Entrepreneur

WHILE MANY social science disciplines have analyzed entrepreneurial behavior, entrepreneurs have been considered most important in economic markets. Yet as a discipline, even economics has not focused much energy on developing theories or empirical data about entrepreneurs. Our task in this chapter is to illustrate how neoclassical economics, especially the model of perfect competition, limited the role of entrepreneurship in the theory of the market. We show that by relaxing the strict assumptions of the neoclassical model, the range of strategic options available to actors in real economic situations increases dramatically, producing opportunities for alert entrepreneurs. Throughout the following discussion, we develop parallels between the strategic options open to entrepreneurs in private markets and entrepreneurs in the political marketplace.

NEOCLASSICAL ECONOMICS AND THE ENTREPRENEUR

Many scholars have argued that neoclassical economics leaves little or no room for entrepreneurs. Neoclassical economists, working in the wake of the "marginalist" revolution built upon the work of Marshall, Walrus, and others, developed the competitive model as an ideal to which real world markets might aspire and to which they could be compared. Like many other highly abstract and powerful models, the model of the competitive market took on a life of its own. Because of its tractability and its elegance, economists often take the basic model of perfect competition as a reflection of reality rather than as an analytic tool.

The core ingredients of the model of the perfectly competitive market are well known. In the idealized model, the competitive market requires a variety of buyers and sellers who trade homogeneous goods about which they have full information. Buyers have freedom to purchase the bundle of goods and services that maximizes their welfare, subject to budget constraints. Given these conditions, the competitive marketplace allocates resources efficiently. However, efficiency is not a dichotomous variable. Rather, markets are more or less efficient and the level of efficiency is ultimately dependent on a variety of factors, including the number of firms in the market, the degree of differentiation between products, and the ease with which firms can enter and exit the market.

Behaviorally, each firm is assumed to seek to maximize profits. Since in the perfectly competitive market any individual firm is so small in comparison to the whole range of producers offering virtually identical goods, firms are price takers, *not* price makers. That is, no firm can artificially inflate the price it charges for the goods it brings to the market—if a firm's price is too high, its market share literally falls to zero. Consequently, and somewhat ironically, in the model of perfect competition there are no true competitors because strategic choices are not possible.

Given the assumption of product homogeneity, firms cannot convince consumers that their product is different or better than that of competing suppliers. All actors in the market are assumed to have complete information about the nature of their transactions. A large number of firms supply the same basic product, using the same basic production technology. Because of competition, firms must accept the market price as a given and each firm earns "normal" profits as returns to their invested capital. Assuming no entry barriers, if firms were earning "excess profits" in a given market, new entrants would be immediately attracted to enter that market and the resulting price competition would force profits back to "normal" levels.

Underlying the model is also the fundamental idea of equilibrium: a situation in which each individual, facing the behavior of others and facing the institutional framework that structures the market, is doing as well as possible. At equilibrium, actors in a market learn that new or different actions do not produce beneficial outcomes. As Kreps puts it:

> [I]ndividuals make individual choices, and the institutional framework aggregates those actions into an aggregate outcome which then determines constraints that individuals face and outcomes they receive. If individuals take a "trial shot" at an action, after the aggregation is accomplished and the feedback is fed back, they may learn that their actions are incompatible or didn't have quite the consequences they foresaw. This leads individuals to change their individual actions, which changes the feedback, and so on. An equilibrium is a collection of individual choices whereby the feedback process would lead to no subsequent change of behavior. (1990: 6)

In developing the foundations for their models of economic behavior, neoclassical economists built on the first principles of methodological individualism and utility maximization. But to make their problems tractable using the calculus and to develop explainable equilibrium states, economists needed to fix as many systemic parameters as possible and to assume that many factors affecting supply and demand were exogenous to the model. Within such constraints and using ever more elegant and increasingly rigorous analytic tools, economists can model how exogenous shocks to a market system affect supply (such as a hurricane that reduces the lime crop) or demand (such as a shift toward lower cholesterol products as consumers focus more on their health). Comparative statics can show how the equilibrium output and price of products in the market are affected by such changes. But fundamentally, in the core model, consumers are *assumed* to have well-specified (and fairly stable) preferences to which firms respond by producing the appropriately valued goods and services. The number of parameters involved is fairly small and many other "real world" conditions are held constant.

MODIFYING THE NEOCLASSICAL MODEL TO REINSERT THE ENTREPRENEUR

This is an admittedly highly simplified version of the perfectly competitive market. However, by simplifying the neoclassical model, we can identify several of the core conditions upon which it is built, including: full information; a multiplicity of buyers and sellers; product homogeneity; low entry and exit barriers; and equilibrium. Each of these core conditions explicitly limits the role of entrepreneurship.

In the following pages, we explore what happens in a market as each of these highly restrictive assumptions is relaxed. Our goal is to produce a more realistic and more textured model of markets (both political and economic). As we do so, we show how these modifications move the highly abstract model of the competitive market closer to real world markets. We specifically show how relaxing each assumption creates opportunities for entrepreneurial behavior that the basic model ignores and we set the stage specifically for our development of a theoretically and empirically important role for entrepreneurs in the local market for public goods. We begin with the issue of full information, the absence of which in many ways lies at the core of opportunities for entrepreneurial behavior.

NEOCLASSICAL ASSUMPTION: THE ROLE OF INFORMATION

In the traditional neoclassical economic model, information and transaction costs are assumed to be zero. In this section, we draw upon several recent streams of research to show that once that assumption is relaxed to allow for the limited information available in most real world transactions, an entrepreneurial role becomes important. We begin our analysis at the micro level, considering specific elements of the profit function and the implications for entrepreneurial action that emerge when the nature of information is no longer taken as given. Following this, we consider the implications for entrepreneurship of asymmetric information leading to transactions costs and management costs. We then step beyond this frame of reference to consider the role of entrepreneurs placed within the broader, macro level operating environment of political-economic institutions.

Perfect Information and the Neoclassical Model

If information and transactions costs are treated as negligible, economic success in the market place can be attributed to the result of correct and swift mathematical calculations and a "blindfolded monkey" can indeed fill the role of the entrepreneur (Pasour 1989: 96). But if there are costs for gathering information, the entrepreneur must attempt to discover market opportunities and cope with constantly changing conditions. Entrepreneurs have a central role in choosing the mix of inputs into the production process: the entrepreneur has to employ some inputs that are necessary for production, but whose exact relationship to the productive process may be underspecified or whose output is indeterminate.

Once the costliness and imperfectness of information is understood, entrepreneurship becomes critical: "Entrepreneurship is little more than profit maximization in a context in which knowledge is costly and imitation is not instantaneous" (Demsetz 1983: 277). Similarly, Leibenstein (1968) argues that in real markets there is always imperfect knowledge about production functions, which creates "market deficiencies" or "gaps" that the entrepreneur sees and fills.

In a perfect market, the price system acts to coordinate the separate and decentralized actions of many different people. Yet, ambiguity always accompanies any particular price change, because it is never clear whether a change in price reflects general inflation, a permanent shift in relative scarcities or consumer preferences, or a temporary fluctuation for which there could be any number of causes. Under such limited information, at best, only a probability distribution for price can be estimated. The entrepreneur lacking full information must decide whether to maximize the expected value of profits or seek a compromise between maximizing profits and minimizing risk (Simon 1969). Price uncertainty and ambiguity, therefore, create opportunities for entrepreneurs to profit from accurately interpreting and forecasting price changes.

Price uncertainty also provides justification for the development of marketing strategies. Improved knowledge of consumer preferences and consumer behavior may help the entrepreneur anticipate various opportunities and determine ahead of time what output quantity will yield the highest expected revenue. Although such action is typically associated with the private sector, it is not unheard of for local governments to undertake surveys of citizens' demands for public services. Of course, as elections near, most politicians engage in some form of "market analysis" to determine what policy rhetoric voters are most willing to "buy" and, in increasingly sophisticated campaigning, politicians use marketing techniques, such as focus groups, which are borrowed directly from marketing experts in the private sector.

Finally, price uncertainty provides justification for entrepreneurial activities aimed at using instruments of government to bring about greater certainty. For firms, such behavior may include lobbying for trade tariffs, rate and entry regulations, and government contracts (see Tullock 1967; Stigler 1971; Buchanan, Tollison, and Tullock 1980). For local governments, parallel strategies may include diversifying the tax base, entering contractual arrangements to provide selected services to other jurisdictions, seeking intergovernmental aid, or seeking higher-level government mandates to restrict the actions of potential or actual competitors. In the words of Cyert and March (1963: 119), all these strategies may be thought of as uncertainty avoidance measures that mitigate against surprises from the market and from competitors by "arranging a negotiated environment."

Perfect Information and the Firm as a Production Function

In the model of pure competition, firms appear as simple production functions rather than as complicated collections of individuals working in complex systems. Absent perfect information, knowledge of the production function can no longer be taken as given. Hence, while managers may be expected to adopt purposeful, self-interested behavior, decisions over what constitutes the best techniques for combining inputs become subject to uncertainty. Although a manager possesses knowledge of existing circumstances, as well as historical information about the market, this will provide no guidance on how to reduce production costs or alter production techniques in response to unfamiliar changes in the operating environment and ongoing competitive pressures. This creates opportunities for entrepreneurs to garner profits by developing innovative management techniques (Simon 1969). Waves of managerial reform are commonplace and have swept through both the private and the public sectors of the United States repeatedly during this century (see, e.g., Knott and Miller 1987). Yet the very nature of the competitive process ensures that entrepreneurs must keep searching both for better ways of applying and combining existing techniques and for adopting wholly new ones to meet ever-changing circumstances.

One arena in which entrepreneurs seek to innovate is by reorganizing the use of personnel to increase the efficiency and the responsiveness of workers. The fundamental problem for any manager is to monitor and coordinate the behavior of his or her subordinates, especially specialized workers whose incentives may lead them in directions other than that desired by the entrepreneur.

This coordination problem is rooted in the very nature of modern complex organizations. The division of labor has the potential to increase productivity by allowing individuals to gain and apply superior levels of expertise and by limiting the amount of information they must deal with at any given time. To achieve these benefits, specialization must be accompanied by coordination (March and Simon 1958: 162).

The key to coordination in organizations is communication. In some instances, the communications task will be trivial, but in many instances—particularly those requiring a high degree of specialization—determining how to ensure a smooth flow of information within an organization may be a complex task (see Hammond 1986). Those managers who are able to design the most appropriate organizational form to meet the tasks at hand may be able to obtain high profits from production where others only achieve normal returns on investments. In government, those managers who are able to develop appropriate organizational forms may be able to realize financial savings where others cannot, and they may gain credit for the savings or increase the flexibility in their budgets to pursue other policies or perks they value (e.g., Dunleavy 1991).

Additional opportunities for entrepreneurship are introduced as a consequence of the transaction costs associated with purchasing inputs and selling output. All production processes could conceivably occur through the use of market coordination. Organizations and firms would not be necessary, and hierarchical bureaucratic organizations would be irrelevant to the functioning of the market. In reality, however, production is often coordinated within firms. Managers can reduce transaction costs (and, hence, the total costs of production) by substituting one contract for the many spot contracts that would be associated with production coordinated through use of the price mechanism (Coase 1937).

Recently, scholars have considered how, at the micro level, measurement and enforcement costs associated with transactions frequently determine the nature of contracts (Cheung 1983) and the structure of economic organizations (Williamson 1985). At the macro or market level, these costs frequently contribute to the development of social, political, and economic institutions (Libecap 1989; Barzel 1989; North 1990; Ostrom 1990). The presence of transaction costs provides opportunities for entrepreneurs in both the private and public sectors to garner profits from establishing contractual arrangements among the owners of inputs that economize on these costs and facilitate mutually beneficial trade.

Scholars such as Olson (1965), Axelrod (1984), and Ostrom (1990) have explored various ways in which informal actions or contractual arrangements (including the establishment of proto-governmental monitoring agents) can develop between individuals and within small groups to facilitate mutually beneficial transactions. Barzel (1982: 42) suggests that firms will form and trade with each other at junctures where output can be easily measured, but where output is difficult to measure, the different steps will be performed within the firm.

This suggests that an entrepreneur may realize economies in transactions costs through the development of a firmlike nexus of contracts.[1] Concern about transactions costs is particularly relevant for the management of government, where many of the public goods that are provided are inherently hard to measure and where production technologies are uncertain.

Williamson (1985) suggests that the form of various economic organizations can be explained as the result of efforts to economize on transaction costs. Williamson's analysis of transaction costs and his identification of the importance of monitoring, reputation, and repeated trades are among the most important recent theoretical contributions to the study of entrepreneurship. Alchian and Woodward (1987) continue this line of investigation, suggesting that in the absence of perfect information, entrepreneurs face many opportunities to profit from decisions concerning what components to buy across markets and what components to make in-house.

Placing transactions within the firm through vertical integration may reduce some transactions costs. But this strategy is no panacea for the pernicious effects of incomplete and asymmetric information. All incentives compatibility problems, such as moral hazard, shirking, and opportunism, can be seen as having their origins in incomplete information. While placing transactions within a firmlike organization may reduce information costs, incentives compatibility problems will remain. Problems of this sort have been investigated by Alchian and Demsetz (1972), and more extensively, within the principal-agent literature that has emerged since the mid-1970s (see Pratt and Zeckhauser 1985 for an overview and Moe 1984 for applications to political science problems).

How entrepreneurs can economize on management costs is the focus of Miller's (1992) analysis of "managerial dilemmas." Miller follows Alchian and Demsetz (1972) in claiming that in team production situations where monitoring is costly and hence shirking is a dominant strategy, hierarchy may be established as an efficiency-enhancing institutional form (1992: 34). Here, the incentive for monitors to perform their task diligently is provided by making them residual claimants for profits from production. However, Miller (1992: 35) notes that the hierarchial solution to the problem of team shirking is not necessarily automatic or final.

Miller suggests that *any* incentive scheme will leave some member of a team reason to shirk in ways that cannot be efficiently discovered and sanctioned (p. 182). Information asymmetries (in the form of monitoring limitations) and production externalities (in the form of inseparable marginal production) make it impossible for managers to achieve full efficiency just through the manipulation of economic incentives. Rather, several possible equilibria, many of which may be Pareto inferior, exist. This introduces a role for managers to create belief systems, norms, or social conventions in hierarchies that will guide individual behavior so that the output of the team as a whole stabilizes at a relatively efficient equilibrium point.

Miller (1992) demonstrates that entrepreneurs may garner profits from not only giving careful consideration to the nature of various contractual arrangements, but also from paying attention to corporate "culture":

> Rather than relying only on a mechanical incentive system to align individual interest and group efficiency, hierarchical leaders must create appropriate psychological expectations, pay the "startup costs" for appropriate cooperation norms, kick-start the secondary norms that will be the primary enforcers of cooperative norms, and create institutions that will credibly commit the leader to the nonexploitation of employee "ownership rights" in the organization. (p. 232; also see Kreps 1990)

In short, the presence of incomplete information raises possibilities for profits to be made through entrepreneurial action within organizations.

THE NEW APPROACH TO INSTITUTIONS

We turn next to the broader context in which firms operate, and how entrepreneurs may profit from actions that lead to changes in their broader operating environment, including politics. Here, we consider the roles—both indirect (via externalities) and direct (via collective action or lobbying)—that entrepreneurs may play in bringing about profit-enhancing changes in various social, political, and economic institutions. North (1990: 63) suggests that institutions are usually devised to reduce the transactions costs for society as a whole. Institutional changes may be "imposed" on business managers through the political process. Yet, the enforcement and compliance requirements of institutions are themselves costly; hence, incentives arise for entrepreneurs to seek reforms that reduce their socially imposed costs of doing business.

Institutional changes can be thought of as a means (explicit or implicit) of assigning or reassigning property rights. Making this analytical simplification allows us to establish the end point to which rational actors aspire. This is the result identified by Coase (1960): if the price system worked costlessly, the ultimate assignment of property rights (which maximizes the value of production) would be independent of the initial assignment.

Ostrom (1990), in her study of common pool resource (CPR) management, notes that improving overall welfare is not easy in the presence of information and transaction costs:

> Given the strong temptations to shirk, free-ride, and generally act opportunistically that usually are present when individuals face CPR problems, overcoming such problems can never be assured. . . . Further, if individuals find rules that work relatively well, they may have little motivation to continue the costly process of searching for rules that will work even better. "If it ain't broke, don't fix it" applies as much to institutional capital as to physical capital. (pp. 210–211)

Ostrom contends that CPR appropriators (e.g., a group of fishing companies) may adopt incremental changes in operational rules when various conditions are met. These conditions require that most appropriators share a judgment that they: will be harmed unless they adopt new rules; will be affected in similar ways by the change; place high value on the continued activities; face low information, transformation, and enforcement costs; share norms of reciprocity and trust; and constitute a fairly small and stable group (1990: 211). Although Ostrom does not use the term, it is clear that such change could be facilitated by a political entrepreneur who uses various strategies to propel institutional changes through which all may benefit.

Libecap (1989) and Barzel (1989) have considered the development and transformation of property rights from a more generalized perspective than Ostrom. These authors tend to be more specific about the motivation for such institutional change. According to Libecap (1989: 12), the "primary motivation for contracting for property rights is common pool losses. Capturing a share of the expected gains from mitigating common pool conditions encourages individuals to establish or to modify property rights to limit access and to control resource use."

Note how limited information lies at the heart of the need to establish property rights. As value accrues to the use of previously common property (e.g., the fishable sea), actors find it in their interest to delineate the boundaries in which they may operate. Those who actively seek the establishment of property rights may be termed entrepreneurs, since they seek to improve the profitability of their own operations, yet—through their actions—they provide a positive externality (determination of property rights) to all actors who share the operating environment (see also Riker and Sened 1991).

The establishment of such property rights is frequently a prerequisite to profitable trade. Hence, entrepreneurs have a strong incentive to determine ways of reducing the costs of establishing property rights. Once a low-cost method (relative to realizable profits) can be determined, property rights should be established or redefined. Libecap (1989: 16) suggests three factors can create pressures to change existing property rights: shifts in relative prices; changes in production and enforcement technology; and shifts in preferences and other political parameters. Barzel further establishes the possibility for (ongoing) entrepreneurial action by noting: "The public domain is ubiquitous; innumerable commodity attributes are placed in it. Any service not fully charged for on the margin is at least partly relinquished to the public domain. . . . Resource owners attempt to maximize the net values of their resources: They attempt to organize their action so that, ceteris paribus, losses to the public domain are minimized" (1989: 114).

We can think of entrepreneurs as those who rise to the challenge of extracting profits from preexisting property rights. But since property rights will always be less than fully specified, entrepreneurs can also seek gains by deliberately eroding those rights not made explicit in current arrangements, changing the rules to their own advantage (North 1990: 87). The latter approach is riskier and more difficult, but may yield higher benefits. And seeking to alter the broad operating environment is even more proactive than the sort of entrepreneurial behavior of firms documented by Cyert and March (1963).

In sum, absent full information, the role of the entrepreneur becomes complex and many opportunities for entrepreneurial profits arise in what may otherwise be viewed as uninteresting areas of production, management, and trade. Opportunities for garnering profits from entrepreneurial actions emerge from almost every aspect of production, marketing, management, and in the broader social-political context of rule-making institutions, or in politics.

Public Sector Organizations and Incomplete Information

While the problem of incomplete information and uncertainty creates numerous opportunities for private sector entrepreneurs operating in the larger political context, it also creates opportunities for entrepreneurs within government. Production indivisibilities inherent in public goods, unclear marginal price signals from unpriced goods, and other information problems are all present in the public sector.

While Miller (1992) showed that solving information problems in profit-making organizations is far from a trivial task, it is even more complex in the public sector. Wilson (1989) argues that the inability of public sector managers to reallocate resources within their organization (including the personnel constraints of civil service personnel rules), the inability to motivate subordinates through the retention of residual profits, and the need to try to achieve multiple goals imposed by multiple political principals makes public management more difficult than private management. Moe (1984) is one of the few political scientists focused on developing a theory of the nature of the constraints that politicians and public sector managers face, compared to those in privately owned organizations. We will discuss this issue more in chapter 8, but for now it is important to recognize that the greater information problems in the public sector can lead to substantial opportunities for entrepreneurship within government.

ASSUMPTION: MULTIPLE BUYERS AND SELLERS

The classical model of the market is built upon a multitude of buyers and sellers. However, there are many other market configurations besides the one on which the purely competitive model is built. In some markets there is only one buyer who faces many sellers—that is, monopsony. While monopsony is an interesting deviation from the competitive market, the context with which we are more concerned is the inverse case where there is only a limited number of sellers of goods in the market: monopoly or oligopoly.

While monopoly markets are at the other extreme from perfect competition, economists have well-behaved models of such markets. In classic monopoly models, monopolists do not make important strategic choices, but rather simply look to the existing demand curve (of which they are assumed to know the shape) for pricing guidance and set a quantity of output that equates marginal revenues to marginal costs

(MR = MC). This maximizes their monopoly profits. Natural monopolies are assumed to be technologically determined and not the product of successful strategic choices by entrepreneurs.[2] Thus, monopoly theory, like that of perfect competition, is simple and elegant, but essentially bloodless in terms of strategic behavior. Just as there is little need for entrepreneurial actors in the static model of perfect competition, there is no need for an entrepreneur in the extreme model of natural monopoly.

A market configuration that has been subject to intense investigation by economists is that of oligopoly, which is characterized by "imperfect competition" between a limited number of sellers. Essentially, oligopolistic competition falls between the two extremes of perfect competition and monopoly and describes the condition of most real world markets.

In oligopolistic markets, strategic choices by firms are critically important. Hyman describes how strategic choices develop in oligopolistic markets:

> Sellers in oligopolistic markets know that when they or their rivals change either their prices or outputs, the profits of all firms in the market will be affected. The sellers are aware of their interdependence. Each firm in the industry is presumed to recognize that a change in its price or output will cause a reaction by competing firms. Individual sellers in oligopolistic markets *must* consider the reaction from their competitors. The response a seller expects from rival firms to a change in its price, output, or marketing efforts is a crucial determinant of its choices. (1989: 421)

As economists focused increasingly on the strategic interactions in oligopolistic markets, a revolution in the study of industrial organization (IO) took place. Historically, the theory of industrial organization was dominated by the famous "structure-conduct-performance" (SCP) paradigm. In this approach, the *structure* of markets (measured by such factors as the dominant production technology, the number of competitors, the degree of product differentiation) affected the *conduct* of the market (e.g., pricing, investment, research and development) which in turn drove the *performance* of the market (especially efficiency, innovation, and product diffusion). The SCP approach was empirical, based on the observation of industries, but was based on weak, mostly ad hoc theories.

By the 1970s, a new wave of interest in IO emerged, a wave propelled by a growing dissatisfaction with the state of theory in the field and driven by the adoption of noncooperative game theory as the "standard tool" for the analysis of strategic conflict (Tirole 1989: 3). Noncooperative game theory brought a unified methodology to the study of strategic choices and allowed innovations and ideas developed in the study of dynamic change and the effects of asymmetric information to be introduced into the study of markets.

These innovations focused the attention of economists on strategic interactions and made the modeling of strategies central to the study of markets.[3] At present, there is a wide (and growing) array of theories of the oligopolistic market and approaches to its study (for example, Cournot duopoly, price leadership, kinked demand curves, the many extensions of Nash equilibrium). While there is at present intense disagreement over which of these theories best describes market behavior, strategic choices are important in all of them. This focus on strategies obviously increases the theoretical role for entrepreneurial actors, but exactly how entrepreneurs enter the theory is yet to be fully specified.[4]

We believe that many if not most government policies are enacted in an environment that resembles oligopolistic markets. And we believe that, in particular, the suburban governments we study provide a milieux in which the theory of oligopoly and theories of politics can interact profitably. As more Americans moved from urban areas to the suburbs surrounding them over the course of the twentieth century, metropolitan areas developed different organization structures. Some (such as the consolidated governments found in Jacksonville/Duval County and Nashville/Davidson County) are built around the concept of a unified system of government, in which government services attempt to tap scale economies of joint provision to the entire metropolitan area. The metropolitan government or consolidation reform movements pushed this type of change, blaming jurisdictional fragmentation for high costs and lack of policy coordination. At the other extreme, other metropolitan areas are highly polycentric, in which many local governments offer local services in implicit, if not explicit, competition with one another.[5]

In a truly monocentric model, there is a single local government that is a monopoly supplier of local public goods and services. The potential role for entrepreneurial strategies is reduced in a monopoly setting, as the neoclassical economic theory illustrates. However, Schneider (1989) shows that more metropolitan areas have characteristics of polycentric systems than of monocentric markets (also see Ostrom, Tiebout, and Warren 1961; Ostrom 1972). And when there are many suppliers, as is the case in most metropolitan areas, and when suppliers are not "fully competitive," strategic behavior by governments is likely.[6]

Thus, most metropolitan areas have an oligopolistic market structure, and we can use some of the techniques and theoretical constructs economists employ to study the supply side of such a market. Strategic choices over the services to offer, the tax price to charge, the way in which to differentiate one community from others (especially for the most attractive segment of potential buyers—such as businesses and high-income families) become critical to local governments in a dynamic polycentric system. In this intercommunity environment, the public entrepreneur can shape a dynamic strategy, manipulating the policy tools local governments bring to the local market for public goods.

ASSUMPTION: HOMOGENEOUS PRODUCTS

In the neoclassical model of competitive markets, products are assumed to be homogeneous. If there are no distinctions between products (that is, they are "commodities"), then buyers will switch freely between goods on the basis of price alone. In contrast, nonhomogeneous products give rise to strategic opportunities as entrepreneurs seek market niches.

Hayek was one of the first modern economists to directly dispute the assumption of large numbers of firms producing homogeneous commodities with the same essential attributes. Hayek argued that homogeneity even within a single market never exists and information asymmetries lead to ongoing problems of reconciling supply and demand (Hayek 1976: 102). In Hayek's depiction of the imperfect market, knowledge is not diffused instantaneously (as in the perfectly competitive market). These lags give rise to the possibilities of entrepreneurial search for opportunities for profit.

Also operating within the Austrian approach, Reekie (1984) developed the concept of a *discrepant market*—a dynamically heterogeneous market that is never cleared and in which full congruence is never attained. For Reekie, the central problem of economics "is to ascertain how human beings in the discrepant marketplace act in order to maximize each other's satisfaction. . . . The answer lies again in differing prices . . . [that] alter or are perceived to alter or to be about to change. Alertness to these perceived price changes results in the commencement of entrepreneurship and the market process" (p. 115).

Earlier, Alderson (1965) also rejected the notion of homogenous demand. Alderson argued that it is artificial to link firms together just because they produce similar products, since firms can actually be serving quite different markets. Thus, analysis should be shifted to how individual firms create a *differential advantage* in their pursuit of markets. Unlike the model of perfect competition, firms can rarely be sure what price is "right" or what product offering is "correct." These discontinuities and the definition of market niches to secure profits leave room for entrepreneurial activity.

In private markets, suppliers try to restrict competition by maintaining control over information, excluding others from the data necessary to profit in a market. Entrepreneurs glean some new piece of information from the environment and then bet on the future based on their insight. However, once this information becomes public, the entrepreneur loses the competitive edge and entrepreneurial profits are bid away. For example, in the process of arbitrage, the entrepreneur sees a discontinuity in the market. Acting on this insight, the entrepreneur enters into a series of profitable transactions. But as the entrepreneur succeeds, the insight becomes more widely known and competitors enter the field, ultimately driving down the entrepreneur's profits. Over time, the entrepreneur's innovation becomes a more-or-less standardized product, yielding only market rates of return.

In the world of applied business studies, Michael Porter identified four stages by which to analyze the life cycle of products: introduction, growth, maturity, and decline. Each stage has associated with it different implications for buyers, product development, marketing, and competition (Porter 1980: 158–161). And each stage has different implications for entrepreneurship. While Porter notes that there are problems in the specific concept of product life cycles, industry evolution is driven by a series of dynamic processes. One of the most important of these processes is learning by buyers. For Porter, products tend to become more like commodities over time as buyers become more sophisticated. This in turn tends to *reduce* product differention over time.

Similarly, over time many markets are characterized by reduction in uncertainty as technologies are tested, buyers are identified, the potential size of markets clarified, and successful strategies are imitated while poor strategies are abandoned. The reduction of uncertainty may lead to new entrants into the market—more risk averse actors can now enter the market, increasing the competition the original entrepreneurs faced. Finally, diffusion of proprietary knowledge can also occur over time, and may be especially fast in the absence of patent protection or other barriers built on proprietary knowledge or specialized technology.

Theoretical problems emerge when the concepts of private information and product differentiation are carried over to the public sector. What, if any, private information can public sector entrepreneurs monopolize? The very nature of public entrepreneurship often requires that at critical times (especially during elections) a political entrepreneur *must* share information with the public, without being able to protect the rate at which it disseminates to competing politicians. In order to raise capital, the private sector entrepreneur may have to share insights with others. But this process of revelation is protected by patent laws, franchising agreements, etc. In the public sector, there is no similar legal protection on sharing information. And while policy entrepreneurs may emphasize the benefits of their proposals and try to hide the negative aspects (Arnold 1990), the public sector entrepreneur must inevitably disclose more information than the private entrepreneur. In large part, this is because a critical task for the private sector entrepreneur is to raise capital—and capital is controlled by a small number of individuals or institutions.

In contrast, most public sector entrepreneurs need votes or support in public opinion to succeed.[7] Building and maintaining a political coalition is critical to the success of a political entrepreneur and revealing information and ideas is central to this coalition process (Doig and Hargrove 1987).[8] Indeed, ambitious political entrepreneurs may seek to have their innovations imitated elsewhere, to develop a broader reputation and to increase the rewards of their entrepreneurial activities.

ASSUMPTION: EASY ENTRY AND EXIT

The fourth critical aspect of the neoclassical model that we examine is the assumption that competitors can easily enter into or exit from specific markets. In fact, the recent development of the theory of "contestable markets" (see Baumol, Panzar, and Willig 1982) has been based largely on the ability of firms to move in and out of markets with minimal cost. When entry and exit are easy, competitors can move quickly to take "above normal" profits away from those who were able to earn them. Thus, strategic competitors must try to erect barriers to entry to protect their profits from those who, by their entry, would reduce them to "normal" levels.

In his analysis of private market competition, Porter (1980) suggests several sources of barriers to entry, including: economies of scale; product differentiation (such as brand identification, customer loyalty stemming from past advertising or customer service); capital requirements; switching costs; access to distribution channels; and cost disadvantages independent of economies of scale (proprietary product technology, favorable access to raw materials, favorable location, or government policies).

Thus, in private markets entrepreneurs try to create entry barriers to earn "excess," or above-normal, profits. Political science has developed a literature on entry barriers that shows a similar process occurs in political markets. Incumbent politicians use many strategies to restrict competition, especially by limiting the ability of challengers to enter political contests. Most of the tools that incumbents use are designed to diminish the number and quality of candidates that might otherwise emerge to challenge the incumbent. Of particular importance may be the ability of incumbents to advance the interests of their constituents by manipulating bureaucratic services and by controlling the flow of legislation constituents and contributors need (Fiorina 1977; Tullock 1965; Parker 1991). The increasing use of personal contact as a form of political advertising also increases the entry barriers challengers face, especially since much of this contacting is subsidized by the government (Parker 1986; Fenno 1978; Cain et al. 1987). While the use of the congressional franking privilege is the most often cited advantage of political office holders, local government leaders also use the more limited perks of their office to send newsletters to constituents and to dominate local news coverage.

In the arena of local government, entry barriers may also be embedded in the "constitutional rules" that structure local political economies (Oakerson and Parks 1988). Rules governing the incorporation of new communities, the annexation of existing ones, and the types of services local government must supply all affect the range of competition local government officials face and the opportunities for entrepreneurial activity (Burns 1991). The degree of fragmentation and diversity in service offerings in the local area can also affect the incentives and actions of incumbent politicians and the potential for entrepreneurial activity (Schneider 1989).

The manipulation of entry barriers to limit challenges to incumbents has been most widely studied in congressional elections, but the effort to protect political incumbency occurs at all levels of government. How local political entrepreneurs overcome existing entry barriers and the extent to which they then try to erect new ones to protect their newly attained positions is a critical dimension of a theory of entrepreneurship in local government.

Exit barriers are perhaps less well understood, but are important to the theory of contestable markets. If large amounts of sunk costs are involved and "hit and run" entry is not possible, the decision calculus of competitors changes, and markets lose their contestable nature. Even if entry is easy, but it leaves new entrants stuck in a market for awhile after incumbents have reacted to them, difficult exit from the market may act to deter entry in the first place.

ASSUMPTION: EQUILIBRIUM/DISEQUILIBRIUM

The fifth and final assumption that we analyze is that of equilibrium in markets. Many of the issues explored above ultimately trace back to the fundamental concept of equilibrium that underlies so much of economic analysis. In this section, we show how the very conception of equilibrium in economics may limit the role for entrepreneurs. But more importantly, we show that many political scientists believe that as a discipline, political science should be more concerned with *disequilibrium* rather than equilibrium.

Many scholars argue that neoclassical economics defines equilibrium as a *state* or condition of "perfect competition." In contrast, the Austrian economists argue that we should be more concerned with the *process* of reaching that equilibrium. According to Kirzner, viewing equilibrium as a state rather than a process makes the concept static rather than dynamic. Further, this mainstream conception of equilibrium has forced entrepreneurship out of their models: "[the] neoclassical approach has . . . squeezed the real-world entrepreneur back into the neoclassical full-equilibrium box" (Kirzner 1985: 8–9).

And once we shift our focus away from dynamic change, entrepreneurs become irrelevant to neoclassical economics (Reekie 1984: 9). Austrian-school economists view change over time as a critical dimension of economics that they argue is often neglected in neoclassical work. For Austrians, "human action is not 'preprogrammed.' Learning occurs, tastes and technologies change, exogenous variables are continuously imparting new shocks to the system" (Reekie 1984: 33). From this perspective, fewer market parameters are fixed than in most neoclassical models. And entrepreneurs both generate the shocks to the system (cf. Schumpeter) and act to take advantage of the changes that accompany such shocks. The concern for change over time and disequilibrium has important implications for the study of politics.

Entrepreneurs and Equilibrium

In the Austrian tradition, entrepreneurs have greater independence of action and market outcomes are less predetermined than in neoclassical economics. However, in both the neoclassical and the Austrian schools of thought, the relationship between entrepreneurs and equilibrium is central.

On one hand, entrepreneurs can be viewed as seizing opportunities in the market to move it toward equilibrium. This essentially is the role entrepreneurs play in neoclassical economics. But Austrians are divided over the relationship between entrepreneurs and equilibrium.

While Kirzner's entrepreneur is defined by an "alertness to disequilibrium" and independently injects new elements into markets, ultimately for Kirzner "the changes the entrepreneur initiates are always toward the hypothetical state of equilibrium" (Kirzner 1973: 73). In contrast stands Schumpeter's idea of creative destruction (1942; also see Shackle 1972). For Schumpeter, entrepreneurial activity is most likely to emerge when a market is approaching equilibrium. In this evolving situation, the successful entrepreneur engages in a series of innovations that move the market first toward disequilibrium and then ultimately to a new market arrangement that is more profitable for the entrepreneur. Schumpeter's entrepreneur engages in creative destruction tearing apart existing political-economic arrangements in order to create new ones.

For Schumpeter, the entrepreneur stands to profit from the successful introduction of new ideas or policies into a market that appears stable to others. After the disruption caused by the innovation, a new stability may emerge. But for Schumpeter, as the market absorbs the last round of innovations to approach equilibrium, the potential for entrepreneurial profits from innovation increases, giving rise to yet a new generation of entrepreneurs.

Disequilibrium in Political Systems

With the renewed interest in institutions propelled by social choice theories in the last decade, political scientists have also begun to explore the relationship between entrepreneurs, innovation, and equilibrium. Since the concept of equilibrium is at the core of so much economic analysis, the extent to which entrepreneurs move private markets toward equilibrium or disequilibrium is theoretically critical for their enterprise. But the concept of equilibrium is also important in the study of entrepreneurs in *political* markets.

Much of the recent analysis of political equilibrium can be traced to the work of William Riker and his argument that political situations are normally characterized by an underlying *disequilibrium* of tastes and that stable equilibria in politics are rare. Riker argues:

> We know from Arrow's theorem that cycles cannot be avoided by any fair system . . . [and] that other methods of voting (e.g., positional methods like plurality voting and approval voting and point counting or electoral methods like proportional representation which are intended to make minorities win) are subject to disequilibria, manipulation, agenda control, etc. in much the same way as majority rule. It seems fairly safe to conjecture, therefore, that equilibria are as rare and fragile as is majority rule. And this rarity and fragility are doubtless as much features of systems based upon coopted committees as of those based on popular election. . . . What we have learned from the study of these alternative systems is thus: Disequilibrium, or the potential that the status quo be upset, is the characteristic feature of politics. . . . There are no fundamental equilibria to predict. (1980: 443)

Riker's contention is built upon and supported by a large and growing number of experimental and formal analyses that have severely restricted the conditions under which equilibrium can be expected. For example, Plott (1967) showed that for a large family of preference profiles, a simple majority equilibrium does not exist. Work by McKelvey (1976, 1979), Schofield (1978, 1983, 1984), and McKelvey and Schofield (1987) established that if equilibrium does not exist, then agendas can lead to almost any outcome (see Austen-Smith 1983 for a review of this work). Yet despite these abstract proofs, stable "equilibrium" outcomes are empirically observable despite the underlying dynamics of instability. This presents a conundrum for political scientists that has turned scholarship toward the study of institutions. Shepsle (1979) was among the first to show how institutions can induce stable outcomes despite the forces pushing toward disequilibrium. For Shepsle:

> [T]he relationship between social choices and individual values is a mediated one. Standing between the individual bundle of tastes and the . . . available social choices are institutions—frameworks of rules, procedures, and arrangements—that prescribe and constrain the set of choosing agents, the manner in which their preferences may be revealed, the alternatives over which preferences may be expressed, the order in which such expressions occur, and generally the way in which business is conducted. (1986: 51–52)

This argument underlies the concept of "structure-induced equilibrium"—that institutions can induce equilibria where, absent these arrangements, no equilibria exist. In a similar vein, using field studies exploring the use of common property resources, Ostrom (1990) shows how a wide variety of societal arrangements can overcome strong inherent tendencies toward disequilibrium driven by conflicts in tastes and strategies.

The idea of structure-induced equilibrium provides a line of argument that addresses a critical part of the equilibrium/disequilibrium conundrum. But this makes Riker's argument linking politicians and equilibrium an even more central issue that must be addressed in any theory of entrepreneurship. For Riker, while equilibrium may appear in political arrangements at any given point in time, such an equilibrium is inherently unstable. This presents openings for Riker's heresthetician—an entrepreneurial political leader who "probes until he finds some new alternative, some new dimension that strikes a spark in the preferences of others" (Riker, 1986: 64). Riker argues that through agenda control, strategic behavior, and, most importantly, the introduction of new policy dimensions to political debate, the heresthetician can break up structure-induced and maintained equilibria to create new and more profitable political outcomes. Further, Riker argues that when institutions stand in the way of rational individuals, individuals will act to change the institution: "insofar as a constitutional system supplies an outcome that is not the same as outcomes that might have been obtained from simple majority rule in the system without [institutions] . . . losers are likely to change the [institutions] . . . in the hope of winning on another day. . . . If institutions are congealed tastes and if tastes lack equilibria, then so do institutions, except for short-run events" (1980: 445).

Thus, while Shepsle stresses structure-induced equilibria to explain stability, Riker's heresthetician resembles Schumpeter's entrepreneur: both engage in creative destruction tearing apart existing political-economic arrangements in order to create new ones. Like Schumpeter's entrepreneur, Riker's heresthetician stands to profit from the successful introduction of new ideas or policies into a market that to others appears stable. After the disruption caused by the innovation, a new stability may emerge. But Riker believes that lurking behind this new stability is still the fundamental disequilibrium of taste that can then be exploited by the next generation of entrepreneurial politicians. Similarly, for Schumpeter, as the market absorbs the last round of innovations to approach equilibrium, the potential for entrepreneurial profits increases, giving rise to yet a new generation of entrepreneurs. Empirically, the outcome of innovations pushed by Schumpeter's entrepreneur or by Riker's heresthetician may thus resemble a *punctuated equilibrium*, a process in which institutions are characterized by long periods of stability punctuated by short bursts of rapid change (Krasner 1982).

North (1990: 90) argues that "such discontinuous change has some features in common with discontinuous evolutionary change (characterized in demographic theory as punctuated equilibrium), but perhaps its most striking feature is that it is seldom as discontinuous as it appears on the surface." For North, while formal rules may be changed quickly, a subtext of informal constraints remain, which makes the change less pronounced. The most recent work on political change based on the concept of punctuated equilibria shows that at times change is more deeply experienced than articulated by North, but does confirm North's observation that informal norms can survive radical realignments of interests.

Punctuated Equilibria: Baumgartner and Jones

In their study of *Agendas and Instability in American Politics*, Baumgartner and Jones (1993) build on Riker's theoretical argument, specifically employing the concept of punctuated equilibria. Their work balances theoretical development with a series of detailed case studies showing how disequilibrium in policy systems can be produced with greater frequency than theories of incremental change or theories of equilibrium would allow.

Baumgartner and Jones ascribe punctuated equilibrium to the nature of any social system in which (quoting Simon): "the environment makes parallel demands on the system, but the system can respond only serially" (Simon 1977: 157). That is, the system is grappling with a large number of issues, but its leaders can attend to issues only one at a time, becoming an information and attention bottleneck. Just what and how issues capture the attention of these decision makers becomes critical. But the result is intermittent performance, characterized by "lurching" and "lulls."

Paralleling the dialogue between Riker and Shepsle, Baumgartner and Jones begin with the supposition that political systems are never in general equilibrium. But this does not mean that there is perpetual chaos. Structure-induced equilibrium and the definition of issues processed by those institutional structures create some stability. However, this stability can be ephemeral:

> The tight connection between institution and idea provides powerful support for the prevailing distribution of political advantage. But this stability cannot provide general equilibrium, because a change in issue definition can lead to destabilization and rapid change away from the old point of stability. This happens when issues are redefined to bring in new participants. Similarly a change in institutional rules of standing or of jurisdiction can rupture an old equilibrium. (1993: 16)

Baumgartner and Jones argue that no single overarching equilibrium is possible in American politics. However, policy subsystems are often institutionalized as structure-induced equilibria in which a prevailing *policy understanding* predominates. Disaggregated decision systems are viewed as linked to institutionally defined structure-induced equilibria: by disaggregating policy decisions, those who control decisions also share values. For Baumgartner and Jones, the role of ideas (or "ideology") is critically important to the maintenance of the status quo. First, a definable institutional structure must exist to limit access to the policy process (a form of entry barrier). Equally important, a powerful supporting idea is associated with this institutional arrangement. Image and rhetoric communicate and reinforce the link between this ideology and core political values.

But the generation of *new ideas* makes many policy subsystems unstable in the long run. Policy entrepreneurs need not change the opinions of their adversaries (a process that Riker defines as rhetoric). Rather, as new ideas begin to take hold, different policy makers and institutions suddenly become mobilized and begin to claim jurisdiction over issues that had not interested them. This expansion of interest swamps the existing status quo, and stability is punctuated with periods of volatile change.

Baumgartner and Jones's analysis rests on the argument that structure-induced equilibria are fundamentally unstable, because entrepreneurial political leaders will eventually find leverage points to upset the status quo. Those excluded from the policy subsystem constitute "slack resources" that can be mobilized by policy entrepreneurs. And mobilization typically occurs through a redefinition of the prevailing policy image.

The destruction of these policy monopolies is almost always associated with a change in the intensities of interest as new actors become concerned with a particular question. For Baumgartner and Jones, this mobilization is typically driven by a new understanding of the nature of the policies involved. This is the introduction of new dimensions stressed by Riker as an element of heresthetics.

Baumgartner and Jones argue that the manipulation of policy images and the shopping around for institutional venues interact to drive punctuated equilibria in politics. These are concrete manifestations of the entrepreneurial instincts so common in American politics (see, e.g., Aberbach, Putnam, and Rockman 1981: 231) and are manifestations of the strategies used by Riker's herestheticians.

Baumgartner and Jones reject cyclical theories of politics in favor of the idea of punctuated equilibria. The institutional changes that are created in the policy process need not bear resemblance to those that existed a generation or two earlier because change is driven by a fresh definition of political issues. "A punctuated equilibrium model of the political system differs dramatically from the type of dynamic equilibrium model implicit in any discussion of cycles . . . new issue definitions are more important sources of change than the action-reaction model of cycles. As such, an evolutionary model is more relevant to politics than is the regularity implied by a theory of cycles" (1993: 245–246).

From this perspective entrepreneurs play a critical role in politics, providing the energy and the new issues that cause dynamic change in the system and tear apart old equilibria. The focus on equilibrium and disequilibrium delineate possibilities for entrepreneurial behavior that can emerge once we relax the restrictive assumptions of the neoclassical models of markets. A less than fully competitive number of suppliers, incomplete and asymmetric information, heterogenous policy ideas, entry barriers, and disequilibrium all interact to create multiple opportunities for entrepreneurs in government.

THE STUDY OF POLITICAL ENTREPRENEURS

Neoclassical economics limited the role of entrepreneurs. However, as the study of markets progressed and as the intellectual and analytic tools available for their study developed, the assumptions of the market model that limited the role of entrepreneurs were identified and relaxed. As a result, the role of strategic entrepreneurial behavior as an independent factor in the functioning of markets is now becoming established. The approach to entrepreneurship found in the other social sciences, including political science, was never as analytically constrained as in economics. However, much of the work in these other disciplines was fixated on the seemingly unique and idiosyncratic behavior of entrepreneurs. In turn, and unfortunately, much of the present social scientific work on entrepreneurship focuses on the actions of a limited number of "exceptional" individuals. In this approach, biography is the tool of choice.[9] Such studies, because they emphasize the uniqueness of the subject, cannot be cumulative.

In contrast, we argue that political entrepreneurship must be approached through systematic attempts to develop a theory of entrepreneurship and that any theory of entrepreneurship must be tested empirically. In the next chapters, we analyze in more detail what entrepreneurs do and the supply and demand conditions that can be associated with the emergence of entrepreneurs.

CHAPTER 3.

The Functions of Political Entrepreneurs in the Local Market for Public Goods

ENTREPRENEURS are found in domains other than the world of private markets. However, scholars who have looked beyond the private market tend to use the concept of entrepreneurship as a loose metaphor rather than as a tightly developed analytic concept. These scholars provide only implicit justification for using the term "entrepreneur," often focusing on just one or two specific actions (such as spotting gaps in policy domains and brokering deals; risking political capital; or creating new coalitions—see, for example, King 1988; Kingdon 1984; Smith 1991), and no sustained effort is made to clarify the extent to which entrepreneurship in the public sector is really analogous to entrepreneurship in the private sector.

Scholars who have compared the public and the private sectors usually focus on questions of management, seeking to identify differences between the environment in which public and private managers operate. The focal point of this management-oriented research differs from our own concern for entrepreneurial behavior, but that debate helps identify some of the differences that structure the behavior of entrepreneurs in different sectors. In the classic statement, Wallace Sayre argued that the public and private management are "fundamentally alike in all unimportant respects" (as quoted in Allison 1982: 184). However, since Sayre's work, scholars have argued that the differences are narrowing. Partly this convergence is associated with the ongoing progressive reforms in American bureaucracy, many of which are obsessed with making government run more like a business (Downs and Larkey 1986; Knott and Miller 1987; Osborne and Gaebler 1992).

Arguments distinguishing public and private management identify both external and internal factors. Most scholars agree that the external constraints on public managers are different than those on private managers, and that they are more difficult to deal with (Allison 1982). This difficulty emerges in part because political institutions often introduce more than one principal to which managers must respond (Moe 1984). But Bower (1983) and others note that American business firms are increasingly subject to political scrutiny and that management in both sectors has a "political face."

There is greater disagreement about differences on internal issues. Some authors suggest that managers in both sectors face essentially the same types of principal/agent problem, a problem that is not necessarily resolved by the presence of external competitors or a bottom-line measure of profit making. Others argue that the constraints of civil service personnel rules and the inability to motivate subordinates with the retention of residual profits makes public management different and much more difficult. Wilson (1989) specifically argues that the inability to reallocate factors of production, especially personnel, the inability to retain profits, and the need to serve goals given by multiple principals make public management different (and more difficult) than private sector management.

Casson (1982: 351), who agrees that there are important differences between public and private entrepreneurs, nonetheless presents a definition of the function of entrepreneurs he believes is essentially "institution-free" (p. 348). We begin with Casson's approach. We believe that, despite obvious differences in the locus of their activities and the nature of their goals, to a considerable degree all entrepreneurs perform particular functions and, in order to do so, share certain characteristics. However, as our argument develops, we add institutional complexity and texture to our argument and show how public sector entrepreneurs (including ones operating in the local market for public goods) face tasks and problems that are different from the problems private sector entrepreneurs face.

We begin by arguing that *all* entrepreneurs perform three functions. First and foremost, entrepreneurs discover unfulfilled needs and select appropriate prescriptions for how those needs may be met—that is, they are alert to opportunities. Second, as they seize these opportunities, entrepreneurs bear the reputational, emotional and, frequently, the financial risk involved in pursuing a course of action with uncertain consequences. Finally, in pursuing these actions, entrepreneurs must assemble and coordinate teams or networks of individuals and organizations that have the talents and resources necessary to undertake change.

DISCOVERING AND FRAMING OPPORTUNITIES

Discovering unfulfilled needs in areas of social and political activity is not necessarily difficult. But selecting the appropriate ways to satisfy those needs often requires exceptional insight. Entrepreneurs must not only define what the unfulfilled needs are, but they must be able to recognize the contextual nature of those needs and establish feasible approaches to meet them.

Needs may be well established or they may be latent. There is considerable evidence that social problems are neither objective nor the specific result of identifiable societal conditions; rather, they exist primarily in terms of how they are defined and how they are conceived of by society (Hilgartner and Bosk 1988). Hence, a clever entrepreneur may seize opportunities to transform social perceptions. In this process, the entrepreneur generates "needs," and then meets those needs with specific responses. If an entrepreneur "frames" the situation appropriately, the entrepreneur can couple the problem with a solution, replace the status quo with a new institutional arrangement, and collect above normal profits (Kingdon 1984; Baumgartner and Jones 1993; on the effects of framing, see Kahneman and Tversky 1979).

Many scholars have documented how political entrepreneurs can frame issues in such a way that their preferred alternatives are transformed into government policy. For instance, Nelson (1984) shows how child abuse was transformed from a private matter to an issue of public concern. Baumgartner and Jones (1993) present similar evidence from several policy domains. Kingdon (1984), McCraw (1984), and Derthick and Quirk (1985) all document how economists in the 1970s, whose analysis had led them to conclude that regulation of the transportation industry served the interests of the providers at the expense of the general public, carefully developed their case for deregulation and achieved considerable success. Derthick and Quirk (1985: 246) suggest that "advice tends to be efficacious insofar as it has two general attributes, which are by no means necessarily related: substantive soundness—the quality and persuasiveness of analysis as judged by the criteria of analysts themselves; and political adaptiveness—the ability of analysis to meet further criteria inherent in the political process and to underlie rhetoric that meets those criteria."[1] At a more theoretic level, Riker (1986: 34) notes that policy success can indeed be built on rhetoric that persuades indifferent people to accept the new idea. But success can also be achieved by introducing a new viewpoint (or dimension) into an ongoing policy debate. For Riker, the defining tool of the heresthetician is the ability to redefine political situations to gain majority support for his or her most preferred alternative. This "ability to shift from moment to moment, poking and pushing the world until it favors the heresthetician's cause" is "the height of the heresthetician's art."

The Importance of Entrepreneurs in Framing Issues

While there are numerous anecdotes and case studies that show how entrepreneurs frame choices, we believe that entrepreneurial action in discovering opportunities and framing issues can be summarized by a limited set of activities that can be displayed along a continuum (see

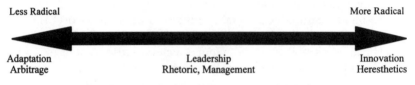

Fig. 3.1. The Range of Entrepreneurial Actions

figure 3.1). On the right side of the continuum are those entrepreneurial activities that have the capacity to produce the most radical change in the markets or arenas in which entrepreneurs operate. On the left side are entrepreneurial activities associated with change that is less radical, but still more than incremental. Figure 3.1 identifies three "generic" categories of entrepreneurial activity: (1) innovation, which can be closely tied to the use of heresthetic strategies; (2) leadership, which includes elements of rhetoric and management; and (3) arbitrage, which includes the adaptation of innovation across different markets or arenas. In figures 3.1.1, 3.1.2, and 3.1.3, we illustrate the operations of entrepreneurs in each of these three classes of activity.

Innovation

The entrepreneurial activity that produces the most radical change and carries the highest risk is innovation. Innovation requires the most extreme form of entrepreneurial alertness and discovery. True innovation is rare but necessary for the development of new products, new services, and new institutional arrangements. In private markets, innovation usually connotes the invention of products or services consumers will want, anticipating consumers' changing preferences. As Reekie puts it: "the entrepreneur notes, ex ante, that the preferences of consumers are different tomorrow from what they are today. He notes, ex ante, that the production techniques of firms are not the same tomorrow as they are today. The Misesian entrepreneur foresees these changes in the market data. It is this foresight which is important" (1984: 50).

In the public sector, entrepreneurs sometimes must create new institutional forms to pursue their vision of the future. For example, Robert Moses achieved many of his goals by creating public authorities with considerable fiscal autonomy. Other public entrepreneurs experiment with combinations of existing or new institutions, creating special districts or other public organizations, getting new enabling legislation passed, and creating interorganizational arrangements to produce new goods and services. Other public entrepreneurs may specialize in creating ways to inspire citizens and government workers to pursue the new product or service the entrepreneur favors. But perhaps the most far-reaching op-

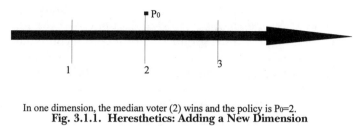

Quantity of services considered in one dimension

In one dimension, the median voter (2) wins and the policy is $P_0=2$.
**Fig. 3.1.1. Heresthetics: Adding a New Dimension
to a Policy Debate**

portunities for public entrepreneurs lie in the fact that they can innovate by developing a new idea or policy and use these innovations to challenge existing institutional arrangements and the terms of ongoing debates.

It is here that Riker's idea of the heresthetic becomes an important component of entrepreneurship. Figure 3.1.1 shows how a heresthetician can add a new dimension to a debate to achieve a preferred outcome on an issue. Suppose three groups (1, 2, and 3) in a town support

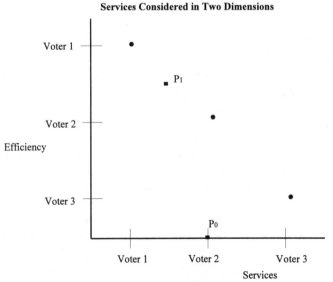

Services Considered in Two Dimensions

**Fig. 3.1.1 (cont.). Heresthetics: Adding a New Dimension
to a Policy Debate**

An entrepreneur can introduce a new dimension to the debate, relating to the efficiency of services that are delivered. The entrepreneur now offers policy P_1. This policy is closer in Euclidean space to both voter 1 and voter 2, who now combine to outvote the previous outcome, P_0.

different levels of services to be provided in the community. The median group, 2, will win when this issue is framed in only one dimension. The policy will be P_0. Seeing an opportunity to disrupt that policy outcome, an entrepreneur, representing group 1, introduces a second dimension into the debate. This new dimension, for example, may focus on the *efficiency* of the service provision, regardless of the *level* of services provided. Given the preferences illustrated here, the entrepreneur can offer policy P_1. Because this new policy proposal is closer in Euclidian space to their ideal point, members of group 2 will find the new alternative preferable to policy P_0. Groups 1 and 2 now outvote group 3 to adopt outcome P_1. This new policy is closer to the goals of the entrepreneur. Granted, this will require skill by the entrepreneur and it may not be easy to maintain the policy at P_1 as members of groups 2 and 3 react strategically themselves.

The critical point is that, unlike other actors in the policy process, entrepreneurs see opportunities to frame issues in a manner that increases the likelihood of building support for their goals. But note that because introducing this new dimension can be perceived as a radical change to existing policy discussions, the entrepreneur pushing for true innovation stands a high chance of failure.

Leadership

Consider next the leadership dimension of entrepreneurship, which we place in the middle of the continuum. Leadership, and the rhetorical and management skills associated with it, is an entrepreneurial activity that leads to less radical change than true innovation, but which can still transform markets or organizations.

Rhetoric is the ability to change the preferences of political actors (Riker 1986) or to tap "latent demand" that others do not even sense (Wilson 1980: 366). But political entrepreneurs not only may be able to anticipate change in electoral preferences, they may also be able to shape that change. The ability to change preferences is far more critical in politics than in economics, where consumer tastes are often taken as fixed and change in preferences is taken as exogenous to the market. Baumgartner and Jones (1993) emphasize the critical role of rhetoric in mobilizing new actors in policy debates. These newly mobilized actors help transform political debates and policy arrangements. Thus, rhetoric has an "external" dimension, as entrepreneurs try to build or mobilize political coalitions.

Because so much economic and political activity takes place in the context of large organizations, such as firms or government bureaucracies, rhetorical skills coupled with managerial skills are an important

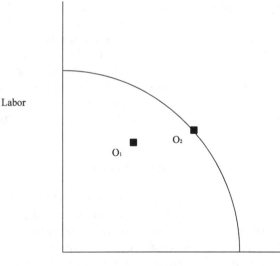

Fig. 3.1.2. Government Production Frontier
The entrepreneur's management (more capital, less
labor) and rhetoric skills increase output from O_1 to O_2.
The production frontier maps a series of data points
that form an "envelope" of what the most efficient
communities are able to achieve.

combination for an entrepreneur. Rhetoric can inspire and motivate
workers and thus attack internal collective action problems within hierarchical organizations. By instilling a sense of mission, some managers
are able to get more outputs than others with the same set of inputs
(Barnard 1938; Selznick 1957; Wilson 1989; Miller 1992; Brehm and
Gates 1993).

Providing such leadership may be even more important for political
entrepreneurs because slack is more likely in public bureaucratic systems. Typically, public bureaucracies are not subject to the discipline
imposed by market competitiveness and tangible individual rewards for
excellent performance are highly restricted. Thus, public sector entrepreneurs face constraints in improving production and performance. In
contrast to private managers, managerial public entrepreneurs cannot
lawfully retain profits, cannot allocate factors of production according to
their own preferences, and must serve some goals not of their own
choice (Wilson 1989). Yet, some entrepreneurs successfully overcome
such constraints and achieve more with less. Exceptional performance in
this arena constitutes what we call entrepreneurial leadership.

Figure 3.1.2 illustrates entrepreneurial leadership. In this example, a
manager combines two inputs, say labor and capital equipment, to pro-

duce a certain level of output. Technology will define the limits on the production function. But not all bureaucratic organizations will be achieving at maximum output—that is, they will not all be on the production possibility frontier. Those "below" the frontier are not combining inputs as efficiently as technologically possible. Only innovation can move output beyond this frontier, but skilled entrepreneurs can use rhetoric and management skills to move their agencies closer to the maximum efficiency on the frontier of the production possibility curve.

Arbitrage/Adaptation

On the extreme left of the entrepreneurial spectrum illustrated in figure 3.1 are less radically transforming and less risky activities, including adaptation and arbitrage. True innovation is rare, but many ideas are borrowed and adapted from somewhere else to a new setting. Policy ideas are often recycled, transformed, and adapted to fit the changing preferences of the electorate (Kingdon 1984; Sanger and Levin 1992). This type of alertness to the value of transferring innovation can yield profits to an entrepreneur.

Arbitrage is an entrepreneurial function that involves recognizing that gains can be made by linking streams of previously separate market activities. Many economic markets are related to one another in ways that are not perceived by "ordinary" market participants. Potential gains from trade across these markets are available to those who see and act upon the linkages. Entrepreneurs in this formulation are special kinds of middlemen (Reekie 1984: 46) who see and exploit potential gains from trade of which others are not aware. A policy entrepreneur may see a problem in one policy domain and suggest a solution to that problem which he or she draws from another policy domain. Both Kingdon (1984) and King (1988) note that policy entrepreneurs tend to be "policy generalists" who take great interest in developments outside of their own narrow area of present interest. Therefore, they are always looking for potential solutions that they may adapt into their area of current policy interest.

Arbitrage thus involves "gap-filling" in the circulation of policy ideas. But this same gap-filling function is also evident in the coalition-building process central to politics. Entrepreneurs can identify common interests across disparate groups and gain from linking these groups into a new larger coalition. Kingdon (1984: 192) combines the arbitrage of ideas with coalition building linking people and groups together in a process he calls brokering: "Entrepreneurs advocate their policies, as in the softening up process in the policy stream, but they also act as brokers, negotiating among people and making the critical couplings."

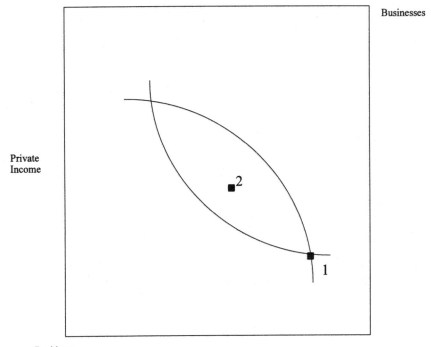

Fig. 3.1.3. Arbitrage as an Entrepreneurial Activity

The entrepreneur brokers a deal to create a business improvement district, moving the outcome from point 1 to point 2.

Both groups (residents and businesses) are better off. Businesses pay more taxes, but get more of the public services they need to improve the infrastructure in their district. Residents get to keep more of their income, while the services they did not want are now diverted to the business district.

This arbitrage activity is demonstrated using an Edgeworth box, which shows gains from trade between two parties. When both parties can move to a higher indifference curve (representing higher utility), they will do so. However, for a variety of reasons, parties may be off the "contract curve" at a point that is not Pareto efficient. The entrepreneur reaps some of the gains from trade by showing both parties how they can be made better off.

Using an Edgeworth box, in figure 3.1.3 we illustrate how an entrepreneur can use arbitrage to improve outcomes for different groups of actors and profit at the same time. Suppose the tax and service situation in a community is at point 1. Businesses want more services but residential taxpayers are reluctant to pay more taxes.

An entrepreneur observes that a business improvement district financed by local firms rather than by residents would provide infrastructure needed by firms presently in the community and improve the ability of the community to attract new economic activity. The entrepreneur is alert to the fact that both businesses and residents would prefer to be at point 2 rather than at point 1 (both would then be on a higher indifference curve of utility).[2] In this situation, businesses will pay more taxes but also get more services from the business improvement district, while residents will pay fewer taxes and see services shifted to the business district. However, residents do not really want to pay for these business-related services. The entrepreneur profits by identifying this opportunity and by negotiating a "deal" between residents and business. The entrepreneur discovers that both groups can be made better off, and by creating a new institutional arrangement (a business improvement district) that improves the situation of both groups, the entrepreneur establishes a reputation that can be used for future political activities.

Discovering opportunities and framing choices is the essential ingredient of entrepreneurial activity. We also identify risk bearing and team creation as two other ingredients of entrepreneurship. We review the risk-taking dimension next and then enter into a much more extensive analysis of the organizational dimension of entrepreneurship.

RISK BEARING

While there is considerable dispute about the degree to which entrepreneurs are defined by their willingness to engage in risky behavior, we argue that all entrepreneurs, no matter what the locus of their activities, must bear the reputational and emotional risks involved in pursuing a course of action with uncertain consequences. In addition, there is usually some degree of financial risk involved in entrepreneurial activity (if for no other reason than there are opportunity costs in pursuing any course of action). In the public sector, many actors in positions to act entrepreneurially face risks if their innovations are rejected. City managers, for example, are not tenured and can be dismissed if their policy fails. Elected officials often derive great pleasure, as well as income, from their jobs, and failure may return them to less exciting and rewarding careers.

The assignment of risk is an important element in entrepreneurial activity. Entrepreneurs often assume the role of residual claimant within a nexus of contracts because their efforts are so difficult to monitor. That is, while entrepreneurs agree to pay all other factors of production a predetermined and fixed amount, they themselves bear most of the risk of variable income attendant on the success of the entrepreneur's actions. Barzel (1987) argues that this willingness to assume risk is taken primarily to signal the entrepreneur's commitment to the activity, reducing the costs of monitoring the behavior of the entrepreneur. By assuming this risk in the short term, the entrepreneur may be rewarded in the longer term by being able to obtain other needed resources at favorable rates (see also Casson 1982: 93).

Similarly, to protect their personal reputation and to encourage continued output from employees, entrepreneurs will honor commitments even if short-term profits can be made by violating them (Demsetz 1988; also see Granovetter 1985). Further, just as individual investors diversify their portfolio of stocks to spread risks, so public entrepreneurs may seek to diversify their stock of human capital and policy proposals. Typically, at any one time, we expect the entrepreneur's portfolio to be heavily weighted toward activities that are low risk. But being able to make a return out of delivering on these low-risk activities may provide entrepreneurs with the leverage to take significantly higher risks in one or two other areas of activity.

That entrepreneurs risk their reputations and their own capital is seen in the realm of electoral politics. But on a less public level, many public entrepreneurs also frequently place their reputations and careers in jeopardy in pursuit of their goals. In her study of the consideration of school choice as a policy alternative in Minnesota, King (1988: 441) suggests that policy entrepreneurs pushing the most innovative options in the area of school choice risked the loss of access to those in formal positions of authority, the loss of political capital (in the form of respect and credibility) accrued through years of public service and a history of policy "victories," and the potential loss of their resource bases to support further policy activities.

While all three of the entrepreneurial activities discussed earlier (innovation, management, and arbitrage) carry with them varying degrees of risk, risk is proportional to the degree to which the actions the entrepreneur proposes differ from the status quo. Thus, innovation carries the greatest risk, while arbitrage is less risky by far.

THE IMPORTANCE OF ORGANIZATION

Besides discovering unfulfilled needs, selecting ways to meet them, and bearing reputational and financial risks, entrepreneurs play a critical role in assembling the human, physical, and financial resources into the groups that are necessary to achieve the entrepreneur's goals. We begin by reviewing the challenges the "logic of collective action" presents for public entrepreneurs, focusing on a critical dimension of the entrepreneurial process—how does the entrepreneur create and maintain an organization?

Every entrepreneur is faced with the problem of assembling resources controlled by others, motivating members of a "team" to work efficiently, and minimizing tendencies to shirk. The public entrepreneur faces a set of organizational problems that can be more severe than those facing the private sector entrepreneur, because compared to his or her private sector counterpart, the public entrepreneur almost always must create and maintain a collective base to mount and sustain challenges to the existing arrangements in the political marketplace. In particular, the political entrepreneur must face squarely the collective action problem, often with a set of tools that are more limited than those the private sector entrepreneur controls.[3]

We explore some of the theoretical propositions developed in the literature on the logic of collective action. Our ultimate goal is to fit these general propositions into our concept of the entrepreneur in the local market for public goods.[4]

"THE" COLLECTIVE ACTION PROBLEM

Recent concern for the collective action problem inevitably traces back to the "logic" of collective action developed by Mancur Olson (1965). Olson defines the problem succinctly: "unless the number of individuals is quite small, or unless there is coercion or some other special device to make individuals act in their common interest, *rational, self-interested individuals will not act to achieve their common or group interests*" (Olson 1965: 2; emphasis in original). Following Olson's work, the formation of groups to pursue collective benefits could no longer be treated as a given (as it was for earlier political scientists like Bentley or Truman)—instead it became a problem central to the analysis of politics.

Despite myriad refinements, the collective action problem has a clear central theme: Olson's "logic" leads directly to the fact that rational individuals have strong incentives to free ride on the efforts of others (e.g., Bendor and Mookherjee 1987; Dawes et al. 1986). The logic of collective action is linked to the tragedy of the commons and the prisoner's dilemma, because at the heart of each is the free-rider problem (Ostrom 1990).

Olson's logic creates barriers to the organization of collective action— barriers that the political entrepreneur must face and overcome in order to organize a political base to pursue new policy goals. Olson's analysis produced two propositions that have been extensively researched and hotly debated. The conditions identified in these propositions affect the ability of entrepreneurs to confront and "solve" the problem of collective action. The first subtheme of Olson's work is the size principle. The second is Olson's "by-product theory," which leads directly to the concern for the role of material and nonmaterial incentives in creating and maintaining groups. Both propositions provide windows through which entrepreneurs can be introduced into the theory of collective action.

The Size Principle

Basically, the size principle has been interpreted as implying that small groups are more likely to organize for collective action. According to Hardin (1982), this seemingly straightforward interpretation of the size principle is not accurate. Hardin argues that the analysis of the size principle has been muddled because there are almost irresistible pressures to merge two different typologies of groups that Olson proposed.[5]

The first of Olson's typologies distinguishes between "privileged groups" and "latent groups." This distinction is based directly on the logic of collective action and is related to the benefit/cost ratio members of groups experience. Groups are privileged if a sufficient number of individuals in the group experience a positive benefit/cost ratio and therefore contribute to the collective good (of course, there are numerous conditions ceteris paribus).

Olson's second typology is based on the actual number of individuals in a group—groups can be small, intermediate, or large. The smaller the group, the lower the organization costs and, hence, the greater the probability that the group will form and be maintained (Olson 1965: 45).

These two typologies get mixed together because *empirical* observation tells us that small groups are more likely to be able to organize successfully to pursue collective actions—empirically they are more likely to be "privileged" than are intermediate or (even more so) large groups (again ceteris paribus).

While the tendency to merge these two typologies has created numerous theoretical problems, there are important insights into the problems of collective action and the entrepreneurial process that can be derived. Small groups are propelled toward their privileged status because they are likely to be more homogeneous in social attributes, reducing transaction and information costs. Small groups can also more easily solve the free-rider problem because they can better monitor the conformity of individual group members to group activities. Monitoring is harder in larger, more heterogeneous groups (Taylor 1982; Dawes et al. 1986; Ostrom 1990).

Privileged groups can also exist if there is at least one group member who is willing to provide the public good, either by unilaterally bearing the cost of provision or by reducing the costs other potential members of a collective group may bear. Making subsidies available to help overcome the obstacles to collective action is a critical role for the entrepreneur. The entrepreneur can reduce information and communications costs, making it easier for challenging groups to organize to contest the status quo (e.g., Frohlich and Oppenheimer 1990).

Walker (1991) stresses the importance of patrons in subsidizing group formation and group maintenance, because the process of political mobilization often is driven from the top down, rather than the bottom up. Many groups are created at the instigation of leaders of corporations or government agencies, who recruit entrepreneurs and sponsor their efforts in order to achieve specific policy goals. According to Walker, the spread of groups during the 1960s and 1970s was a direct result of the increase in the number and types of patrons who could subsidize nascent groups.

These factors all affect the privileged status of different groups, by helping entrepreneurs create privileged groups out of latent ones. In turn, they give entrepreneurs resources to mount challenges to the status quo in a variety of issue domains, significantly broadening the range of issues represented by interest groups.

The size principle and the concept of privilege have a direct bearing on our concern for local government. When used in the analysis of American politics, the term "privileged" often refers to the primacy of capital (see, e.g., Lindblom 1977; Elkin 1985). This privileged position is even more pronounced in local politics because of the mobility of capital and the reliance of local governments on property tax resources. The size principle increases even further the importance of local business: Given the homogeneity of interests and the small number of business actors involved in local communities, business interests may constitute a "privileged" group in Olson's sense as well as in Lindblom's. In short, in the local market for public goods, the two forms of "privilege" reinforce one another. This bias creates barriers to public entrepreneurs who might seek to challenge the probusiness orientation underlying many local policies; at the same time this privileged status may present other probusiness entrepreneurs easy solutions to the collective action problem.

In this light, consider the potential role of neighborhood organizations as a basis for a political entrepreneur in local government. First of all, neighborhoods may meet the small-size criterion and they certainly tend to be more homogeneous than entire cities or geographic regions. Moreover, neighborhoods are usually characterized by frequent interpersonal interactions between members. Further, to the extent that neighborhoods respond to threats, such as a proposal for a new highway exchange or a new shopping mall, their shared interests are enhanced.

These conditions will enhance the likelihood that neighborhood groups can become privileged, easing the problem of collective action.

We argue in chapter 7 that neighborhood groups do in fact perform two critical functions in the careers of some entrepreneurs. First, because they are small and relatively homogeneous, neighborhoods provide a relatively "cheap" base for collective action for policy proposals. Second, they provide a critical mechanism for "certifying" the credentials of an entrepreneur, thereby allowing an entrepreneur to move from a small neighborhood group to a larger collectivity, which may be necessary to implement broader political changes. Success at the neighborhood level certifies the individual entrepreneur's reputation as an honest broker who can be trusted.

The By-product Theory and the Incentives That Entrepreneurs Control

Olson's "by-product theory" highlights the range of incentives that entrepreneurs can manipulate to solve the collective action problem. In his analysis, Olson identified two classes of benefits that derive from group membership: collective benefits and selective ones. Collective benefits are received jointly and excluding noncontributors is thus difficult. In turn, collective benefits may be insufficient inducements for overcoming the free-rider problem. Selective incentives are targeted on contributors and can thus motivate membership activity. In this way, selective incentives help solve the collective action problem by improving the benefit/cost ratio of collective action. The by-product theory suggests a loose coupling of collective and selective incentives: Members are tied to a group by selective incentives and leaders are therefore free to fashion policy positions without fear of losing members. This component of Olson's and related work highlights the importance of selective incentives, which entrepreneurs can manipulate, and it explains why entrepreneurs may have considerable autonomy in their policy actions once they have identified and mobilized a group.[6]

But the by-product theory has been hotly debated. From our perspective, the most important aspect of this debate on the by-product theory is the finding that entrepreneurs can manipulate a whole range of nonmaterial incentives to overcome problems of collective action.

Olson's analysis emphasizes the importance of economic incentives in decisions about whether or not to contribute to collective action. But nonmonetary incentives can also drive the decision of individuals to join a group and to participate in collective action. The effort in political science to identify these other incentives traces to the work of Wilson (1973) and Clark and Wilson (1961).

Wilson argues that in addition to material rewards, other nonmaterial benefits include solidary benefits, such as fun and friendship that derive from working with others, and purposive (or "expressive") benefits, which are intangible rewards from contributing to the group because of its stated goals.[7] Entrepreneurs can use both of these goods to overcome collective action problems.

The Nonmaterial Incentives Available to Entrepreneurs

The policy goals an entrepreneur advocates may themselves be important in mobilizing people to join and contribute to an organization (Hansen 1985). The collective goals of the organization are a unique asset which can play a central role in the marketing strategy of the public entrepreneur. These collective benefits give entrepreneurs a differentiated product that distinguishes the organizations they create from private firms offering only material benefits—that is, the entrepreneur offers policy benefits that may be coupled with competitively priced services. While selective benefits can induce more people to join the interest group, the political benefits cause consumers to *choose* to join a particular group rather than simply purchasing the selective benefit in the private market. Thus, collective goals must be central to the public entrepreneur's marketing strategy.

But from our perspective, even more important is that the entrepreneur can change the beliefs that people have about their importance in an organization. By using a variety of interpersonal skills and by forcefully advocating a compelling vision of the future, a successful entrepreneur can make people feel engaged in a "team" production process. The successful entrepreneur can make people feel that their contributions are important. To the extent an entrepreneur can do this, individual incentives to free ride (or shirk) fall, monitoring costs are reduced, and groups can be motivated into "privileged" status.

As Taylor (1987: 25) argues, "the entrepreneur is *not* just 'an innovator with selective incentives,' or someone who simply concentrates or centralizes resources. What is perhaps more characteristic of public entrepreneurship is its role in changing beliefs—beliefs about the public good itself, about what others have done and are likely to do and about others' beliefs." Similarly, according to Rothenberg (1988), during the "experiential search" process he believes characterizes the retention decision members of organizations must make, members gather information about the benefits/costs of membership and then decide whether or not to remain in the organization.

Entrepreneurs can affect this search process. Most importantly, Rothenberg argues that many individuals overestimate their own importance and are induced to remain members of the organization even though an "objective" benefit/cost analysis might induce them to quit or free ride. The entrepreneur encourages people to think that their contribution is critical, thus affecting decisions about membership and contribution.

In short, the entrepreneur can provide selective incentives to help overcome the collective action problem. And the entrepreneur can also provide the required monitoring to make conditional cooperation possible. But the entrepreneur can also manipulate collective benefits and psychological variables to change the benefit/cost ratio members and potential members of groups experience.

This manipulation of the benefits and costs of cooperative behavior is at the core of the analysis of entrepreneurs developed in transaction cost economics, a perspective that is beginning to reshape the study of political leadership. Transaction cost economics shows that the problems facing the private sector entrepreneur trying to organize a joint production processes overlap with the problems of public entrepreneurs trying to solve collective action problems.

Transaction Costs, Contracting, and the Role of the Entrepreneurs

Alchian and Demsetz (1972: 783) define the entrepreneur by the right: "(1) to be a residual claimant; (2) to observe input behavior; (3) to be the central party common to all contracts with inputs; (4) to alter the membership of the team; and (5) to sell these rights." While the team-building task of the private sector entrepreneur is assisted by the ability to control the nature of the "nexus of contracts" that constitute firmlike coordination, contracting is by no means a panacea for overcoming problems associated with free riding and shirking (Jensen and Meckling 1976; Demsetz 1988). Much of Williamson's (1985) analysis concerns the ability of various contractual arrangements to align the incentives of different actors in various contexts. Yet, contracts can never be fully specified and contracting parties must frequently rely on reputation, trust, and other nonmaterial incentives.

The private sector entrepreneur improves coordination, communication, and commitment within firmlike contractual arrangements. Commitment to the continuing association of the same people makes it easier for firm-specific and person-specific information to be accumulated and reduces monitoring costs.

Entrepreneurs with exceptional interpersonal and team-building skills will have an edge in assembling teams in an efficient manner. Often, such teams are expected to be short term because of the uncertainty inherent in the task at hand. The entrepreneur, then, must find ways of establishing good communication flows and high levels of commitment while at the same time retaining the organizational flexibility that is required to make the most of changing opportunities. Often the successful execution of these tasks is a direct result of the interpersonal skills of the entrepreneur.

Bianco and Bates (1990) use a transaction costs perspective in their game theoretic approach to the study of political leadership. They argue that there are two known solutions to the collective action problem. The first is iteration and retaliation. Here the game theoretic results are clear and compelling: In many forms of repeated games it is possible to sustain cooperation, and free riding is no longer *the* dominant strategy[8] (also see Axelrod 1981; Hardin 1982; Taylor 1987; Bendor and Mookherjee 1987). Alternately, leaders or entrepreneurs can also produce cooperative outcomes. The entrepreneur has a central role in negotiating contracts, monitoring conformance with these contracts, and enforcing penalties for defection. But central to the analysis developed by Bianco and Bates is the importance of the capabilities of the leader. One component of capability is "reputation"—the beliefs followers have about the leader's trustworthiness and the ability to enforce contracts.

Beyond carefully tailoring contractual arrangements, entrepreneurs improve the productivity of teams and firms by creating appropriate psychological expectations, demonstrating trustworthiness, and paying attention to corporate culture. Miller (1992) specifically argues that no matter how smart the manipulation of material incentives, psychic rewards and internal commitment/motivation are always more effective tools for getting cooperative behavior (see also Kreps 1990; Brehm and Gates 1993).

In short, for the successful entrepreneur solidary and expressive benefits are as important as material ones. And the most successful entrepreneurs efficiently reduce free riding (and associated monitoring costs) by manipulating nonmaterial incentives to create a teamlike atmosphere where individuals feel they are important to the achievement of the goals and objectives of the group.

Networks and Entrepreneurs

Another solution to the organizational dilemmas that entrepreneurs face is to make use of networks of firms and individuals. According to Powell (1991: 271), networks are "lighter on their feet" than hierarchies. In networks, transactions occur neither through discrete exchanges nor by administrative fiat, but through individuals engaged in reciprocal, mutually supportive actions. Again, like any productive relationship, networks take considerable effort to establish and sustain, and this may constrain both partners' ability to adapt to changing circumstances. A mutual orientation—knowledge which the parties assume each has about the other and upon which they draw in communication and problem solving—is established (Granovetter 1985).

Networks are particularly apt for circumstances in which there is need for efficient, reliable information (Powell 1991: 272). This makes networks particularly useful to entrepreneurs, who must make the best use of available information if they are to achieve high profits (see chapter 9). But given the loose nature of the relationships established in networks, trust is vital, just as it is to the maintenance of high-performance firmlike arrangements.

For public entrepreneurs, developing trust in relationships and support networks is vital to the pursuit of their goals. According to King (1988: 461), the impact of entrepreneurs in the domain of school choice was enhanced by their networks and relationships. These networks "magnified the individuals' influence, pooled resources, and created synergism." Public entrepreneurs capitalize on their connections, to establish and maintain supportive networks within their particular policy communities (Kingdon 1984: 189–190; Heclo 1978; Smith 1991). Of course, these actions are not simply taken for purely instrumental reasons. Kingdon (1984: 130) suggests that much of the reward of public entrepreneurship comes from "solidary" incentives, and from simply playing the policy game: "They enjoy advocacy, they enjoy being at or near the set of power, they enjoy being part of the action. They make calls, they have lunch, write memos, and draft proposals, probably for the other [e.g., instrumental] reasons we have discussed . . . but in combination with the simple pleasure they take in participating." This evidence suggests there are many pecuniary and nonpecuniary rewards for entrepreneurs who are adept at assembling and coordinating teams, or becoming skilled networkers, no matter what their locus of activities.

Entrepreneurs thus are defined by their vision of opportunities, their willingness to take risks to pursue their vision of the future, and their ability to organize collective groups or teams to pursue that vision. The public entrepreneur brings these talents and related proposals to the public marketplace. That market is structured by supply and demand factors, which we consider in the next chapter.

We now turn to the empirical portions of the book, in which we test these theoretical concepts of entrepreneurship in local politics and policy.

_____ **Part Two** _____

THE DECISION CALCULUS
OF THE PUBLIC ENTREPRENEUR

IN THIS PART, we explore empirically the conditions that affect the probability that an entrepreneur will emerge in different communities in our sample of suburbs. We focus on the interplay between the structural conditions of elections, organizations, budgets, and fiscal resources in a community and how these factors create opportunities and resources that can entice a potential entrepreneur into the public sector.

The costs of entrepreneurship are partly a function of the collective action problem entrepreneurs face and the ease with which this problem can be solved. Similarly, the benefits (or "profits") entrepreneurs reap are a function of the rewards available from winning office. Some of the rewards are obviously psychic—related to the joys of creating new policies and affecting change. In this part, we show that as the costs of public entrepreneurship drop and the benefits rise, entrepreneurs are more likely to be found. We lay out this argument in chapter 4, in which we construct a model of the market for entrepreneurs.

In this part, we begin our empirical analysis. We root this analysis and the identification of the benefits and costs of entrepreneurship firmly in the local market for public goods, in which local services are delivered by multiple municipal governments in packages that are paid for using a revenue system in which local property taxes are central. In this arena, governments are in competition with one another and use their taxes and services to lure desirable households and business firms.

In chapter 5, we present an analysis of the factors that affect the emergence of all the public entrepreneurs we identified. In chapters 6 and 7, we focus on one of the central areas of policy and politics that preoccupy the suburban governments we study—the politics of growth. We show how the changing conditions of suburban growth and changing public attitudes toward growth produce opportunities for political entrepreneurs. In chapter 8, we turn to the study of managerial entrepreneurs. In many cities, city managers play an important role in developing new ideas and energizing local bureaucracies.

In each of these chapters we seek to identify empirically those factors that increase the likelihood of finding an entrepreneur.

CHAPTER 4.

The Market for Entrepreneurs

JAMES Q. WILSON (1989) argued that it is impossible to model the process through which public entrepreneurs emerge—that the emergence of entrepreneurs is a rare event driven by idiosyncratic factors that are hard to identify and to model systematically. Earlier, Shackle (1972) questioned the ability of social scientists to model the emergence of private sector entrepreneurs. In fact, few economists have examined the factors associated with the supply and demand of private sector entrepreneurs. The most notable exception is Casson (1982), who developed an explicit model of the market for private sector entrepreneurs. In this chapter, we develop components of a theory of a market for public sector entrepreneurs and we use this market approach to identify systematic regularities in both the supply of and the demand for entrepreneurs.

In chapter 2, we showed that when key assumptions of the neoclassical model of the market are relaxed, the *potential* for entrepreneurship increases. Our theoretical analysis in that chapter and as we developed it further in chapter 3 identified various conditions that *may* affect the probability that an entrepreneur will emerge in the local market for public goods. While strong theory is obviously a sine qua non of good research, ultimately, we confront what we consider to be another fundamental task of social science: testing strong theoretical propositions with empirical data. Our work is informed by the need to specify the conditions affecting entrepreneurship developed in our theory in a manner that can be empirically tested. Thus, our *theory* identifies the factors that *may* affect entrepreneurship, our *empirical work* is designed to identify those factors that *actually* have an effect. As we move from the domain of theoretical exploration to the domain of empirical work, we specify more exactly the institutional milieux in which local entrepreneurs operate, examining how the forces structuring the supply and demand for public entrepreneurs are embedded in the local market for public goods.

By specifically identifying the factors that shape the emergence of public entrepreneurs, we return to a fundamental task proposed by Kirzner (1979: 12): we seek to identify the "institutional settings that are most conducive to opportunity discovery." Our research focus resonates with North's argument that the "kinds of information and knowledge required by the entrepreneur are in good part a consequence of a particular institutional context" (North 1990: 77).

MODELING THE MARKET FOR ENTREPRENEURS

We begin with a simple market model for entrepreneurs, building on the work of Casson (1982). While Casson was specifically concerned with modeling entrepreneurship in the private market, his analysis identifies challenges facing all entrepreneurs, including ones in the public sector. For Casson, entrepreneurs are motivated by profit, but the extent of entrepreneurial profits is driven by the nature of the goods the entrepreneur is introducing and the ability of the entrepreneur to control competition in the market. In the private sector patent protection, monopoly control over information or raw materials, and the creation of entry barriers all increase the potential for entrepreneurial profits. But entrepreneurs in the public sector face additional problems rooted in the institutional milieux in which they operate.

In particular, public goods have many characteristics that present problems that fundamentally affect both the supply of and the demand for public entrepreneurs. More specifically, the nature of public goods, especially the well-known problems of exclusion and free riding, increases the challenges public sector entrepreneurs face. Exclusion is based on the custody of physical property and the right of the "owner" to defend such property from others who have not paid for its use. Maintaining the custody of public goods is difficult and laws governing the assignment of property rights for public goods are far murkier than for private goods. Moreover, the pecuniary profits public entrepreneurs can gain are limited. These factors reduce the potential reward for public sector entrepreneurship. Moreover, many of the mechanisms private sector entrepreneurs use to make new markets and to protect their profits have very few public sector counterparts (Casson 1982: 150–152).

The identification of these types of institutional factors that affect the supply and demand conditions in the market for public sector entrepreneurs is theoretically critical. In the following sections, we add contextual details of the institutional setting public sector entrepreneurs face, with the goal of ultimately applying the analysis to the study of entrepreneurship in the local market for public goods.

CASSON'S MARKET FOR ENTREPRENEURS

Casson argues that entrepreneurs specialize in "judgmental decisions" that coordinate scarce resources to produce and manage change (1982: 23). Coordination problems emerge even in the most smoothly functioning markets because information is never perfect and uncertainty and transaction costs always make coordination costly and incomplete. Opportunities emerge as new information becomes available, making the existing allocation of resources inefficient. Thus, change is inevitable, leading to opportunities for entrepreneurs to bet on alternative futures that yield higher profits.

Casson builds on these fundamentals to develop the idea of a market for entrepreneurs. In general terms, Casson's market brings together judgmental decisions and entrepreneurs (p. 327). In so doing, this market performs three important functions. First, on the demand side, the market identifies judgmental decisions—that is, it identifies opportunities where some discontinuity in the market exists and where some entrepreneurial profits are possible. Second, the market identifies entrepreneurs and helps determine the supply of entrepreneurs. And third, the market matches potential entrepreneurs to judgmental decisions: that is, it establishes a clearing mechanism reconciling the demand for entrepreneurs with their supply. Thus, the "good" being exchanged in this market is a matching service that ultimately leads to the "correct" entrepreneurial decision being made. But since the entrepreneurial decision is a highly heterogeneous good, the matching process is always difficult and the market itself may be subject to uncertainty and inefficiencies. In Casson's analysis, one of the key factors in the market for entrepreneurs is the difficulty in screening out "false" entrepreneurs, individuals who seek the rewards of entrepreneurship without making the proper judgments. Most markets, especially markets for complex goods, rely on intermediation to facilitate adjustments and, most importantly, to screen for quality. But since entrepreneurship is not a routine "commodity," screening for the quality of entrepreneurs is obviously difficult. We argue later that the reputation of entrepreneurs, garnered through repeated political "trades," is a critical factor in the local market for public goods (on the issue of reputation see Williamson 1975; Barzel 1987; and Bianco and Bates 1990). But first we look at the fundamentals of the demand for and the supply of entrepreneurs in this market.

THE DEMAND FOR ENTREPRENEURS

The demand for entrepreneurs can be viewed as fundamentally a function of two factors: (1) the rate of change in the technologies of production and (2) the rate of change in the preferences of consumers. More rapid change in either of these factors leads to a greater demand for entrepreneurs to present new alternatives. These factors are often exogenous to a given market: technology or tastes change for reasons outside a specific market and the entrepreneur seizes the emerging oppor-

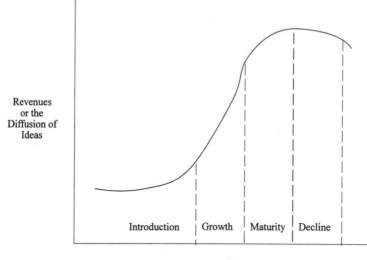

Time

Fig. 4.1. The S-Curve of Innovation

tunities. But in many markets, entrepreneurs do not wait for change. Instead they introduce new products and create new preferences—that is, the demand for entrepreneurial products can be endogenous to a given market.

While change can occur in a variety of ways and at a variety of speeds, one widely used model of industry and product evolution is the simple "S-curve."[1] Porter's model of the S-curve is typical. As illustrated in figure 4.1, Porter divides the product life cycle into four critical stages: introduction, growth, maturity, and decline (Porter 1980).[2] The concept of product life cycles has been used by economists to study private sector goods, and the S-curve has also been widely used by political scientists in the study of the diffusion of public policy innovations (see, e.g., Gray 1973; Menzel and Feller 1977; Clark 1985; Glick and Hays 1991).[3] In the following discussion, we use the term "products" to encompass concrete goods and services as well as more abstract political ideas and policy proposals.

Each stage of product development presents different implications for competition and for the opportunities presented to potential entrepreneurs. At the introduction stage of product development, truly creative entrepreneurs experiment with alternate and sometimes radically different visions of the future. The risks here are high and the probabilities of success low. But those entrepreneurs whose vision of the future is correct and who "bet" on the right alternative stand to earn the highest entrepreneurial profits. Individuals who innovate and create at this stage may constitute the "dynamic few"—the focal point that motivates so many biographical studies of entrepreneurs.

At the growth stage of product innovation, the likelihood of entrepreneurial activity is at its maximum. At this stage, the opportunities for entrepreneurial profits through arbitrage and the adoption of innovation are greatest. As products enter this rapid growth phase, discontinuities emerge as some sectors of the market get "stuck" in old patterns of demand or consumption, while new alternative goods or policies transform other sectors. Entrepreneurs can seize the opportunities inherent in these discontinuities. During the growth stage, an entrepreneur need not invent a new product but can reap profits by introducing an innovation to a new market segment. Given the geographical segmentation and the corresponding spatial nature of local politics, this growth stage is particularly important in studying the local market for public goods. For example, an entrepreneur can advocate the introduction of a policy found in a neighboring community into his or her own community and gain credit for the diffusion of an already established idea.

As policies and products move through the growth phase, opportunities for entrepreneurship begin to disappear. For example, as the diffusion of innovation unfolds, buyers become more acquainted with these (now not so new) products. The products themselves become more standardized. Markets that trade homogeneous commodities have fewer possibilities of product differentiation and entrepreneurial activities. In short, over time, the "commoditization" of goods, services, and ideas reduces entrepreneurial profits.

Porter has identified other changes that further restrict entrepreneurial profits at this stage of the product life cycle. As products mature and become more like commodities, technologies are tested, potential buyers are identified, and the size of markets established. Successful strategies are imitated and poor strategies abandoned. The resulting reduction of uncertainty leads new entrants into the market and risk averse actors enter the market to compete with earlier, more entrepreneurial entrants.

Entry barriers built on proprietary information and specialized technology tend to erode, as do barriers caused by shortages of qualified, specialized personnel. Porter argues that the rate of diffusion of proprietary technology depends on the particular industry: "The more complex the technology, the more specialized the required technical personnel, the greater the critical mass of research personnel required, or the greater the economies of scale in the research function, the slower proprietary technology will diffuse. When heavy capital requirements and economies of scale in R&D confront imitators, proprietary technology can provide a lasting mobility barrier" (1980: 173). In the local market for public goods, most of these barriers are low, allowing for rapid diffusion of new ideas and narrowing the window during which the local entrepreneur can maintain extraordinary profits from new ideas.

Finally, at the maturity stage, the profits from marketing the product are pushed down to "normal" market-level returns, and the opportunities for entrepreneurship continue to dwindle as the market approaches a state of equilibrium. For many products, a phase of decline occurs sometime later.

In Schumpeter's analysis, as markets approach these final stages of maturity and decline, a new burst of entrepreneurial activity can erupt as energetic individuals seeking higher profits than can be obtained within the existing arrangements create new markets and new products. This is Schumpeter's "creative destruction": existing products, ideas, markets, and the institutions based on them, are swept away by the next wave of entrepreneurs seeking opportunities for higher profits.

There are many variants of the S-curve used in analyzing the development and the diffusion of policy innovation. The relevant stages have been divided up in different ways. For example, Schon (1971) and Van de Ven (1986) argue that issues often develop after a disruptive event. In the next stage, solutions surface, policy networks galvanize, and debate occurs. Some ideas become legitimated and reach the "agenda." Ultimately, the idea becomes institutionalized: it is taken for granted and creates entry barriers against new and possible better ideas. Unfortunately, these models lose explanatory power at a critical stage, providing no answer to one of the most important questions: Why do some ideas reach the agenda and become legitimated while others do not? We believe that in many cases a successful entrepreneur can make the difference, by attracting support to the idea and giving it currency.[4]

Most important to our argument, however, is that the pattern of diffusion means that those entrepreneurs active in the early stages of diffusion of an innovative idea are most likely to bear greater risks, but they are also more likely to achieve higher rewards for success. In contrast, entrepreneurs entering the policy cycle later earn corresponding lower returns.

The Demand for Public Entrepreneurs

While there is a paucity of information about the demand for private sector entrepreneurs, the demand for public entrepreneurs has been studied even less. In perhaps the best-known work in political science that addresses the demand for new policies, Kingdon (1984) analyzes the role of entrepreneurs in discovering "policy windows" and in joining the multiple "streams" of the policy process. Once a window opens, policy entrepreneurs seize the resulting opportunities. The entrepreneur couples what Kingdon calls the problem stream and the political stream, in the process grafting the entrepreneur's policy idea (or "product") onto the resulting flow.

For Kingdon, demand is largely exogenous. Indeed, since Kingdon relies on a variant of Cohen, March, and Olsen's (1972) "garbage can" model, few elements of policy change are predictable. In contrast, we believe that the demand for public entrepreneurs can be understood using a more structured approach derived from a framework similar to that for private sector entrepreneurs. More rapid change in production technologies or in political preferences creates more demand for entrepreneurial policies, and thus, for public entrepreneurs.

In addition to responding to emerging changes in political preferences, public entrepreneurs can themselves be catalysts of change, leading and mobilizing demand, rather than simply following it. In chapter 2, we argued that entrepreneurs are primarily defined by their alertness to opportunity. If demand is obvious to many observers of a market, then an alert entrepreneur is not required to respond to such obvious demand—any politician can sense demand and the political support for new policy proposals. Risks in such a situation are low, and the returns from acting to satisfy such demand would also be low.

However, the nature and intensity of political demand is often not obvious. Tastes and political preferences, to the extent that they are well formed by most of the citizenry, are changing all the time (see, e.g., Stimson 1991). So too are objective economic and political circumstances. Entrepreneurs are alert to *latent* demand that is not fully formed or not yet well understood by others. Wilson (1980) uses this approach to define entrepreneurial politics, specifically in regulatory politics; but his argument is applicable to a broader range of policy arenas. For Wilson (1980: 370), an entrepreneur "takes advantage of a crisis or scandal . . . mobilizes latent political support . . . and uses the media to put opponents on the defensive by associating the preferred solution with widely shared values." In the context of the local market for public goods, a crisis might be engendered by high taxes, deteriorating services, or overly rapid growth. The entrepreneur senses an emerging demand from citizens to do *something* about the problem and then uses his or her entrepreneurial skills to change preferences.

This latent or anticipated demand approach to modeling entrepreneurial behavior has parallels in the political science literature on agenda setting. Cobb, Ross, and Ross (1976) suggest three models of agenda setting: "outside access," in which citizens are the major source of issues; a "mobilization model," in which politicians or bureaucrats seek to create the appearance of mass support for their policy; and "inside access," in which outside support is not critical and political insiders control the issue. Milward and Laird (1990) argue that entrepreneurs use one or more of these approaches to bring favored issues to the forefront of the policy agenda. Wilson's latent demand model of entrepreneurial politics combines elements of the first two models; entrepreneurs sense latent demand and they attempt to mobilize and to create not only the appearance of mass support, but also true mass support.

In the context of multiple local governments, many problems, ideas, and solutions are common to different communities. Solutions often come from the "bottom" and percolate upward, rather than from the top down (Osborne and Gaebler 1992). Entrepreneurs generate innovative local policies and, if these policies are popular and/or successful, the innovations are taken up by other politicians. This process has been modeled using the S-curve described previously. We model some of these conditions in our empirical analysis in the following chapters.

THE SUPPLY OF ENTREPRENEURS

The supply of entrepreneurs is determined by the size of the population of potential entrepreneurs, by the benefits and costs of engaging in entrepreneurial action, and by any economic, political, cultural, or religious barriers that limit their emergence. Thus, two classes of questions pertain to the study of the supply of entrepreneurs. First is the question of the size of the *potential* population of entrepreneurs. Second is the question of the factors that affect the rate at which these potential entrepreneurs are *converted* into actual entrepreneurs.

The range of issues under debate concerning the supply of entrepreneurs is as extensive as the agreement is small. For example, for Schumpeter entrepreneurial skills, like any other special trait, has a distribution in a given population that is "Gaussian—though more plausibly a skew-law" (1939: 99). However, Schumpeter did not have any empirical evidence to support this claim. Moreover, he did not address the underlying conditions that created his hypothesized distribution, although in his later work he did express concern that the supply of entrepreneurs was declining. On the conversion side, based on empirical historical evidence, Schumpeter argued that waves of entrepreneurship tend to clump together. But his theory did not explain why this empirical pattern occurs.

Schumpeter's failure to provide definitive answers to these theoretically important questions is not surprising—more than forty years after his seminal contributions, the debate still continues. As Livesay argues in his overview of the history of the study of entrepreneurship, after "an enormous expenditure of effort by the 'new economic historians' (as well as present-oriented economists) has produced a lot of debate, not much factual information, and little if anything in the way of satisfactory explanatory theory" (1982: 12). While Livesay was concerned mostly with the discipline of economics, in fact, there are diverse perspectives on the supply of entrepreneurs; many of these perspectives are driven by the boundaries and paradigms of different disciplines.

In the following discussion, we review briefly some of the most important perspectives on the underlying supply of entrepreneurship. The distinguishing characteristics of these works is how little agreement there is across studies of the supply of entrepreneurs.

The Psychology of the Entrepreneur

An entire genre of work has focused on the psychological and sociological characteristics of entrepreneurs. Max Weber, in his classic work on *The Protestant Ethic and the Spirit of Capitalism,* presented the first systematic attempt to identify the preconditions of modern entrepreneurship. Weber argued that the Protestant ethic provided a necessary but not sufficient condition for the rise of capitalism. One of the most important elements in the Protestant ethic that Weber identified was the shift in the attitude toward work. Under Calvinism work became the means of salvation, and success in this world became an indicator of success in the next. Moreover, Calvinism's emphasis on honesty transformed contracts and commerce, by reducing transaction costs and increasing certainty in the contractual dealings underlying any modern market. These mores allowed trust to be developed outside of kinship ties.

But Weber's concept of the Protestant ethic is disputed. Shapero and Sokol (1982: 75) argue that: "There is nothing in Protestantism which leads automatically to capitalism; its importance was rather that it undermined obstacles which the more rigid institutions and ceremonies of Catholicism imposed. The capitalist spirit is as old as history."

Despite such reservations, the study of the transaction costs of kinship, the importance of "modern" values, and various aspects of religious beliefs in propelling entrepreneurship form a continuing theme in the work of cultural anthropologists studying the economic transformation of the economies of less developed countries (see, e.g., the articles in Berger 1991).

Schumpeter also paid attention to the psychology of the entrepreneur. Schumpeter argued that the entrepreneur is driven by strong psychological needs, including the dream of creating a private kingdom, the will to conquer, and the inordinate joy of accomplishing tasks and creating new products, ideas, and institutions. A good deal of work exploring the psychology of entrepreneurial behavior has developed since Schumpeter (1942) and McClelland's (1961) work is the bedrock upon which most of the subsequent studies of the psychology of the entrepreneur has been built. McClelland's research is based on a link between entrepreneurial behavior and the need for achievement (termed "Nach"). Causally, in McClelland's work people with high needs are driven to become entrepreneurs.

Other psychological work (e.g., Rotter 1966; Brockhaus and Nord 1979) looked in more detail at the "locus of control" (that is, whether the outcome of events is perceived as being within or beyond personal control), risk-taking, problem-solving style, values, and other characteristics of entrepreneurs. Welsh and White (1981) summarized many of these studies to identify eleven personal characteristics that were needed for successfully launching a business venture. However, in an excellent review of this literature, Brockhaus and Horwitz conclude that from the viewpoint of psychology there is "no generic definition of the entrepreneur" (1986: 42).

In reviewing the literature on leadership, Van de Ven (1986) concluded that "no empirical evidence was found to support that there are a finite number of characteristics or traits of leaders and that these traits differentiate successful from unsuccessful leaders." Van de Ven further warned that the effort to identify the traits and personality traits of leaders was chimerical. Brockhaus and Horwitz (1986) believe that similar efforts to identify such traits in entrepreneurs are likely to fail.

McClelland's work is also criticized because it is not rooted in the historical or cultural milieux in which entrepreneurs operate (Gasse and d'Amboise 1981). Many sociologists and anthropologists stress the importance of the marginality of certain ethnic groups in encouraging entrepreneurship. The high rate of entrepreneurship among Jews is a longstanding empirical fact, often explained by their marginal position in so many of the societies in which they have located. More recently the overseas Chinese and Indians have joined the "club" of ethnic groups that supposedly support high levels of entrepreneurship. The conditions of their diaspora, and the resulting marginality, conditions similar to those experienced by Jews, are credited with creating a large potential population of entrepreneurs in these groups (see, e.g., Berger 1991). However, the number of ethnic groups that support disproportionate numbers of entrepreneurs is in fact so extensive as to dilute any reasonably sound theoretical argument. Shapero and Sokol (1982) list about a dozen ethnic groups with high rates of entrepreneurship, including Jews, Lebanese, Ibos, Parsis in India, Bataks in Indonesia, the Mendocinos in Argentina, the Cubans in Florida, and the "pied noires"—the displaced French colonists from Algeria, Tunisia, and Morocco. Not surprisingly, some economists have made forays into this debate. For example, Ronen argued that the supply of entrepreneurial talent is endogenous to the economic system and can be "stimulated by a climate that will ensure the entrepreneur's freedom to innovate, to choose his means, and most importantly, to reap his due reward" (1983: 3). Psychologists and cultural anthropologists have problems with this typical economic approach to entrepreneurship. Many anthropologists argue that the supply of entrepreneurs and especially the conversion process that turns potential entrepreneurs into actual ones is much more complex than the benefit/cost analysis underlying Ronen's approach.

For example, Berger (1991) argues that while economists view the supply of entrepreneurs as the product of market forces, "anthropologists, historians, psychologists, and sociologists emphasize in varying and often contradictory terms, the influence of noneconomic factors, such as social norms and beliefs, psychological motivations for achievement, the legitimacy of entrepreneurship, questions of social 'marginality,' and the 'internal fit' between any and all of these and the rise of modern entrepreneurship" (pp. 3–4).

From this cultural anthropological perspective, entrepreneurship is rooted in a cultural process and the very innovativeness that defines entrepreneurship can only be understood in the context of culturally imposed boundary conditions that define newness and propriety. Lavoie develops this idea:

> The entrepreneur is typically pictured as a loner bucking the crowd, a maverick who sees things differently from everybody else. This view contains an element of truth, of course, in that the entrepreneur comes upon a new reading of his situation that may be qualitatively different from the readings other have been able to make. But his ability to read new things into a situation is not primarily due to his separateness from others but, indeed, to his higher degree of sensitivity to what others are looking for." (1991: 49; also see Landa 1991)

In this light, social and cultural networks, social institutions, legitimacy, and the distribution of psychological characteristics supporting innovation are critically important in driving the conversion of potential entrepreneurial energies into actual entrepreneurship.[5] Berger argues that it is culture that determines the way in which entrepreneurial energies are channeled: "In one type of culture, individuals high on the entrepreneurial motivation scale may become successful businessmen, and in another type, they may invent a new twist in the ritual of shamanism" (1991: 21).[6]

While Mark Granovetter, a sociologist, hasn't extended his analysis of the embeddedness of entrepreneurs in social networks to include the option of shamanism, he has articulated a well-received version of the effects of networks on the conversion of potential to actual entrepreneurs. For Granovetter, "attempts at purposive action are embedded in concrete, ongoing systems of social relations" (1985: 487). Using the example of trust in business dealings and attempting to reinterpret Williamson's theory of transaction costs from a sociological perspective, Granovetter argues that "social relations between firms are more important, and authority within firms less so, in bringing order to economic life than is supposed in the markets and hierarchies line of thought" (p. 501).

Aldrich and Zimmer (1986) use this network perspective to help explain patterns of entrepreneurship. They conclude that "entrepreneurship is a social role, embedded in a social context. Investigators cannot treat entrepreneurs in isolation as autonomous decisionmakers or lump them together with others with similar social characteristics, without regard to context." Instead, they argue we should be concerned with "the effects of social networks in facilitating or inhibiting the activities of potential entrepreneurs" (p. 20).

Political scientists have not been drawn into these debates. In turn, very little work has been done identifying the conditions that define either the underlying supply of public entrepreneurs or the mobilization of potential public entrepreneurs into actual ones. We acknowledge the value of these inquiries by other social scientists, but we also see them as doing little to facilitate rigorous empirical testing. In our view, progress in developing theories of entrepreneurship can best be made by focusing on objectively verifiable regularities, such as the costs and benefits to entrepreneurship. We take this approach throughout the remainder of the book. However, in chapter 9, we do extend our analysis to consider aspects of the embeddedness/network argument.

THE BENEFITS AND COSTS OF PUBLIC ENTREPRENEURSHIP

Potential entrepreneurs have energies and talents they could invest in alternate spheres of activity. The rate at which they are attracted to the local *public environment* (as compared to some other domain such as private business) is a function of the costs they face in entering the public arena and the benefits they garner if they succeed as entrepreneurs. In our approach, public sector entrepreneurs compare their expected benefits (defined in terms of power, financial rewards, policy influence, or other rewards) to the expected cost of entrepreneurial activity (defined in terms of money, time, energy, and opportunity costs). This calculation ultimately informs the decision to allocate energies and resources to public sector activities or to invest these scarce resources in other domains.

The level of many of these costs and benefits is embodied in measurable facets of local government. For example, we argue that many of the costs facing public entrepreneurs are a function of the collective action problem and the ease with which this problem can be solved. In turn, the costs of solving the collective action problem in local government are a function of the institutional arrangements of that locality, in particular the structure of the local electoral system, which affects the costs of organizing a political base for entrepreneurial politics.

Similarly, the benefits (or "profits") entrepreneurs reap are a function, among other things, of the powers they can hold and resources they can control should they win elective office. More specifically, in local government, the tax base and the budgetary slack of their local community may be able to provide the opportunity for a successful entrepreneur to reallocate resources to achieve policy goals.

Limiting the Supply of Entrepreneurs: Barriers to Entry

Suppliers in any market have strong incentives to limit entrepreneurship. New entrepreneurs can disrupt existing business practices, challenge existing products with new ones, reduce profits, and drive current market participants into bankruptcy or other forms of exit. Even entrepreneurs develop strong incentives to limit the entry of other entrepreneurs into the market.

Casson's analysis shows the competitive threat to entrepreneurs from other entrepreneurs:

> [I]f two or more entrepreneurs compete to exploit the same opportunity, then normally neither of them will obtain any reward. . . . The reason why competition eliminates rewards is that the information exploited by the entrepreneur is an indivisible good. Once the information has been acquired, the additional cost involved in its exploitation is zero. Thus so long as a positive reward accrues to the information, it pays each entrepreneur to bid away from his competitors the resources required to exploit it. Consequently competition between entrepreneurs bids down the reward for information to zero. (1982: 109)

In short, existing suppliers have incentives to limit the entry of new entrepreneurs *and* even entrepreneurs have incentives to limit the entry of other entrepreneurs. This, according to Baumol (1968: 42), helps explain the fluctuating wavelike supply of entrepreneurs identified by Schumpeter. For Baumol, there are random outbursts of entrepreneurial activity that drive the economy away from stagnant equilibrium. However, as entrepreneurs become successful, opposition by losers emerges, and these losers in turn organize to impose restraints on entrepreneurial activity, mostly by erecting entry barriers to limit competition. In Baumol's analysis, institutional restraints on entrepreneurship are thus neither exogenous nor historical accidents. He argues that the very success of entrepreneurs stimulates the imposition of laws, rules, and regulations that constrain future entrepreneurial activity.

The Supply of Public Entrepreneurs

Perhaps most important for our analysis is that government institutions, rules, and regulations all affect the costs and benefits of public entrepreneurship. It is well known that private sector actors often seek public sector regulation to gain higher than market rates of returns or "rents" (Tullock 1967; Stigler 1971; Krueger 1974; Buchanan, Tollison, and Tullock 1980). Public sector actors can also pursue a rent-seeking strategy by erecting entry barriers to limit competition. Among the most important political entry barriers are the rules and regulations of elections (registration, timing, access to the ballot, etc.) that favor some groups over others. Entrepreneurs often shop between alternate institutional and political venues to find lower entry barriers (Baumgartner and Jones 1993). They sometimes even have to change the "rules of the game" in order to eliminate the entry barrier.

There are public sector parallels to other entry barriers private sector firms enact to limit competition. (Porter 1980 describes a whole range of these business strategies.) For example, private sector firms try to erect entry barriers by differentiating their product in terms of innovative features and by convincing consumers that these features are worth higher prices. Public entrepreneurs often stress their unique experiences, their concern or commitment, or some other personal quality. And certainly, the presumed uniqueness of the policy ideas the entrepreneur is advocating may be the defining characteristic of entrepreneurial politics.

Entry barriers are also related to the "switching costs" that consumers absorb as they change products. In the local market for public goods, these costs can be incurred if a community changes its politicians or its policies. Moving from established and well-known policies to new and innovative ones may maximize switching costs. Incumbent politicians facing challenges by entrepreneurial politicians often suggest that switching costs are high and that their own policies should be given more time to work. Entrepreneurial politicians may succeed in convincing the public that the added costs (often embodied as higher risk) associated with the new policies are worth paying for because of long-term gains and improved quality of life.

The importance of access to distribution networks is critical to success in the private market: success is often contingent on getting your products to consumers. Similarly, in the public sector access to citizens is critical, and this is done increasingly via the media. Politicians must get their ideas before legislators or bureaucrats, and, often more importantly, voters. Incumbent politicians at all levels have advantages in gaining access to citizens, for example, through mailings at government expense and the ability to get press coverage easily (Parker 1991).

The institutional structure of government in the metropolitan region may affect entry costs. In regions with fewer and hence larger governments, the costs of "advertising" innovative ideas and creating coalitions large enough to propel change are higher. The effects of the size of political units are better documented in the study of electoral systems, which have a very specific role in affecting entry barriers to political entrepreneurship in the local market for public goods. Local governments use two basic forms of representation: district systems versus at-large systems. Research demonstrates how these alternate electoral systems impose different costs on groups seeking access to the ballot and the policy-making process (see, e.g., Lineberry and Fowler 1967; Morgan and Pelissero 1981). We extend that line of analysis by showing that compared to district systems, at-large systems pose higher entry costs to political entrepreneurs. Entrepreneurial politicians operating in an at-large system must contact and attract a larger number of voters to challenge incumbents than they would face in a district election system. We show this relationship empirically in chapters 5 and 6; in figure 4.2 we illustrate it graphically.

Figure 4.2 shows the demand and supply curves for entrepreneurship in the local market for public goods. The flat part of the SS curve is, according to Casson, driven by the alternate wage rate—that is, there is some point on the axis labeled "expected rewards to entrepreneurial activity" below which entrepreneurial activity will not occur. This is similar to Porter's concept of the "entry deterring price."

Figure 4.2 presents two alternative paths for the supply curve after the rewards exceed the minimum level. Using the example of different elec-

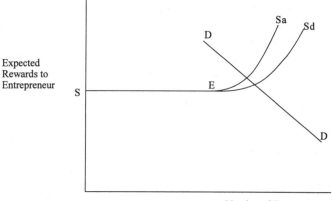

Fig. 4.2. The Supply of and the Demand for Entrepreneurs
The portion of the supply curve from S→E is below the reservation
or the entry deterring price, which is determined by opportunity
costs and any other expected costs of failed entrepreneurship.

   The SS'_d is the supply curve in a municipality with district elections, while SS'_a is the supply curve in a municipality with at-large
elections. For any given level of demand, the supply of entrepreneurs will be lower in the at-large city because of entry barriers and
the higher cost of mobilizing challenges to the status quo.

toral systems, SS_d represents the supply of entrepreneurs in a district
system and SS_a the supply of entrepreneurs in an at-large system. For any
given level of demand, the supply of entrepreneurs is higher in the district election system, because the costs of entrepreneurship are lower.
Any entry barrier that affects the costs of entrepreneurship will act in a
similar manner to reduce supply.

TESTING THE MODEL IN THE LOCAL MARKET
FOR PUBLIC GOODS

Thus far in this book, we have developed a theory of public entrepreneurship informed by theoretical discussions emerging from several social science disciplines. In particular, we have found economists' discussions of entrepreneurship to be most useful for helping us to think about
the process of public entrepreneurship. Creating strong social science
theory is difficult, but actually translating the concepts and propositions
of a theory into testable hypotheses is harder still. We are empirical so-

cial scientists and we believe that any theory must be put to empirical tests. This is the task we undertake in the rest of the book.

As we translate our theory into testable hypotheses, "slippage" inevitably occurs. For example, the most rigorous testing of our theory of public entrepreneurs would take our supply and demand framework and translate it into a model containing the precise identification and specification of the factors that define each function. These functions would then be estimated simultaneously. However, as our review of the literature shows, neither the supply- nor the demand side research identifies the indicators that should be included in either function. And, the variables that do appear in the analysis of the demand side (mostly from economics) do not even share the same disciplinary roots as the variables that most frequently appear in the supply-side literature (drawn mostly from sociology, cultural anthropology, and psychology).

Our modeling work, our empirical testing of our models, and our interpretation of our empirical results are all consistent with the theory of the supply and demand for public entrepreneurs that we have developed here. We are aware, of course, that our empirical work falls short of the ideal standards that could conceivably be achieved using a more elegant mathematical approach to testing an integrated model of the supply and demand of entrepreneurs. But we make no apology for that. Inevitably, if we are to make advances in our understanding of empirical reality, we must be prepared to make a trade-off in our modeling techniques between their methodological sophistication and their appropriateness, given the empirical data we have to work with. Consequently, in the empirical analysis that follows, we look at the emergence of entrepreneurs in local governments as a function of conditions found in three domains. First, we believe that some entrepreneurs are highly attentive to the changing demographic and economic conditions of communities. In particular, the changing racial composition of suburbia and differences in the rate and composition of growth provide opportunities for entrepreneurial activity (e.g., Eisinger 1988; Clarke 1990; Schneider and Teske 1993). Second, we believe that the service levels and taxes of local government is another domain that provides opportunities for entrepreneurship. Beginning in the 1970s, the entire fiscal and service environment of local government has been subjected to continued assaults from repeated recessions, declining levels of intergovernmental aid, and changing expectations about services and taxes. While some local entrepreneurs have linked social and fiscal issues (Clark and Ferguson 1983), most have treated these domains as separate "markets." Third, we believe that the responses of entrepreneurs to opportunities are affected by the nature of the political system and the costs and benefits that the political system imposes on potential entrepreneurs. Finally, given the highly decentralized nature of local government in the United States and the wide-ranging differences across metropolitan areas, we root our empirical analysis in the specific regional milieux which strongly structure the opportunities and policy tools available to the entrepreneur.

CHAPTER 5

The Emergence of Political Entrepreneurs

ALMOST SINCE its incorporation in 1920, the village of Malverne, Long Island was controlled by the Independent Party. And Cathy Hunt was sick and tired of it. Although Hunt had been active in many civic organizations, including co-founding and leading the Malverne Civic Association and chairing an "Adopt-A-Station" committee to improve commuter rail station conditions, she had never run for elective office. But Hunt knew that Malverne faced serious problems; its tax rate was among the highest in the county and had reached the legal maximum. As a result, the village had to borrow funds to pay for current services.

In 1987, Hunt, a forty-year-old high school–educated former executive secretary, led a group of concerned citizens to form a new party, the "Home Pride Party," to challenge the long-entrenched status quo. Their opponents in the Independent Party had not faced a contested election for twenty-one years. The Home Pride slogan was "We are not politicians! We are concerned citizens!" Hunt promised to be a full-time mayor, even though the position paid only $7,500. She argued: "Today government must be run like a business. Can you imagine a successful business where the boss is never around?"

The central issues in their campaign included road repair, long-range planning to improve the local budget, and opening up the governmental process to more citizen input. As the incumbents tried to protect their positions, the campaign turned aggressive and even "dirty." After the election, Hunt filed multimillion-dollar libel and slander suits against her opponents for the misleading information she claims they disseminated during the campaign.

To her surprise, Hunt won the mayoralty race and her supporters won half the seats on the board of trustees. After winning, Hunt replaced several entrenched village employees from the old regime, hired a consultant to recommend solutions to the road repair problem, looked for new sources of external grant funds, and addressed rapidly increasing solid waste disposal costs. She also planned to meet with all village employees to seek their input in solving these problems. She worked to reduce both the $300,000 accounts payable deficit and the $2 million in long-term debt the previous regime left behind.

Using an innovative new political party and her own energetic leadership, Hunt transformed the politics and policies of Malverne. Despite these changes in local politics and policies, Hunt wanted to do more. She told the regional newspaper, *Newsday:* "I'm finding that government works slowly and that's frustrating to me. I'm a compulsive person."

In Naperville, Illinois, a rapidly growing suburb outside of Chicago, Mayor Margaret Price was also pursuing entrepreneurial policies. Naperville's rapid growth had long been supported by a strong progrowth coalition, but as growth accelerated, opponents emerged and coalesced into an antigrowth group that was able to elect three council members in 1985.

Price brokered compromise solutions to the disruptions of growth, by advocating "managed growth." She argued that the city needed to annex new growth areas to control density and the type of development in the community. The *Chicago Tribune* quoted her as defending developer impact fees: "unless you have some mechanism for sharing development costs, a community will become no-growth because of high taxes." In the course of balancing Naperville's contending coalitions, Price spearheaded the drafting of a much needed master land use plan. Price sought to broker a compromise between competing interests by changing attitudes and improving communications. Price told the *Chicago Tribune:* "I've tried to dispel the 'we-versus-they' attitude and tried to achieve better communication between our business community and homeowners."

The fifty-three-year-old Price was first elected as mayor in 1983, winning by a two-to-one margin over the eight-year incumbent, a real estate agent who had helped Naperville become the fastest growing town in Illinois. When three strongly antigrowth council members were elected in 1985, the level of political conflict in the town accelerated greatly. As a political response to this challenge, in 1987, Price supported a council coalition that won a fierce electoral fight, and she was reelected, again by a two-to-one margin. Price told the *Tribune:* "All the council candidates who won have experience in city government and can take part immediately without a transition." They included a county personnel director and a planning commission chair.

Although Price had substantial experience in public service, she, like Cathy Hunt in Malverne, New York, never expected to be at the center of such a political storm. According to the *Tribune,* she noted: "If anyone had told me 10 years ago that I would be sitting in the mayor's chair, I would have laughed at them."

Price originally got involved in civic affairs to protect the ambience of her adopted town: "Naperville had the feel of a small, Midwest town, not a suburb. It looked like home." Her civic career started slowly; she helped found the Maplebrook II Homeowners Association in 1968. Next she observed council meetings for the League of Women Voters and helped the League successfully champion a city manager reform government structure. She served for seven years on the planning commission. She ran unsuccessfully for council twice. But persistence paid off: she finally won election in 1978. According to the *Tribune,* she noted: "I decided to run because there was discussion about changing our form of government from the council-manager form back to a commission form of government. I thought that would be a giant step backwards." In a sense, she wanted to protect new institutional rules of the electoral game.

Price, like Cathy Hunt, is a part-time mayor, who essentially serves full time. With a $15,000 annual salary, it is clearly not pecuniary rewards that are motivating her entrepreneurship: "I'm not complaining, I chose this job and I enjoy it. . . . Actually, I feel that serving in local office is more of a public service-type job than political. I see my mayoral position as a progression of my involvement in community service organizations." This progression is not finished. Following the same strategy she used to launch her career at the city level, offering extensive service in neighborhood organizations to build a base of support, Price extended her entrepreneurial actions to the regional level: she worked with officials in neighboring suburbs to procure Lake Michigan water sources. Price argues: "With the present growth in DuPage County, cooperation between suburbs becomes even more important."

LOCAL POLITICAL ENTREPRENEURS

These stories are not unusual and they give flavor to the nature of entrepreneurship occurring in local governments across the United States. Indeed, in our nationwide survey of local government, we found literally hundreds of examples of public entrepreneurs, both women and men, African-American and white, young and old, who were challenging local politics in similar fashion to Hunt and Price. Their goals, issues, techniques, and results were different: some entrepreneurs fought for economic development, some opposed further growth, some fought to reduce taxes or to improve the delivery of government services, while others were concerned with managing ethnic changes in their communities. What they have in common is that they advocated *dynamic political change* in their community.

Hunt, Price, and others in our study are not "great figures" in history. Outside of their towns and neighboring communities, probably few people have ever heard of them. They may not seek or achieve higher political office outside of their community. In part, that *is* our point about local political entrepreneurs—they need not be national figures like Admiral Rickover or Robert Moses, about whom whole books have been written. They are, instead, individuals who are acting to take advantage of the opportunities for entrepreneurial activity that are abundant in American local politics. This is especially true in the setting of the many small and moderate-sized suburbs that lie outside of most American cities.

Throughout our history, Americans have shown a persistent propensity to tinker with their local government. In turn, there is almost always demand for political and administrative change at the local level (see, e.g., Hofstadter 1955; Knott and Miller 1987). And this demand for change might have increased in the particularly difficult fiscal environment facing local governments in the 1980s. In some cities, citizens who otherwise might not have become involved in politics pursued the opportunities presented in these turbulent times by forming new organizations or by running for office. In some towns, especially when politicians did not respond to the need for change, high-level bureaucrats, especially city managers, pursued these opportunities. But in other cities, no entrepreneur emerged. In this chapter, we try to identify and model the elements of local political institutions and environments that shape the benefit/cost calculations public entrepreneurs make in pursuing such opportunities.

Our goal is to identify the conditions that affect the probability with which an entrepreneur emerges in any given community. In previous chapters, we argued that the costs of entrepreneurship are partly a function of the collective action problem entrepreneurs face and the ease with which this problem can be solved. Similarly, the benefits (or "profits") entrepreneurs reap are a function of the rewards available from winning office. In the case of Mayors Hunt and Price, the rewards are not monetary, as they work long hours for low pay. Some of the rewards are obviously psychological—related to the joys of creating new policies and affecting change in the communities to which these people are strongly tied. The potential for these rewards may be measured by, among other things, the budgetary slack of their local community, which affects the entrepreneur's ability to reallocate resources to achieve policy goals and by the structure of the electoral process that affects the costs of winning public office and the likelihood that the office possesses the resources to affect change.

These factors affect the decisions made by *individual* entrepreneurs. But these individual decisions can have wider effects. At a more *systemic* level, entrepreneurs can affect the political equilibrium within and across communities in metropolitan areas, introducing new ideas and policies that other communities adopt or emulate.

Types of Entrepreneurs in the Local Market for Public Goods

In the local market for public goods with which we are concerned, bundles of local services are delivered by multiple municipal governments. And these services are paid for using a revenue system in which local property taxes are central.[1] In this arena, governments are in competition with one another and use their taxes and services to lure desirable households and business firms (Peterson 1981; Schneider 1989). In the resulting competition, some forms of local political entrepreneurship may temporarily create disequilibrium, upsetting existing local public service and tax arrangements and altering the relationship between communities in a region. However, over time, many entrepreneurial innovations are absorbed and institutionalized into new political arrangements and a new balance between communities emerges. The tax/expenditure limitations movement of the 1970s (e.g., Clark and Ferguson 1983), the concern for economic development policies of the 1970s and 1980s (e.g., Eisinger 1988), and the antigrowth movement of the 1980s and 1990s (e.g., Schneider 1992; Logan and Rabrenovic 1990) may all be examples of opportunities seized by entrepreneurs in local government and whose actions created the dynamics of punctuated equilibria.

Oakerson and Parks (1988) argue that in local politics, entrepreneurship often occurs in the context of professional associations that link managers across different local governments. Clearly, much entrepreneurial activity concerning local service efficiency is managerial—especially with regard to the introduction of new technologies within a given service domain. However, in our work, we found the emergence of elected politicians in entrepreneurial roles was more common than the frequency of managerial entrepreneurship (we discuss this pattern in more detail in chapter 8).

One of the most important types of local political entrepreneurs active in recent years exploited the opportunities emerging from the politics of growth. We divide these "growth entrepreneurs" into several subclasses. First, we found a significant number of entrepreneurial politicians who were in favor of growth and who advocated using the vast array of traditional tools of local government (such as tax abatements and debt financing) to lure business firms. These politicians had their greatest successes in the 1970s and early 1980s. But eventually what Blair, Fichtenbaum, and Swaney (1984) called the "market for jobs" became so fully developed that most opportunities for political entrepreneurs advocating these traditional tools were identified and entrepreneurial profits bid away in the intense interlocal competition for economic development that characterized the 1980s (Milward and Newman 1989; Schneider 1992). Indeed, so many of these traditional local progrowth tools are so routinized that they are now handled by a cadre of bureaucratic managers (e.g., Blair, Fichtenbaum, and Swaney 1984; Eisinger 1988). This policy "life cycle" clearly replicates the S-curve pattern of innovation in private markets: over time innovative products (in this case, growth policies) are transformed into standard "commodities," competition dissipates initial high entrepreneurial profits, and entrepreneurial leadership is replaced by routine processes handled by bureaucratic managers. Duplicating well-documented patterns found in private sector markets, as the profits of traditional progrowth policies dwindled, a new class of growth entrepreneurs is now emerging advocating a whole new range of what Eisinger (1988) calls demand-side policies to promote economic development.

This evolution in policy tools is perfectly congruent with our theory of entrepreneurship in local government—as the last set of innovative tools became "traditional," the payoffs dwindled and a new generation of political entrepreneurs emerged to create policies with potentially higher rewards. Over time, we expect the life cycle of these new demand-side policies to replicate the life cycle of the last round of innovative growth policies: to the extent that new demand-side policies are successful, political entrepreneurs in other communities will advocate them. As this occurs, the political profits derived from these innovative policy tools will decline and they too will become standardized bureaucratic products. However, while this process unfolds, many political entrepreneurs will make their careers and, at the systemic level, the entire package of growth policies local governments offer will be transformed.

This new generation of entrepreneurs, advocating innovative approaches to economic development, supports local growth. But as the Naperville, Illinois case illustrates, even more radical challenges to traditional patterns of local politics are emerging from antigrowth entrepreneurs—entrepreneurs whose political careers are built on questioning the very value of growth itself (Logan and Molotch 1987; Logan and Zhou 1990; Schneider 1992). In the following chapters, we explore in more detail these types of progrowth and antigrowth entrepreneurs.

While the politics of growth is clearly one of the richest sources of opportunities for entrepreneurship in local government, another type of political innovator that we found in our study was concerned more with local services and taxes, emphasizing efficiency enhancing reforms. These entrepreneurs arose in response to the changing fiscal and service needs of the last decade, conditions described in one of the most recent popular studies of public entrepreneurship, Osborne and Gaebler's *Reinventing Government*. Osborne and Gaebler argue that there were fundamental structural changes in the environment during the 1980s that increased the need for flexible and adaptable responses on the part of both public and private organizations. At the local level, the cutbacks in federal and state aid, coupled with property tax revolts and the steep recession of 1982, combined to drive these governments into despair.

But the crisis presented many opportunities for innovation. Osborne and Gaebler argue that local governments were the first governments to face these challenges and entrepreneurs in many local governments emerged to seize the opportunities inherent in the revolution in demands and constraints in the local market for public goods. According to these analysts, given these circumstances: "local leaders had no choice but to change the way they did business. Mayors and governors embraced 'public-private partnerships' and developed 'alternative' ways to deliver services. Cities fostered competition between service providers and invented new budget systems. Public managers began to speak of 'enterprise management,' 'learning organizations,' and 'self-reliant cities.' States began to restructure their most expensive public systems: education, health care, and welfare" (1991: 17). Many of these innovations are in various stages of testing and diffusion, and the entrepreneurs pushing them are also in various stages of seizing the profits (or suffering the risks) of policy innovation.

No matter the type of entrepreneur and no matter what the exact factors that motivated his or her emergence, to be successful the entrepreneur needs to create a political coalition by which to challenge the status quo. Local entrepreneurs concerned with fiscal conditions seized on dissatisfaction with rising local taxes and the middle class predisposition for the norm of efficiency to challenge existing political/bureaucratic alignments. Often these fiscal reformers not only challenged the existing political leadership in their communities but actually changed the rules of the game. For example, through initiatives and referenda some entrepreneurs created a requirement that extraordinary legislative or voting processes be followed to allow higher taxes. The entrepreneurs identified by Osborne and Gaebler mobilize citizens, redefining them as customers who are empowered to demand change. Many of these entrepreneurs radically change the institutional structure of the bureaucracies they govern, often by engaging in decentralized participatory management to mobilize, motivate, and energize their employees. In so doing, these entrepreneurs fundamentally shift the rules of the game in favor of citizens and away from entrenched organizations.

Similarly, to be successful, the antigrowth entrepreneur must fracture the existing progrowth political alliance found in many communities and create a new political alliance. Neighborhood and community organizations that are faced with rapidly accumulating costs of growth usually provide the organizational basis for the antigrowth entrepreneur. This alternate organizational base is often mobilized as the antigrowth entrepreneur introduces a new dimension in local debates over growth, a dimension that emphasizes what Logan and Molotch (1987) call the "use value" of land, replacing the traditional concern for its exchange value (Schneider and Teske 1993).

STALKING THE LOCAL POLITICAL ENTREPRENEUR

No simple theory exists to explain entrepreneurship in the private market. And any useful theory of public entrepreneurship is necessarily complex. In the previous chapters, we developed a core set of ideas that must inform any theory of public entrepreneurship. Many components of our theory are empirically testable. Starting with this chapter we engage in such empirical analysis. In the empirical analysis presented here and in the next chapters, we begin to identify the conditions that affect the emergence of entrepreneurs in the local market for public goods. Following our theoretical developments earlier in this book, we believe that entrepreneurs are motivated to enter the public arena (ceteris paribus) by the benefits and costs of political entrepreneurship. More specifically, we argue that entrepreneurs are more likely to emerge in the local market for public goods when there are factors that make entrepreneurial profits more likely and where local conditions facilitate a solution to collective action problems. We now seek to test these links empirically.

In constructing empirical tests of our theory, we faced the difficult problem of discovering the extent of entrepreneurial activities in local governments around the country. Rather than drawing on secondary source materials, such as the Innovation Awards of the Ford Foundation, the numerous case studies reported in works such as Osborne and Gaebler (1991), or program-specific innovations that are being developed around the nation (such as reported in *Governance* magazine), we surveyed municipal governments directly. We created a sample of all incorporated suburban municipalities greater than 2,500 population in the largest 100 metropolitan areas in the nation. With certain restrictions on the selection of communities, this produced a set of about 1,400 communities in over twenty states.[2]

We developed a questionnaire that we sent to city clerks in each of these communities. We chose to survey clerks because we believe that they are knowledgeable about the politics and political history of their communities. Moreover, as part of their jobs, they are usually given the responsibility of responding to inquiries about their communities. In short, they make more than credible respondents.

Since asking city clerks to identify local leaders who are "alert to disequilibrium" or who engage in "creative discovery" stretched the norms of language (even if the phrasing would be more theoretically pure), we asked clerks if, during the past several years, there had been any individual in their community whose "policy proposals and political positions represented a dynamic change from existing procedures."[3] If clerks identified such a person, we then asked a series of questions about what that person did that made them entrepreneurial. We also asked all of the clerks about the political structure of their community and we asked them to rate the relative political strength of various groups in the community. With three follow-up letters, we received nearly 1,000 responses. We then matched the information we received from the clerks with data published by the U.S. Census and various state and local reports covering a wide variety of demographic, fiscal, economic, and political factors. Because our field work was conducted during 1991 and our questionnaire asked clerks to name entrepreneurs who emerged over the last several years, we use specific conditions of communities from the early 1980s to predict the emergence of an entrepreneur.

From the original set of communities, we received 953 usable responses, of which 257 clerks nominated someone as a political entrepreneur. Thus, entrepreneurs were found in approximately 30 percent of the cities in our sample.[4] Of these entrepreneurs, 43 percent were mayors, 26 percent were members of the city council, 23 percent were city managers or bureau chiefs, and the remainder were from business or from other private activities.[5]

In the analysis of political entrepreneurs in this chapter and the next, we use probit analysis to identify the conditions that affect the likelihood of finding an entrepreneur in a community. We analyze the emergence of a local entrepreneur as a dichotomous (0,1) variable (with 1 meaning an entrepreneur was reported in the community). Probit is an appropriate technique when a dependent variable takes on only two values. Probit analysis also has a very nice feature: the probit coefficients can be manipulated to show how a change in an independent variable affects the probability of finding the event measured by the dependent variable. In our work, we thus identify not only the objective local conditions that affect the probability that an entrepreneur was found in a given community, using probit to conduct "sensitivity analysis," we also measure how various local conditions affect the likelihood of finding an entrepreneur.

In our empirical work, we investigated four specific classes of community conditions to see how they affected the probability of finding an entrepreneur. These are outlined in the following pages.

Regional Location

It is well known that patterns of political practices, local government services, and demographic change in localities varies markedly across regions of the country. We control for regional location in two ways. First, and most simply, we divide our communities into the four largest geographic regions defined by the census: the South, West, North Central, and Northeast. We create a series of dummy variables noting regional location and include these dummy variables in our probit analysis. At minimum, we use regional location as a control variable. However, in the analysis we present in the chapters on the politics of growth, these variables have important substantive implications.

Second, to correct for more specific regional differences in the distribution of community conditions, all the independent variables have been adjusted by metropolitan means and standard deviations (that is, they have been turned into z-scores based on patterns found in the metropolitan statistical area in which the community is located). Through this transformation, the independent variables reflect the standing of a community relative to its neighbors (Schneider 1989).

Political Factors

We model explicitly many of the political conditions that affect the benefits and costs of entrepreneurship in the local market for public goods. We focus on two sets of political conditions—the electoral conditions in a community and the structure of the office of the chief political executive.[6]

We believe that the office of the mayor is a critical institutional position for many local political entrepreneurs, as it maximizes access to the resources necessary to implement the programs and policies the entrepreneur desires in the pursuit of his or her vision of the future. If the office of the mayor is full time, the rewards of the office are even greater. We thus create a variable that is set to the value of 1 in cities with a full-time mayor and 0 in cities that have either a part-time mayor or no mayor at all.

There may be entry barriers facing an entrepreneur who seeks to win election to office as mayor. For example, the term of office for mayor in the local governments in our sample is almost evenly divided between two- and four-year terms. While a longer term may make the office a more valuable resource for the entrepreneur, it also reduces the frequency of electoral opportunities an entrepreneur has to challenge the established coalition. Similarly, considerable variation is found across communities in the rate at which the mayor's office is vacated. We include in our analyses the length of the term of office and the number of different mayors a community had during the last ten years, using these measures to reflect entry barriers facing the entrepreneur.

Previous studies have documented that the extent of structural political reform affects local politics. Following the established literature, we assess the effects of three aspects of reform on the emergence of local entrepreneurs; however, we reinterpret these conditions through our theoretical lens. First, we assess the effects of the office of city manager on the emergence of entrepreneurs. The office of city manager, like the office of mayor, may increase the probability of finding an entrepreneur, by providing a visible, attractive springboard for the pursuit of alternate policies. City managers sometimes are themselves entrepreneurs, seeking to accumulate a record of success in order to move on to larger and more prestigious communities. Moreover, a city manager may provide expertise and advice to an entrepreneurial mayor. We thus include a dummy variable reflecting the office of manager.

Second, we are concerned with the nature of the local system of representation. Because collective action problems are easier to overcome in smaller constituencies than in larger ones, we believe that cities using district elections rather than at-large elections will be more likely to provide organizational opportunities for an antigrowth entrepreneur. The relative ease with which collective action problems can be surmounted in these smaller constituencies expands the "profitable" opportunities available to an aspiring antigrowth entrepreneur, increasing the likelihood that an entrepreneur will emerge.[7]

In addition to a city manager and at-large elections, the third most common reform of the political structure is the adoption of nonpartisan elections. We examine the effects of this reform on progrowth entrepreneurship, although we have no a priori expectation about the effects of this political variable on entrepreneurship.

We are concerned with the organizational milieux in which local politicians operate and the extent to which different groups in a community may provide a springboard for political entrepreneurship. All political entrepreneurs must assemble a coalition to support their proposed policy changes. We want to assess how the strength of various political groups in the local environment affects the emergence of entrepreneurs. We asked the city clerks to rate the political importance of a variety of local groups on a scale of 1 to 5 (with 1 being not very important and 5 being very important). We relate the strength of four key groups to the emergence of the entrepreneur. First, we measure the importance of local political parties, which may provide an avenue through which the entrepreneur can launch a career. Second, we measure the strength of local business groups, such as the chamber of commerce. Business groups are themselves in a privileged position in local government; they control many resources that politicians need and they can help provide selective incentives to help overcome collective action problems. Thus, they can reduce the costs of entrepreneurship. However, they may also be strong supporters of the status quo putting limits on entrepreneurial politics.

Taxpayer groups constitute our third group. Taxpayer groups often provide a launching platform for politicians in cities where unhappiness over taxes and services is high. These groups are frequently found in local governments and have been particularly important in recent years as cities have felt the pressure of declining intergovernmental aid and rising taxes. We believe that these groups may act as a "safety valve" in local politics, channeling energy and potential discontent, thus substituting for new entrepreneurial activity.[8]

Finally, and of great theoretical importance, are neighborhood organizations that can act as a springboard for the entrepreneur. By lowering organizational costs and providing a mechanism by which to build a reputation as a reliable and trustworthy political actor, neighborhood groups can directly ease the costs of entrepreneurship.[9]

We believe that there is an important relationship between neighborhood groups and the form of election. Neighborhood organizations and district systems of representation both increase the spatial representation of interests (Welsh and Bledsoe 1988), and thus may be substitutes for one another. In contrast, at-large electoral systems downplay spatially defined concerns. Consequently, in at-large systems of representation, neighborhood groups may represent a major avenue by which an entrepreneur can minimize start-up costs. To reflect this contingent relationship, in the probit model we include an interaction term between the form of election and the reported strength of neighborhood groups in a community. This interaction term assumes a value of 0 in cities with district elections, but is the reported strength of the neighborhood group in cities with at-large elections.

Fiscal and Budgetary Factors

The local tax base of a community is a fundamental fiscal resource that can attract public entrepreneurs. A strong tax base gives communities a wide range of policy options for the entrepreneur to pursue. Since communities with a strong tax base can provide good services at a moderate tax rate or moderate services at a low one (Schneider and Logan 1982), a strong tax base represents a public resource entrepreneurs can use in pursuing their vision of the future.[10]

A second fiscal variable, the comparative local tax rate, is more likely to reflect the community's potential support for an entrepreneur. When local taxes are high relative to the taxes of other communities, an opportunity may exist for an entrepreneur to advocate innovations that increase the efficiency of local services, limit expenditures, or redirect patterns of growth that residents might associate with higher taxes. Thus, we hypothesize that both a higher comparative tax base and a higher tax rate will increase the probability that an entrepreneur will emerge in a given community.

Entrepreneurs will also be attracted by the possibility of redeploying local budgets to achieve the policy goals they prefer. Following Peterson (1981), we divide local expenditures into three categories: developmental, allocational, and redistributive.[11] According to Peterson, within the types of expenditures that constitute local budgets, allocational expenditures are the most unconstrained. In Peterson's analysis, cities have little leeway in their expenditure decisions over redistributive services (which they must avoid) and over developmental expenditures (which they must pursue in a nonpolitical professional manner). This leaves allocational expenditures as the domain over which local politicians have the most influence. From our perspective, high allocational expenditures create slack resources that increase public sector opportunities for entrepreneurial profits—these slack resources can be most easily reallocated by the entrepreneur to pursue preferred policies.

Demographic Factors

The probability that an entrepreneur emerges will be related to the demographic makeup of the community. Demographic conditions reflect opportunities for the entrepreneur to advocate new policies and reflect the relative ease with which entrepreneurs can organize the citizenry into collective political action. One important variable affecting the ease of organizing for collective action is the stake that individual citizens have in local tax and service issues. We hypothesize that communities with a greater concentration of renters, individuals without a location-specific investment in property, will be harder to organize than communities with a larger concentration of more firmly anchored homeowners (Cox 1982).[12]

Donovan and Neiman (1992) identify what they call a "social bias" theory linking social status with the political skills and economic resources that facilitate mobilization against development (also see Baldassare and Protash 1982). Thus, communities with lower median income may present greater organizational barriers to an entrepreneur.

As we noted earlier, conflicts over growth are endemic to local politics. Rapid growth can strain existing services, increase pressure on taxes, and mobilize local citizens who see the quality of life in the community changing. We thus test the effects that rapid growth in a community has on the emergence of a political entrepreneur.

We also believe that the growing racial heterogeneity of suburban communities may create the conditions for political entrepreneurship by providing a base for new political demands or by countermobilizing existing residents to the demands of a growing racial minority population. Specifically, we hypothesize that a larger black population can add a new racial dimension to local politics that can increase the probability of local entrepreneurial political behavior. We also include the distance a suburb is from the central city as a control variable, since this condition is often directly correlated with a variety of economic and social conditions of suburban communities (Dye and Garcia 1978).

THE EFFECTS OF COMMUNITY CONDITIONS ON THE EMERGENCE OF ENTREPRENEURS

In the following section we estimate separately the effects of each of the categories of these variables on the probability of finding an entrepreneur. We experimented with a variety of models that combined classes of variables into large equations containing increasing numbers of indicators. The problem with this approach is multicollinearity: as more and more indicators were added to our estimating equations, we became uncomfortable with the increasingly complex interactions between the independent variables. Given multicollinearity—which is a reflection of reality and cannot be solved (either mathematically or empirically) by adding more cases—we opt for the less than perfect solution of reporting three separate probit analyses (we incorporate the regional variables into the other models). Following the analysis of each probit equation, we report a sensitivity analysis that shows how manipulating specific important conditions affects the likelihood of finding an entrepreneur. By comparing across these sensitivity and probit tables, the relative importance of various conditions becomes clear.

Table 5.1.1 reports the results of a probit estimation of the effects of local political conditions on the emergence of a local entrepreneur controlling for region, and table 5.1.2 reports the corresponding sensitivity analysis.[13] Two variables stand out as the most important. First, where cities have a full-time mayor, the probability of finding an entrepreneur

TABLE 5.1.1

The Effects of Political Conditions on the
Probable Emergence of an Entrepreneur

	Coefficient	Std. Error	p > t
Full-time mayor	.31	.14	.03
Turnover	.08	.10	.41
Term length	.01	.10	.92
Manager	.30	.11	.01
At-large	.01	.28	.97
Nonpartisan	−.05	.14	.74
Parties	.01	.04	.81
Business groups	.09	.04	.04
Taxpayer groups	−.10	.04	.02
Neighbor groups	.06	.06	.32
Interaction	−.02	.08	.71
West	.02	.18	.88
North Central	.18	.13	.16
South	.01	.17	.97
Constant	−.96	.26	.00

Source: Survey of city clerks. West, North Central,
South: four main geographic regions delineated by U.S.
Bureau of the Census (Northeast is the omitted cate-
gory).

Notes: Number of observations: 787. Chi square: 25.43
(14 degrees of freedom). Prob > chi square: .03. Full-
time mayor: 1 = full-time mayor; 0 = part-time mayor.
Manager: 1 = city manager; 0 = no city manager. At-
large: 1 = at-large elections; 0 = district elections. Nonpartisan: 1 = nonpartisan elections; 0 = partisan. Term
length: 0 = 2-year term; 1 = 4-year term. Turnover: the
number of different mayors in the last 10 years. Business
groups: reported strength of business groups such as
the chamber of commerce: 1 = not very important;
5 = very important. Taxpayer groups, Neighborhood
groups, Parties: same as Business groups. Interaction: =
0 in district cities; = value of neighborhood group in
at-large cities.

increases dramatically. In fact, this variable has the single largest effect of
variable in any model we test. Ceteris paribus, the probability of finding
an entrepreneur in cities with full-time mayors is almost 11 percent
higher than in the sample as a whole. As we noted earlier, entrepreneurs
in general are defined by a vision of the future that differs from present
conditions and by their energy and commitment to changing existing
policies to fulfill that vision. In the private sector, entrepreneurs often
build new companies or take over existing ones. However, in the public

TABLE 5.1.2

Sensitivity Analysis: The Effects of Political Variables on the Probability of
Finding an Entrepreneur

	Full-time Mayor	Manager	Chamber of Commerce	Taxpayer Groups	Joint Probability
Maximum effect	.40	.35	.34	.35	.54
Minimum effect	.29	.24	.27	.26	.16

Note: In the set of communities for which this particular probit was estimated, the mean probability is .31. To estimate the maximum effect, we set the dichotomous variables (Full-time mayor and Manager) to 1. We set them to 0 to estimate the minimum probability. The two group variables have a range of 1 to 5. We estimate the minimum and maximum probabilities by setting the variable to either + or −1 standard deviation from the mean (depending on the direction of the sign). The joint probability manipulates all four conditions simultaneously.

sector, entrepreneurs usually face established organizations and building new local government agencies de novo is difficult (see Lewis 1980; but see Caro's 1974 study of Robert Moses). In turn, entrepreneurs are attracted to the office of mayor, the equivalent of the local political CEO, as a means of pursuing their vision. Moreover, if the mayor's office is full time rather than part time, the attractiveness of the office to a progrowth entrepreneur increases, because the entrepreneur's ability to pursue alternate preferred policies is enhanced.

Similarly, the office of city manager increases the visibility and the resources of launching an entrepreneurial career. City managers are important in increasing entrepreneurship, about as important as a full-time mayor's office. There is an 11 percent increase in probabilities associated with a full-time mayor's office, and the probability of finding an entrepreneur increases by about 11 percent in cities with managers.

Two groups affect the emergence of entrepreneurs. Strong business groups increase the likelihood of finding an entrepreneur. Following Stone (1989), we believe that business groups reduce the costs of solving collective action problems in communities and, therefore, reduce the costs facing local entrepreneurs. In the next chapter, we will show that the emergence of one kind of entrepreneur, the progrowth entrepreneur, is particularly linked to a strong chamber of commerce. In contrast, strong taxpayer groups lessen the likelihood of a political entrepreneur emerging.

Note that the joint effects of these four political conditions on the probability of finding an entrepreneur is quite strong. Setting the conditions to maximize the likelihood of finding an entrepreneur, the probability of finding an entrepreneur in a city with a full-time mayor, a city manager, strong business groups, and weak taxpayer groups is .54, over 75 percent higher than the sample mean. Similarly, in cities with either

TABLE 5.2.1

The Effects of Fiscal and Budgetary Conditions on the
Probable Emergence of an Entrepreneur

	Coefficient	Std. Error	$p > t$
Allocational expenditures	.11	.06	.08
Developmental expenditures	−.06	.06	.30
Redistributive expenditures	−.16	.06	.01
Tax rate	.08	.05	.13
True value	.09	.06	.13
West	.14	.15	.36
North Central	.20	.12	.11
South	.07	.17	.70
Constant	−.66	.10	.00

Source: True value, Tax rate: state and local sources, adjusted for differences in assessment practices. Expenditures: 1982 Census of Governments, Finance, File A. West, North Central, South: four main geographic regions delineated by U.S. Bureau of the Census (Northeast is the omitted category).

Notes: Number of observations: 658. Chi square: 17.31 (8 degrees of freedom). Prob > chi square: .02. All variables are z-scores standardized by MSA means and standard deviations; that is, they are measures of the position of a community on that condition relative to its neighbors.

TABLE 5.2.2

Sensitivity Analysis: The Effects of Budgetary Variables
on the Probability of Finding an Entrepreneur

	Allocational Expenditures	Social Expenditures	Both
Maximum effect	.34	.35	.39
Minimum effect	.26	.24	.20

Note: In the set of communities for which this probit was estimated, the mean probability is .30. To estimate the maximum effect we set the variables at either + or −1 (since these are z-scores the mean = 0, the standard deviation = 1).

a part-time mayor or no mayor, with no city manager, weak business groups, and strong taxpayer groups, the probability of finding an entrepreneur is only .16, just about half the sample mean.

Tables 5.2.1 and 5.2.2 report the effects of fiscal and budgetary variables on the likelihood of finding an entrepreneur. Empirically, two variables affect the emergence of an entrepreneur. Using the appropriate one-tail significance test, as predicted, the size of slack budgetary resources measured by allocational expenditures does increase the likelihood of finding an entrepreneur. In contrast, high social expenditures

TABLE 5.3.1

The Effects of Demographic Conditions on the
Probable Emergence of an Entrepreneur

	Coefficient	Std. Error	$p > t$
Median income	.00	.06	.96
Renter percent	−.11	.05	.06
Distance	−.07	.05	.16
Growth 1980s	.11	.05	.02
Black percent	.12	.05	.02
West	.17	.14	.22
North Central	.26	.11	.02
South	.07	.14	.61
Constant	−.68	.08	.00

Source: Renter percent, Black percent, population 1980: 1980 Census of Population and Housing. Population 1990: counts generated by PL 94-171. West, North Central, South: four main geographic regions delineated by U.S. Bureau of the Census (Northeast is the omitted category). Distance: maps.

Notes: Number of observations: 829. Chi square: 18.61 (8 degrees of freedom). Prob > chi square: .01. All variables are z-scores standardized by MSA means and standard deviations, that is, they are measures of the position of a community on that condition relative to its neighbors. Median income: Relative community income 1980. Growth 1980: z-score of Population 1990/ Population 1980.

reduce the likelihood of an entrepreneur emerging. From Peterson's perspective, cities that are high spenders on these social consumption goods could be viewed as "inefficient" by their residents—that is, they are spending their money on activities that are not in the city's interests. As in any market, offering goods that are not wanted should give rise to entrepreneurs who would argue for cutbacks in "unnecessary" and "uncompetitive" services. However, our empirical evidence is to the contrary—that cities that invest in human capital seem less likely to support entrepreneurial politicians. Investments in human capital and local community development may make sense in suburbs where outlays for such services are low (Schneider 1989) and where, because the extent of redistribution is limited by the relatively narrow income range in many communities, conflict over these services may be lower (Schneider 1986).

Next we turn to the effects of demographic factors, most of which reflect the extent of demand for entrepreneurial activity (see table 5.3.1). As we hypothesized, higher concentrations of renters reduce the probability of finding an entrepreneur, because these renters present

TABLE 5.3.2

Sensitivity Analysis: The Effects of Demographic Variables on the
Probability of Finding an Entrepreneur

	Renter percent	Black percent	Growth	Joint Probability
Maximum effect	.33	.34	.28	.42
Minimum effect	.26	.25	.21	.19

Note: In the set of communities for which this particular probit was estimated, the mean probability is .29. To estimate the maximum effect, we set the variables at either + or −1 (since these are z-scores the mean = 0, the standard deviation = 1).

higher organization costs. However, more affluent communities that may be easier to organize are not more likely to support entrepreneurs. We also found that the more rapid growth was associated with a higher incidence of entrepreneurship—that the disruptions caused by such growth increase the opportunities available to entrepreneurs.

But of the demographic variables, the sensitivity analysis in table 5.3.2 shows that the percent black is the most important variable—that communities with large black populations were more likely to support entrepreneurs than communities with smaller black populations. We believe that increasing opportunities for entrepreneurial activities emerge in communities that must come to terms with increasing ethnic diversity.

A DETAILED LOOK AT THE CHARACTERISTICS OF LOCAL POLITICAL ENTREPRENEURS

More than 50 of the 257 entrepreneurs named by city clerks were government bureaucrats, mostly city managers coupled with a handful of other high-ranking bureaucrats. Since these managerial entrepreneurs do not directly stand for elections and since they work full time in career government positions, we examine the conditions affecting their emergence, strategies, and constraints separately in chapter 8. The remaining "political" entrepreneurs have one thing in common: they act in the larger political and electoral environment of their community, seeking and often winning election to office.

To learn more about the characteristics, goals, and strategies of political entrepreneurs, we sent a second wave survey to the same city clerks of the nearly 200 political entrepreneurs who identified an entrepreneur in the first wave. With three follow-up letters, we received 117 usable responses (a response rate of close to 60 percent). From these surveys, we developed the following aggregate profile of political entrepreneurs in the local market for public goods.

THE BACKGROUND AND PERSONAL QUALITIES
OF THE POLITICAL ENTREPRENEUR

Not surprisingly, most of the entrepreneurs we identified had roots in local businesses: 8 percent of the entrepreneurs were from the law profession, 4 percent from real estate, 4 percent from insurance, and 33 percent from other business activities. In a later chapter, we explore in more detail the relationship between the composition of the local business environment and local public entrepreneurship. Close to 14 percent of the entrepreneurs came from careers in education and 15 percent came from public administration. Very few entrepreneurs built their careers entirely within the political sphere (only 3 percent). Yet once they were bitten by the "political bug," they kept on going: 81 percent of the entrepreneurs ran for another local office; 8 percent ran for a county office; and 6 percent ran for either a state or national office. By demonstrating energy, commitment, and new ideas, entrepreneurs may view their present activities as a springboard for career advancement.

In line with the need for high levels of energy, public entrepreneurs were fairly young: the 30–40 age group is the modal category, followed by the 40–50 age group. These entrepreneurs were highly educated: two-thirds of them had at least a college degree. The modal category was "finished college" (42 percent), followed by the category "an advanced degree"—21 percent. Not surprisingly, given the racial makeup of most suburbs, James Garner, the black mayor highlighted in the accompanying box, was an exception: almost all the entrepreneurs in our study were white (95 percent).

Given the characteristics and activities of entrepreneurs that we discussed in chapter 3, it is not surprising these entrepreneurs ranked high on such personal qualities as self-assuredness, intelligence, energy, and a sense of civic obligation. Despite the importance of the concept of the Protestant ethic in Weber's discussion of entrepreneurship, religious conviction was not ranked high compared to other politicians.

USE OF RHETORIC, IMAGES, AND IDEAS

We have argued that the successful use of rhetoric to persuade and change preferences is a critical aspect of entrepreneurial leadership. Correspondingly, the communications skills of the entrepreneurs were rated highly. Over two-thirds of the clerks said that, compared to other politicians in surrounding communities, the entrepreneur was "much

MAYOR JAMES GARNER:
A CASE OF BLACK POLITICAL ENTREPRENEURSHIP

In many cities, members of racial minorities are taking an entrepreneurial role in spearheading policy change. An excellent example is provided by Mayor James Garner in Hempstead, New York. In 1987, Garner became the first black mayor ever elected in any community on Long Island. He faced a situation in his village of 50,000 people described by *Newsday* as having "one of the most serious drug problems on the Island, a depressed economy, a faltering school system, declining real estate prices and high taxes." In contrast to affluent suburbs in Nassau County that are among the greatest concentrations of wealth in America, the village of Hempstead includes many low-income residents, and a population that is nearly two-thirds black. The *New York Times* quoted Garner: "It's the only village on Long Island with a racial mix like this."

Garner grew up in rural North Carolina and migrated to Hempstead in 1969, taking a position as a cargo agent at JFK airport. He showed entrepreneurial tendencies, by opening his successful Grand Central Exterminators business in 1977. Then-mayor George Milhim appointed Garner to the Board of Trustees in 1984, and he was elected to the board in 1985. Disenchanted with the two-term Milhim's policies, Garner defeated him in the Republican primary in 1989 and then defeated Milhim, running as an Independent, and a black Democratic candidate, winning over 50 percent of the votes. In the election, Garner received considerable help from the National Republican Committee, which was seeking stronger ties with black voters. After his election, Garner met with President Bush several times.

Like many of our entrepreneurs, Garner was not a career politician. *Newsday* quoted Garner as saying, "I never thought I'd be a trustee, let alone mayor. I got interested in politics as a businessman because I saw that politics and business should go hand in hand."

Garner campaigned strongly by focusing on what have traditionally been urban rather than suburban issues: crime and drugs. After his victory, he stated: "This was not a campaign, this was a movement. We have a message and our message is that we will stamp out all drug dealers in Hempstead." Indeed, Garner's

GARNER (cont.)

first important policies were aimed at improving local law and order. He added eighteen new police officers to the village base of ninety, passed a local ordinance to allow the aggressive elimination of "crack houses," and pushed to publish the names of prostitute's clients to reduce the prostitution problem. Garner's goal was to reduce Hempstead's reputation for crime and to bring new business into the village to stimulate the economy. This was difficult; like many other firms, Abraham & Straus, after occupying what was once the largest suburban department store in the nation in downtown Hempstead, moved to more affluent suburbs in the early 1990s.

As a result of his popularity in Washington, D.C., Garner aggressively sought federal funds to fight crime in Hempstead. He has faced a difficult challenge in trying to work with, but maintain some independence from, the strong Nassau County Republican political machine, which has traditionally not been aligned with black Long Islanders. This problem was exacerbated by the strong association of all four Village Board of Trustees members with the county party machine.

Thus, Garner shows how minorities in older, less affluent suburbs are beginning to come to political power, just as minorities in central cities did a generation ago. Former mayor Milhim ran a campaign that many considered racially divisive (especially as he faced two black challengers), but it did not succeed. That Garner is a black Republican made him all the more exceptional, but his entrepreneurial background in business illustrates the important link between such activities in the public and private spheres.

higher than average" in public speaking ability and the ability to use newspapers to communicate with the citizens of the community. These types of more local communication media are more important than television in most suburbs.

While some entrepreneurs introduced true innovations, others relied more on adaptation of ideas from elsewhere. Nearly 40 percent of the clerks said that the images and ideas offered by the entrepreneurs were totally new to their community. But 51 percent said that these ideas were major modifications of existing programs. Almost one-third of the clerks reported that the entrepreneur's ideas were very different from the ideas raised in political campaigns in neighboring communities and over 20 percent said that these ideas were very different from the ideas raised in campaigns in other communities in the state or region.

Congruent with our theory, political entrepreneurs clearly emphasize visions of the future in the messages they send. Almost 61 percent of the entrepreneurs frequently used images of the future in their appeals. In contrast, only 28 percent frequently compared the present state of their communities to the past and only 19 percent frequently compared the conditions in their communities to other neighboring communities.

What were the specific components of the images political entrepreneurs most frequently used? The most commonly used theme was the general quality of life in the community (used "frequently" by 81 percent of the entrepreneurs). This was followed by the quality of the neighborhoods in the community, the quality of parks, and the quality of infrastructure, which were all used frequently by about two-thirds of the entrepreneurs.

THE GROUP BASES OF LOCAL ENTREPRENEURSHIP

All entrepreneurs must solve collective action problems. Political entrepreneurs must form coalitions in order to be elected and to govern. The local political milieux offers a broad range of groups upon which political entrepreneurs can base their careers and from which they can assemble political coalitions to support their policies. Here, we study the relationship between several types of local groups and the careers and coalitions of political entrepreneurs.

Some groups reflect the traditional power bases of local politics. Business groups, such as the chamber of commerce, represent one of the most enduring bases for political power in local communities. Other groups, such as good government groups and taxpayer groups, have also been historically active in local politics over most of this century. More recently, neighborhood groups and environmental groups have increased their visibility and impact on local politics, providing new issues and new organizational possibilities for political entrepreneurs.

There are several other groups that affect politics in some communities, especially large central cities, whose effects in suburban communities may be muted. In cities in the Northeast and Midwest, political parties can be critical to the career of any politician. While the decline of local party organizations has been well documented, political parties still represent a major source of labor and money for many politicians. And while local elections in many cities are officially nonpartisan, local parties still control access to the ballots in a large number of communities. (See the box on Thomas Tarpey and his use of the local political party organization in River Grove, Illinois.)

MAYOR THOMAS TARPEY

Thomas Tarpey is an example of a local entrepreneur who used his energy, his persistence, his personality, and a strong organization to change politics in his community. Tarpey is the part-time mayor and a retired police chief of River Grove, Illinois, a middle-class suburb with about 10,000 people, which sits just twelve miles west of Chicago's downtown loop.

In 1980, after several policy disagreements, incumbent Republican Mayor Elmer Wolf demoted Tarpey from his position of police chief and placed him on the midnight shift. A few years later, Tarpey decided to fight fifty years of Republican control in River Grove and narrowly defeated the twelve-year incumbent Wolf in 1985. According to the *Chicago Tribune*, Tarpey believed that: "Nobody gave me a fiddler's chance in hell."

Once elected, Tarpey moved to improve the reputation and working of local government. According to the *Tribune*: "He has fashioned himself a reformer who made public records at the village hall readily accessible and no longer allowed his predecessor's son-in-law a lucrative contract to annually grade the suburb's alleys."

Tarpey soon gained positive media exposure from his adept handling of the town's response to a major flood of the Des Plaines River in 1986. His performance propelled him to the Democratic nomination for state representative in 1986 and prompted the Republicans to try to get him to switch parties. He dropped out of the race, mysteriously, in part because of rumors surfacing about his former drinking problem (he was a publicly announced recovering alcoholic).

Tarpey has been particularly skillful at maintaining his power by using political skills more often seen in urban machines than in the suburbs. According to the *Tribune*: "What has boosted Tarpey's value as a political commodity, his supporters say, is his grassroots political organization and his unassuming style. . . . Tarpey has survived by making an effort never to miss a baptism or a wake, pressing the flesh with the skill of the best ward heeler. . . . While some local political parties vanish between elections, his TEAM party has a permanent headquarters, claiming a membership of 150 and meetings every Monday."

According to one former village official: "Tom is a damn good public relations man." A local real estate broker says: "Our mayor is visible. Like Mayberry's sheriff, Andy Taylor, he's out there walking door-to-door."

TARPEY (cont.)

Tarpey ran unopposed in his last mayoral contest and contin-ues to have a vision of the future for his town: "I've got a million goals. . . . I'm willing to go along with anything if the town wants it."

Municipal workers can also provide a base of support for political cam-paigns and for launching new policy positions. Again, the effects of municipal workers is well documented in the study of central cities, and Schneider (1989) shows that in suburbia an organized local public sec-tor work force can also be a significant political force. Similarly, studies of central cities have clearly documented the importance of racially based alliances in launching political careers and policy changes. While these studies are mostly oriented toward the study of central cities, the growing racial diversity of suburbia and the increasing number of black families finding homes in suburban communities is transforming the demographic makeup of many suburban communities and creating new possibilities for racially based politics.

We identified eight specific types of groups and asked our respon-dents to judge the role these groups played in the political lives of the political entrepreneurs. The groups we identified include: business groups; taxpayer groups; good government groups; neighborhood groups; environmental groups; political parties; municipal employee or-ganizations; and racially based groups. We asked two questions designed to assess the group basis for entrepreneurial careers. First, we asked city clerks to judge how important each of these groups was in the career of the political entrepreneur.[14] We then asked the clerks if each of these groups was part of the coalition that the political entrepreneur assem-bled in order to win election.[15] While we recognize the absence of com-parative information for nonentrepreneurial politicians, we present the following information to illustrate the group basis for entrepreneurial careers in local politics.

The Importance of Different Groups in the Careers of Political Entrepreneurs

Neighborhood groups are the single most important group in the ca-reers of the political entrepreneurs we studied. Across the entire set of entrepreneurs, the mean importance assigned to neighborhood groups was the highest of all eight groups. Moreover, there was no regional var-iation in this pattern: in all four of the major census regions, neighborhood groups were always ranked the most important group. Even more telling, if we look only at the high end of the scale—that is, where a particular group was *very important* for the career of the entrepreneur—the pattern is even more pronounced: over half of the clerks judged neighborhood groups as very important for the careers of the political entrepreneur.

We believe that neighborhood groups play several roles in entrepreneurial politics at the local level: they minimize the costs of collective action; they provide a relatively low cost milieu from which entrepreneurs can launch challenges to the status quo; and they serve as intermediary organizations that can screen out opportunistic behavior and provide the entrepreneur with a reputation as a trustworthy leader.

Following the singular importance of neighborhood groups, business groups and taxpayer groups also were judged important in the careers of these entrepreneurs. The role of business groups in local governments is well understood and their importance in propelling entrepreneurs is confirmed in the empirical data presented earlier in this chapter. In contrast, the role of taxpayer groups needs further research.

At the bottom of the scale are racially based groups, with an average score just half that of neighborhood groups. While many central city politicians have launched careers and challenges to the existing power structure in their communities, the demographic makeup of suburbia has historically reduced the opportunities of politicians to launch race-based challenges to the status quo, but with the changing demography of suburbia, new opportunities may be emerging.

We examined the regional pattern for responses to each of the eight groups and discovered some differences. Among the most important is the greater role of racial groups in the South—a region where there has historically been a larger black population in suburbia. Neighborhood and environmental groups are more important in the West than in other regions. As we will show in the next chapter, this may in part be driven by the importance of antigrowth entrepreneurs in the West. In the Northeast, parties and municipal employee organizations are significantly more likely to have been important to the careers of political entrepreneurs than entrepreneurs in other regions. In contrast, these groups are particularly weak in the West, a difference in part explained by the strong nonpartisan tradition in the West and the strong history of local parties in the Northeast.

Groups and the Coalitions Entrepreneurs Assemble

In addition to the role each specific group played in the entrepreneur's political career, we also asked clerks whether or not each group was part of the coalition the entrepreneur assembled. Obviously there is an overlap between this question and the previous measure: entrepreneurs are likely to bring groups that were important to their career into their electoral coalition. Paralleling the previous analysis, we found that neighborhood groups are the most commonly included group in entrepreneurial coalitions. Racially based groups are by far the least common.

While taxpayer groups were important to the careers of many entrepreneurs, they are not included as often in entrepreneurial coalitions as we expected. While taxpayer groups ranked as the second most important group in career patterns, they were ranked third from last in terms of their inclusion in coalitions. In contrast, good government groups were included in a much higher percentage of coalitions than would be expected from their importance in the careers of entrepreneurs, ranking second in their frequency of inclusion in coalitions.

This difference between good government and taxpayer groups may reflect the stability and continuing involvement of good government groups in local politics—they have reputations to protect and may be reliable coalition members. In contrast, in the post–Proposition 13 world of tax revolts, taxpayer groups may be politically volatile and pose difficult problems for entrepreneurs who may need to finance new policies.

Techniques for Holding Coalitions Together

Our data provide some insight into how political entrepreneurs maintain their coalitions. First, and most important, political entrepreneurs emphasize feelings of "solidarity": 72 percent of our respondents reported that the entrepreneur made individuals feel like they were part of a team that was trying to accomplish an important job for the community. Similarly, 66 percent used the friendship of individuals in the coalition to maintain group support. But the coalition was also driven by the importance of specific "purposive" policy goals: 56 percent of the entrepreneurs stressed public policy goals to maintain their coalition.

In contrast, selective benefits were much less important. Only 35 percent of the entrepreneurs reportedly relied on the dissemination of information through newsletters. Less than one-quarter (22 percent) relied on possible professional or personal benefits people might gain from being part of a winning coalition, and only 6 percent offered very specific selective benefits such as group insurance or travel discounts.

These results show that selective benefits or the promise of some political patronage from the entrepreneur's victory do not form the core strategy for holding the entrepreneur's political coalition together. Instead, a vision of policy success and the feeling of being part of an important and cohesive team are the most common strategies entrepreneurs used to solve collective action problems. This evidence parallels the conclusion that Miller (1992) reaches in his analysis of assembling and maintaining teams in hierarchical organizations.

THE FUNCTIONS AND THE BASES OF
PUBLIC ENTREPRENEURSHIP

We have argued that every entrepreneur faces three specific tasks. Entrepreneurs must discover or create opportunities, they must assume some risks in assembling the resources to develop and pursue alternatives to the status quo, and they must overcome collective action problems to achieve those alternatives.

In the local market for public goods, our data show that opportunities for entrepreneurship emerge from a variety of factors. For example, we found that rapid growth and racial diversity in communities systematically create opportunities for political entrepreneurship. But the opportunities created by these and other conditions must be seized by entrepreneurs, and the rate at which entrepreneurs emerge to seize these opportunities is a function of the rational pursuit of power, motivated by the probabilities of profit and policy success: that is, some opportunities will be seized because the benefits outweigh the costs of entrepreneurship, while similar opportunities in other communities will not be seized because the political or social structure imposes high costs.

Thus, while entrepreneurs assume risks, they do not do so casually. Rather they calculate the extent of risks and the possible rewards for entrepreneurial activity. When the potential benefits for entrepreneurial success in a community are high, such as occur in communities with slack budgetary resources or in communities with a more rewarding full-time office of mayor, entrepreneurs are more likely to emerge. When the costs of organizing collective action are relatively low, as in communities with higher concentrations of homeowners or with strong business groups, entrepreneurs are also more likely to emerge. In solving these collective action problems entrepreneurs use their superior skills of rhetoric and organization to create a sense of teamwork. And they provide a vision of a new future to motivate their supporters.

In the next chapter, using these insights, we look in more detail at entrepreneurial activity in a domain that is at the center of local politics: the politics of growth.

CHAPTER 6

Entrepreneurs, Policy Dimensions, and the Politics of Growth

IN THIS CHAPTER, we show how the politics of local growth provide myriad opportunities for political entrepreneurship. Previously, we argued that entrepreneurs can affect political outcomes by manipulating the ideas underlying policy debates. In this chapter, we show how the politics of local growth can be understood as a conflict over the way in which citizens think about growth. We start this chapter by reviewing the role that entrepreneurs can play in defining the ideas that structure policy debates. We then turn to the literature on the growth machine and regime politics, emphasizing the link between institutional arrangements and ideology inherent in these approaches to the study of local politics.

Using a property rights perspective, we show that at the core of these two models of local politics is the assignment of the rights to control growth to business interests. We then argue that the politics of the entrepreneurial state, documented, for example, by Eisinger (1988) and Clarke (1990), and the politics of no-growth, documented, for example, by Logan and Molotch (1987) and Schneider (1992), can be understood as conflicts over the assignment of these property rights. Finally, we present empirical evidence showing the conditions under which different types of entrepreneurs concerned with the politics and ideology of growth emerge in suburban municipalities.

POLITICAL ENTREPRENEURS AND THE MANIPULATION OF IDEAS

Ideas are important. They help structure the options individuals, organizations, and entire policy systems consider and they help create and maintain political equilibria. North (1990) argues that institutions make it possible for individuals to avoid thinking about problems or confronting choices. For North, the corresponding incomplete processing of information attendant to institutional practices:

> [A]ccounts for ideology, based upon subjective perceptions of reality, playing a major part in human beings' choices. It brings into play the complexity and incompleteness of our information and the fumbling efforts we

make to decipher it. It focuses on the need to develop regularized patterns of human interactions in the face of such complexities, and it suggests that these regularized interactions we call institutions may be very *inadequate* or very far from optimal in any sense of the term. (1990: 23)

Regularized behaviors, such as the use of heuristics and standard operating procedures, that are embedded in institutional arrangements save computational time. And the inertia of these routines helps maintain the status quo even if present outcomes are far from optimal. But this, of course, means that extraordinary profits can be reaped by challenging the status quo and creating new arrangements.

Entrepreneurs often try to force people to think about a wider set of alternatives than they ordinarily consider. The resulting mobilization of otherwise quiescent individuals can disrupt existing political arrangements and create profits for entrepreneurs. But to seize these opportunities, entrepreneurs must overcome the inertia built into the status quo and overcome the active resistance of the groups that benefit from present institutional arrangements.

Political entrepreneurs can challenge the status quo by using rhetoric and heresthetics to make people think differently about political institutions and practices and to lead people to challenge what may otherwise seem like fixed parameters in the political world. One way entrepreneurs can do this is by reframing choices. As Tversky and Kahneman (1981) show at the individual level, reframing can break through existing routines and lead people to rethink their choices, behaviors, and habits.[1] At the organizational level, introducing new management styles or creating a new institutional "ethos" can break through established operating procedures and cause new, energetic, and more efficient production and provision of services. Osborne and Gaebler's (1992) study of local governmental innovations is full of examples of reinvigorated decision making and policy innovations brought about by the reconceptualization of the strategies, choices, and options available to local governments. Riker (1986), Derthick and Quirk (1985), and Baumgartner and Jones (1993) all demonstrate how political choices can be reframed creating dramatic systemic changes and causing seemingly stable policy systems to change rapidly.

Entrepreneurs are critical to this reframing process. By reframing problems and recasting the terms of political debates, entrepreneurs challenge institutional regularities and change political systems. By breaking up "regularized patterns" of interaction, entrepreneurs make people think about new solutions to problems, and in so doing, mobilize forces that can reshape the world to look more like the entrepreneur's vision of the future.

We accept Riker's (1986) distinction between rhetoric and heresthetics. Using rhetoric, a politician tries to change the outcome of a policy debate by shifting preferences within the existing dimensions of current policy discussions. To use Riker's terms, rhetoric seeks to relocate people's "ideal points" on existing parameters and it involves the use of persuasion to make people change their minds and their tastes (1986: 54). An entrepreneur using rhetoric will try to create a new constellation of opinion within the parameters of present debates. That is, rhetoric tries to shift *people* within the parameters of existing policy conceptualizations rather than changing *alternatives*.

The goal of the entrepreneur as heresthetician is different. Rather than trying to move people within an existing spatial configuration, heresthetics changes "the space or the constraints on the voters in such a way that they are encouraged, even driven, to move themselves to the advantage of the heresthetician" (Riker 1986: 47). The heresthetician thus redefines the ideas underlying the debates that are taking place. This is most dramatically accomplished by introducing new dimensions to ongoing debates: "the distinguishing feature of the heresthetic is that voters are induced to change sides, not by persuasion, but by reinterpretation of the issue" (p. 49). Compared to the goals of rhetoric, the goals of heresthetics are more ambitious because the heresthetician does not accept the terms of a debate as "given."

As Riker called attention to the fundamental instability of political arrangements brought about by the ability of herestheticians to induce policy changes and to disrupt equilibria in a wide range of circumstances, other analysts responded by noting that stability is in fact much more common and more enduring than Riker's analysis predicts. The most commonly offered solution to this disjunction between the widespread disequilibria predicted by theory and the widespread stability discovered by empirical observation is that institutions built on standard operating procedures limit choices and create stability despite any underlying disequilibria of tastes (the foundation of this argument is the idea of "structure-induced equilibrium" introduced by Shepsle 1979).

Building on Riker's concern for the ever-present potential for change, but recognizing the importance of structure-induced equilibrium, Baumgartner and Jones argue that ideas (or to use North's term, "ideologies") are central to policy stability and policy change. Baumgartner and Jones argue that policy stability is linked to a definable institutional structure that limits access to the policy process. The effectiveness of such an institutional arrangement requires a powerful supporting idea that legitimizes existing policies and limits political challenges. Politicians who benefit from this status quo use positive images and rhetoric to reinforce the link between policy ideology and the existing core political practices. The "tight connection" between institution and ideas provides support for the prevailing distribution of political advantage and creates the conditions for a structure-induced equilibrium.

However, stability is not permanent, in large part because the ideas that people hold about issues can change or, more importantly, these ideas can be changed. For Baumgartner and Jones, "change in issue definition can lead to destabilization and rapid change away from the old point of stability. This happens when issues are redefined to bring in new participants. Similarly a change in institutional rules of standing or of jurisdiction can rupture an old equilibrium" (1993: 16). The destruction of policy monopolies, and the equilibrium that these structures induce, is almost always associated with a change in the intensities of interest that groups have in an issue. By reframing issues, entrepreneurs lead people to look at existing policies in a new light, changing intensities of interest and mobilizing political forces to challenge the status quo.

We use the politics of local growth, a central issue of local politics, to explore the role of entrepreneurs in changing ideas and challenging existing institutional arrangements based on those ideas. In the next section, we explore the nature of property rights and we show how the assignment of the property rights to growth has created an institutional arrangement tightly linking ideology to political arrangements. We then show how challenges to these property rights lead to opportunities for entrepreneurial politicians.

ENTREPRENEURS, PROPERTY RIGHTS, AND THE POLITICS OF LOCAL GROWTH

We begin with Libecap's (1989) definition of property rights and with his description of the link between these rights, political power, and policy outcomes:

> Property rights are the social institutions that define or delimit the range of privileges granted to individuals to specific assets, such as parcels of land or water. Private ownership of these assets may involve a variety of rights, including the right to exclude nonowners from access, the right to appropriate the stream of rents from use of and investments in the resource, and the right to sell or otherwise transfer the resources to others. Property rights institutions range from formal arrangements, including constitutional provisions, statutes, and judicial rulings, to informal conventions and customs regarding the allocations and use of property. *Such institutions critically affect decision making regarding resource use.* (p. 1; emphasis added)

As Libecap argues, the assignment of property rights affects the distribution of the benefits and costs of assets and, by allocating decision-making authority, these rights determine the standing of actors in economic and political systems and define the resources they bring to negotiations over programs, laws, and policies.

Conflict emerges because property rights are usually underspecified. According to Barzel: "Because of the complexity of transactions and the costliness of metering and policing the attributes [of many goods], not all attributes are priced. . . . Because it is costly to measure commodities fully, the potential of wealth capture is present in every exchange. The opportunity for wealth capture is equivalent to finding property in the public domain; in every exchange, then, some wealth spills over into the public domain, and individuals spend resources to capture it" (1989: 3).

We believe that these abstract ideas find very real manifestations in the politics of local growth. As growth occurs in suburban communities and as land values rise, property rights may become more valuable. And as growth occurs, the assignment of property rights almost certainly becomes more contentious.

Consider, for example, the conversion of land from agricultural to residential use. Over generations, farmers may have assumed the right to spray their property with pesticides or herbicides in order to pursue their livelihood. When surrounded by other farmers or by undeveloped land, this property right may go unchallenged. As suburban growth proceeds and properties bordering farms are converted to residential use, the new property owners will often contest the rights of the farmer to continue using the chemicals the farmer needs. The specific right of farmers to use pesticides and the right of residents to be free from the spillovers of such use must now be negotiated and more fully specified in what can be a highly contentious political process as the "range of privileges" granted to individual property owners must be renegotiated.

Similarly, consider the "rights" of neighborhoods to be free of traffic congestion. As development occurs and as land is converted to more intense commercial or industrial activity, local traffic inevitably increases. Neighborhoods that have been accustomed to quiet streets with light traffic may now find themselves surrounded by shopping malls or commercial development. And they may find themselves swamped by the new traffic resulting from this growth. Who has the property rights to the streets: the neighborhoods that want quiet or the businesses that want more intense development and higher profits? This disagreement often ends up driving zoning decisions and local elections.

The point is clear: there are perpetual conflicts as individuals or groups seek to assign or modify property rights. This political process can be highly intense, because the assignment of property rights ultimately affects the distribution of wealth and the ability of actors to shape the outcomes of future political conflicts.

As this process unfolds, groups with vested interests in the status quo often have significant advantages in political bargaining because they have often used the present assignment of property rights to solve collective action problems—for example, farm organizations are often highly powerful politically even as the demography of a region shifts to more urban uses. Moreover, existing interests will have established ties to politicians and other political actors, further reducing the costs of collective action (Libecap 1989: 6). Thus, groups already benefitting from the present distribution of wealth are more likely to be organized politically. Conflict over property rights can be even more lopsided in favor of established groups because their perceived threat of loss tends to be weighed more heavily than the benefits of potential gain motivating challengers: that is, challenges to the present distribution of property rights threaten to remove a benefit already enjoyed by established interests. These groups are even more likely to mobilize their resources more effectively in defense of the status quo (Walker 1991; on prospect theory in general, see Quattrone and Tversky 1988).[2]

Libecap identifies three factors that increase pressure to change the existing assignment of property rights: shifts in relative prices; technological changes in production or enforcement; and, for our purposes most important, *shifts in preferences and other political parameters*. In our analysis, the first two factors are largely exogenous to the politics of local government. However, shifting preferences and changing political parameters is *exactly* what political entrepreneurship is all about.

Political entrepreneurs can use rhetoric to change preferences. More ambitiously, they can introduce new dimensions to political debates to fracture the existing equilibrium. And they can help solve collective action problems and mobilize new groups to challenge the prevailing distribution of power embodied by existing groups supporting the status quo. While technological changes or other social trends may increase the opportunities for successful challenges to the status quo, ultimately an entrepreneur must identify these opportunities and seize them.[3] We illustrate these themes using the local politics of growth.

THE GROWTH MACHINE AND THE POLITICS OF PROPERTY RIGHTS

At the core of many contemporary models of local politics is the alliance of local business interests and politicians united in the pursuit of growth and economic development. This alliance was termed the *Growth Ma-*

chine by Harvey Molotch in 1976. The businesses forming the core of the growth machine are ones that profit most directly from intense local land use and the associated profits of growth. These businesses include real estate, insurance and construction companies supported by banks, utilities, and the local media. The intensity of their shared interests and the resources they control make a business-based coalition a relatively unified force in local politics that can attract the participation of local politicians who then enact laws and policies to nurture growth. This political arrangement has a strong supporting ideology in the long-standing American belief that growth is good and that it is associated with "human progress" (see Molotch 1976; Logan and Molotch 1987; Elkin 1985; Garreau 1991).

The Growth Machine and the Property Rights of Growth

The growth machine is a political arrangement that assigns the property rights of growth to those advocating development and shifts political power toward land speculators, developers, and what Logan and Molotch (1987) call "rentiers"—individuals and groups concerned with land as a commodity—and shifts power away from "ordinary" citizens who gain enjoyment from their use of land.

There are reasons businesses have been able to capture the property rights to growth. Cities operate at the cusp of the demands of capital and the practices of a democratic society. As Elkin (1985), Stone (1989), and others have argued, in our democratic capitalist system the basis for all political authority in local governments rests on balancing two fundamental and often contradictory forces: the popular control of the formal machinery of government (embodied most obviously in the electoral process) and the private control of capital. For local governments, who are given responsibilities for raising money to support services by taxing local wealth, the balance between these forces gives rise to a fundamental corollary—local government conduct is constrained by the need to promote investment activity in an economic system dominated by private ownership.

This accommodation is biased by what Lindblom has called the "privileged" position of business in American politics resting in the dominant ideology of markets and the sanctity of capital. This privileged position is even more pronounced in the local political scene because of the mobility of capital and the reliance of local governments on local property tax resources. The nature of collective action may give local business added advantages. In particular, the "size principle" may increase the importance of business: Given the homogeneity of interests and the small number of business actors involved in local communities, business interests may constitute a "privileged" group in Olson's sense.[4]

The concept of privilege is central to Stone's analysis of regime politics. For Stone, in the day-to-day political environment of urban politics, coalitions are motivated by the importance of what he calls "small opportunities"—that is, most people are not motivated or propelled by a grand vision but by the pursuit of particular discrete projects. Any group that has the capacity to help others achieve these small opportunities is in a strong position to attract allies. There are many types of resources, including organizational support (such as money, credit, donations, business contacts, prestigious endorsements), technical expertise to allow the in-depth analysis of problems, and media coverage, that can enable individuals to seize the small opportunities that motivate them. As such, these strategic resources are incentives that cement political coalitions.

Note that these types of resources are always distributed in favor of business groups. The control of these selective incentives keeps business elites at the center of almost all local governing coalitions. Thus, in local politics, Olson's concept of "privilege" reinforces Lindblom's and the juxtaposition of strategic resources and ideology creates the enduring position of the growth machine.

The core *idea* uniting the growth machine is that growth is good, because it brings jobs, enhances the tax base, and pays for local services at moderate tax prices. The *resources* of the growth machine include selective incentives that allow it to solve collective action problems. And the core *institution* of the growth machine encompasses "downtown" business interests that maximize their profits with local growth.[5] In the city as growth machine, initial entitlements over the use of land are assigned to the members of the growth machine. In turn, progrowth policies de facto have high legitimacy.

While Stone (1989) argues that cities have a wider range of choices than the "corporate regime" of the growth machine and proposes two alternatives: "caretaker regimes" and "progressive regimes," his analysis shows how hard it is to transfer power away from corporate progrowth interests. But entrepreneurs always face established patterns of interests and successful entrepreneurs develop strategies to overcome entrenched current market configurations.

We believe that despite the difficulties presented by the entrenched growth machine, local political entrepreneurs can challenge the status quo by reconceptualizing the terms of the debate between the interests of capital and the interests of residents. Challenges can be mounted by entrepreneurs who can solve the collective action problem of neighborhood groups, allowing them to overcome the inherent privileges of local business interests. These challenges to the assignment of property rights can open up windows of opportunities for entrepreneurs to negotiate a new arrangement between established business interests and emerging claimants to power and policy. In short, challenging the equilibrium of the growth machine can create opportunities for extraordinary profits and opportunities for the political entrepreneur who can develop strategies for challenging the existing assignment of property rights.

PROGROWTH AND ANTIGROWTH ENTREPRENEURS

Our goal is to look in detail at progrowth entrepreneurs and then at the relatively new phenomena of challenges to the growth machine and the emergence of antigrowth entrepreneurs. We begin with an analysis of *progrowth* entrepreneurs. As we argued earlier, progrowth policies and the growth machine are established fixtures of local politics. Nonetheless, some entrepreneurs still seek to capitalize on the resources of the growth machine and the ideology of growth.

We then move to the analysis of entrepreneurial politicians who are seeking to create new innovative progrowth policies. We are particularly concerned with the emergence of a small number of politicians who are seeking to *shift* the debate about growth policies by introducing the more entrepreneurial approaches to growth identified by Peter Eisinger (1988; also see Clarke 1990). The analysis of the progrowth entrepreneur and of politicians advocating new growth policies demonstrates a fundamental point: while the interests of capital and the growth machine are the dominant sources of power in local politics, entrepreneurial politicians can still seek profits by stressing the importance of growth and probusiness activities and by defining new opportunities within the established progrowth policy space.

But some challenges transcend the boundaries of that policy space. In the following chapter, we analyze the more dramatic challenges to the present progrowth equilibrium that are embodied in the emergence of *antigrowth* entrepreneurs. These individuals engage in more risky behavior, seeking to *redefine* the terms of the policy debate of growth. Antigrowth entrepreneurs often introduce a new dimension to the debate over local growth and they organize new groups to challenge the privileged position of the business groups at the heart of the growth machine. By so doing, these entrepreneurs challenge the "tight connection" between ideology and political institutions that structures so much of local politics and that assigns the property rights to growth to members of the growth machine.

THE PROGROWTH ENTREPRENEUR
IN LOCAL GOVERNMENT

While business interests form the privileged core of local political coalitions, they cannot succeed in the local political scene on their own. Most importantly, the business community must create a link to political leaders in order to have their preferences translated into local public policies. One important link in this translation are entrepreneurs who propose progrowth policies and create coalitions to overcome resistance to such policies (Mollenkopf 1983; Elkin 1985, 1987; Logan and Molotch 1987; Stone 1989). There are payoffs to be garnered by successful progrowth entrepreneurs: they can advance their political careers by claiming credit for job creation and any tax stabilization resulting from economic growth. Perhaps more importantly, progrowth entrepreneurs gain access to the "selective incentives" controlled by business and can use these incentives to solve the organizational problems facing all entrepreneurs.

In their search for political advantage, progrowth entrepreneurs can propose that policies found in other communities be introduced into their community. This aspect of entrepreneurship is evident in the diffusion over time of what have become "standard" progrowth tools (such as tax abatements and industrial revenue bonds) in a process studied by Eisinger (1988), the ACIR (1981a), and others. Progrowth entrepreneurs can also propose that more innovative economic development policies be tried. For example, Eisinger (1988), Clarke (1990), and Goetz (1990) show that recently entrepreneurial politicians have begun to advocate and experiment with more innovative progrowth policies that go beyond the standard tools of economic development. But even if their policy positions or "products" are new, these progrowth entrepreneurs are motivated by the desire to gain political profit by their policy positions.[6]

We look first at the emergence of progrowth entrepreneurs. We are interested in identifying the factors associated with the emergence of progrowth entrepreneurs as a class. Following Eisinger, we then divide progrowth entrepreneurs into those who advocate the use of more-or-less standard tools of economic growth (what Eisinger calls "supply-side" policies) to attract development and those entrepreneurs who use the new generation of "demand-side" progrowth tools. In an analysis limited by a small number of communities with these types of entrepreneurs, we identify some of the conditions that may affect the emergence of these specific types of entrepreneurs.

THE BASIS FOR PROGROWTH ENTREPRENEURSHIP

Recall that in our survey we asked clerks if in the 1980s there had been any individual in their community whose "policy proposals and political positions represented a dynamic change from existing procedures." We then asked clerks a series of questions about the policy positions the entrepreneur took. In this analysis, we define a progrowth entrepreneur as an individual (a) who was identified by the clerk as an entrepreneur and (b) who advocated programs to attract new businesses or to retain existing ones.

Using this definition, progrowth entrepreneurship is a fairly common form of entrepreneurial activity: about 15 percent of the communities we surveyed had a progrowth entrepreneur and almost 60 percent of the entrepreneurs in our sample advocated progrowth policies of some kind.[7] (See the box on Eugene Moses, a fairly typical progrowth entrepreneur.)

The first goal of this chapter is to identify the factors that affect the probability that a progrowth entrepreneur will be found in a suburb. Paralleling our approach in chapter 5, we analyze the emergence of a local progrowth entrepreneur as a dichotomous (0,1) variable (with 1 meaning a progrowth entrepreneur was reported in the community) and we use probit analysis to identify the local conditions that affect the probability that a progrowth entrepreneur was found in a given community. We use the same variables and procedures reported in chapter 5 and measure the likelihood of finding a progrowth entrepreneur as a function of regional location, and political, fiscal, and demographic factors.[8]

The Regional Distribution of Progrowth Entrepreneurship

We begin by examining the regional distribution of progrowth entrepreneurs. Empirically, there is a regional pattern in the distribution of progrowth entrepreneurs; but this regional pattern is quite different from the distribution of antigrowth entrepreneurship we will show in the next chapter and that is documented in previous research (Logan and Zhou 1990; Donovan and Neiman 1992; Schneider and Teske 1993). Across the four major geographic regions delineated by the Census Bureau, the suburbs of the North Central region are significantly more likely to host a progrowth entrepreneur than are suburbs in other regions.

Among the suburbs in our sample, 21 percent of the suburbs in the North Central region had a progrowth entrepreneur, compared to 12

EUGENE MOSES:
A PROGROWTH ENTREPRENEUR

In 1982, midway through his four-year council term, Eugene Moses was elected mayor of Azusa, California, a suburban city outside of Los Angeles. Azusa had experienced considerable decline and its downtown had become the most run-down in the San Gabriel Valley; Moses called it "almost a skid row." Although Moses emerged as a progrowth entrepreneur with a focus on downtown, he faced significant opposition on his own city council. For example, Councilman Decker argued: "Nothing has been done down there for the past 30 years. The downtown area is gone. May Company (department store) is not going to move in." Moses countered: "If we aren't going to bring new businesses in, then we should really help the existing businessmen improve and renovate their property."

Upon taking office, Moses dismissed a redevelopment consulting firm the Azusa Community Redevelopment Agency (CRA) had retained for showing no progress in upgrading the downtown area over the previous six years. Again, Moses received little council support and expanded the scope of the issue by circulating petitions among the citizens. After getting 500 names on his petition, Moses stated: "I think the council will have to listen to this. There are just too many people who want something done downtown."

His plan to improve the downtown included building new shops, theaters, and restaurants that would not only serve the people of Azusa, but more importantly would attract tourists. Although his ideas were not fully adopted, he advocated successfully a historical-cultural commission to designate sites and to seek low-interest rehabilitation funding from the CRA, which he called "one of the most important things to happen in Azusa in years." His goal was to improve the town's aesthetic and historical appeal, the better to buttress his promotion of Azusa as the "Recreational Gateway to the [San Gabriel] Foothills."

In addition to this downtown-oriented progrowth approach, Moses developed other innovations. For example, he saved over $125,000 annually by contracting with the county for provision of fire and paramedic services, and emphasized efficiency in local government operations. Moses's entrepreneurial reach exceeded Azusa's boundaries; he fought for a national nuclear weapons freeze, arguing that small cities like Azusa need to speak out on national issues.

percent in the Northeast, 15 percent in the South, and 17 percent in the West.[9] Thus, while the West has been the geographic center of the highly visible antigrowth movement of the last ten years, suburbs in the North Central region have apparently concentrated on trying to attract business growth. This may be the direct result of the economic trends sweeping the regions during the 1980s, a time during which economic growth in metropolitan areas in the "rust belt" of the Midwest fell behind other regions. The pattern may also be the result of differences in historical attitudes toward growth.

THE EFFECTS OF LOCAL CONDITIONS ON PROGROWTH ENTREPRENEURSHIP

Political Conditions

In chapter 5, we showed explicitly how structural conditions of local government affect the benefits and costs of entrepreneurship and thus change the probability with which entrepreneurs are found across local governments. Here, we find once again that a full-time mayor and the office of manager are associated with the emergence of a progrowth entrepreneur (see table 6.1.1). Other variables that reflect the structure of elections do not affect the emergence of progrowth entrepreneurs.

The effects of group activity are important. First, and theoretically most relevant, there is a positive relationship between the reported strength of local business groups (such as the chamber of commerce) and the emergence of the progrowth entrepreneur. Local business groups stand to benefit directly from new programs that attract new businesses or implement policies to retain existing ones. And business groups can provide the resources to subsidize an entrepreneur advocating probusiness policies, in part by providing the resources necessary to overcome collective action problems and create political organizations.

We found a negative relationship between taxpayer groups and progrowth entrepreneurship. On one hand, taxpayer groups may be directly interested in progrowth policies that can lead to stabilization of tax rates. However, Barnekov and Rich (1989), Logan and Molotch (1987), and Schneider (1992), among others, argue that there are declining payoffs to local taxpayers from progrowth business policies. Taxpayer groups may have discovered this during the 1980s, putting brakes on the efforts of entrepreneurial politicians who promise programs designed to deliver benefits to taxpayers, but that in reality benefit mostly local businesses. To the extent that tax abatements and other concessions to businesses fail to stabilize local residential property taxes and represent "give

TABLE 6.1.1
The Effects of Political Conditions on the
Probable Emergence of a Progrowth
Entrepreneur

	Coefficient	Std. Error	p > t
Full-time mayor	.54	.15	.00
Turnover	.17	.11	.13
Term length	.01	.11	.88
Manager	.26	.13	.04
At-large	−.12	.31	.71
Nonpartisan	−.01	.15	.91
Parties	.02	.04	.57
Business groups	.09	.05	.07
Taxpayer groups	−.10	.05	.05
Neighbor groups	−.04	.08	.58
Interaction	.08	.09	.35
West	−.02	.21	.93
North Central	.33	.15	.02
South	−.03	.19	.86
Constant	−1.31	.29	.00

Source: Survey of city clerks. West, North Central, South: four main geographic regions delineated by U.S. Bureau of the Census (Northeast is the omitted category).

Notes: Number of observations: 788. Chi square: 32.45 (14 degrees of freedom). Prob > chi square: .003. Full-time mayor: 1 = full-time mayor; 0 = part-time mayor. Manager: 1 = city manager; 0 = no city manager. At-large: 1 = at-large elections; 0 = district elections. Nonpartisan: 1 = nonpartisan elections; 0 = partisan. Term length: 0 = 2-year term; 1 = 4-year term. Turnover: the number of different mayors in the last 10 years. Business groups: reported strength of business groups such as the chamber of commerce: 1 = not very important; 5 = very important. Taxpayer groups, Neighborhood groups, Parties: same as Business groups. Interaction: = 0 in district cities; = value of neighborhood group in at-large cities.

aways" to business, taxpayer groups may now present barriers to progrowth entrepreneurship.

There is no relationship between the strength of neighborhood groups and progrowth entrepreneurship. A growing literature traces antigrowth sentiments to conflict between neighborhoods and "downtown" interests and in the next chapter we show a direct relationship

TABLE 6.1.2

Sensitivity Analysis: The Effects of Political Variables on the Probability of
Finding a Progrowth Entrepreneur

	Full-time Mayor	Manager	Chamber of Commerce	Taxpayer Groups	Joint Probability
Maximum effect	.33	.21	.21	.22	.45
Minimum effect	.17	.15	.16	.16	.09

Notes: In the set of communities for which this particular probit was estimated, the mean probability is .19. To estimate the maximum effect, we set the dichotomous variables (Full-time mayor and Manager) to 1. We set them to 0 to estimate the minimum probability. The two group variables have a range of 0 to 5. We estimate the minimum and maximum probabilities by setting the variable to either + or −1 standard deviation from the mean (depending on the direction of the sign). The joint probability manipulates all four conditions simultaneously.

between the strength of neighborhood organizations and the emergence of antigrowth entrepreneurs.

The sensitivity analysis of table 6.1.2 shows clearly that these factors matter. The effect of the office of mayor is particularly important—a city without a full-time mayor has only a .17 probability of housing a progrowth entrepreneur. In cities with full-time mayors, the probability literally doubles. Together the four political variables have a large combined effect. Setting all these political variables to maximize the likelihood of finding a progrowth entrepreneur, the probability rises to .45. Setting all the variables to minimize the likelihood of finding a progrowth entrepreneur, the probability falls to .09.

The Effects of Fiscal Conditions

Using a one-tailed test of statistical significance, fiscal conditions significantly affect the probability of finding a progrowth entrepreneur in the way we predicted: higher taxes increase the likelihood of finding an entrepreneur, as does a weaker tax base (see tables 6.2.1 and 6.2.2). Citizens in communities with high taxes and a weak tax base may be more likely to endorse progrowth policies as a means of coping with high costs. We argued above that the relationship between economic growth and taxes may be tenuous at best and that organized taxpayer groups may no longer avidly support probusiness policies. Nonetheless, high taxes may create an opportunity for entrepreneurs to advocate policies to alleviate these costs. And given high enough taxes, the lure of such promises may be compelling, despite the experiences of other communities.

TABLE 6.2.1

The Effects of Fiscal and Budgetary Conditions on the
Probable Emergence of a Progrowth Entrepreneur

	Coefficient	Std. Error	p > t
Allocational expenditures	.05	.07	.45
Developmental expenditures	−.00	.06	.97
Redistributive expenditures	−.05	.06	.35
Tax rate	.09	.05	.09
True value	−.12	.07	.09
West	.11	.17	.55
North Central	.28	.14	.04
South	−.04	.19	.83
Constant	−1.07	.11	.00

Source: True value, Tax rate: state and local sources, adjusted for differences in assessment practices. Expenditures: 1982 Census of Governments, Finance, File A. West, North Central, South: four main geographic regions delineated by U.S. Bureau of the Census (Northeast is the omitted category).

Notes: Number of observations: 659. Chi square: 13.78 (8 degrees of freedom). Prob > chi square: .02. All variables are z-scores standardized by MSA means and standard deviations, that is, they are measures of the position of a community on that condition relative to its neighbors.

TABLE 6.2.2

Sensitivity Analysis: The Effects of Fiscal Variables
on the Probability of Finding a Progrowth
Entrepreneur

	Tax Rate	True Value	Both
Maximum effect	.20	.21	.24
Minimum effect	.15	.15	.12

Note: In the set of communities for which this probit was estimated, the mean probability is .18. To estimate the maximum effect we set the variables at either + or −1 (since these are z-scores, the mean = 0, the standard deviation = 1).

The Effects of Demographic Conditions

In tables 6.3.1 and 6.3.2, we turn to the effects of local demographic conditions. To explore the possibility of a relationship between income and progrowth entrepreneurship, we examine how local wealth (measured by community median income in 1980) affected the probability of

TABLE 6.3.1

The Effects of Demographic Conditions on the Probable Emergence of a Progrowth Entrepreneur

	Coefficient	Std. Error	$p > t$
Median income	−.23	.08	.00
Renter percent	−.05	.06	.40
Distance	−.11	.05	.06
Growth 1980s	.05	.06	.39
Black percent	.09	.05	.11
West	.19	.16	.26
North Central	.39	.12	.00
South	.07	.17	.65
Constant	−1.17	.09	.00

Source: Renter percent, Black percent, population 1980: 1980 Census of Population and Housing. Population 1990 counts generated by PL 94-171. Distance: maps. We , North Central, South: four main geographic regions delineated by U.S. Bureau of the Census (Northeast is the omitted category).

Notes: Number of observations: 829. Chi square: 27.99 (8 degrees of freedom). Prob > chi square: .03. All variables are z-scores standardized by MSA means and standard deviations, that is, they are measures of the position of a community on that condition relative to its neighbors. Median Income: Relative Community Income 1980. Growth 1980: z-score of Population 1990/Population 1980.

TABLE 6.3.2

Sensitivity Analysis: The Effects of Demographic Variables on the Probability of Finding a Progrowth Entrepreneur

	Distance	Median Income	Joint Probability
Maximum effect	.19	.23	.26
Minimum effect	.14	.11	.09

Notes: In the set of communities for which this particular probit was estimated, the mean probability is .17. To estimate the maximum effect, we set the variables at either + or −1 (since these are z-scores the mean = 0, the standard deviation = 1).

finding a progrowth entrepreneur during the 1980s. Indeed, higher income communities are less likely to support progrowth entrepreneurs (thus, communities with high-income residents and with a strong tax base—that is, communities that are already winning in the competition between cities—are less likely to support entrepreneurs who may seek to change policies that citizens already believe are working well).

We also relate the emergence of progrowth entrepreneurship to recent patterns of local growth. One possibility is that rapid rates of growth may reduce the likelihood of progrowth entrepreneurship—as communities absorb the costs of rapid growth (Logan and Molotch 1987; Feagin 1988), they may feel it necessary to curtail further expansion or certainly to reduce their support for more progrowth activities. However, rapid growth during the 1980s had no effect on the likelihood of finding a progrowth entrepreneur. Apparently, recent population growth does not necessarily turn communities away from support of progrowth business policies.

THE PROGROWTH ENTREPRENEUR

Local business forms a privileged core for most local political coalitions, and the resources they control give businesses extraordinary advantages in local politics. But business leaders must ultimately negotiate with politicians in order to translate their preferences into public policies. A critical political actor in this translation process is the progrowth entrepreneur—an individual who is willing to advocate new progrowth policies and who is willing to invest resources to construct a political coalition to enact these policies. This entrepreneur is attracted to progrowth policies for a variety of reasons. At one level, economic growth may be consistent with the entrepreneur's personal vision of the future. Progrowth entrepreneurs may also believe that the programs they advocate are beneficial to the community, for example, by creating jobs and by increasing the flow of tax revenues.

But there are other incentives that attract a progrowth entrepreneur. The rate at which potential entrepreneurs are attracted to the political arena is a direct function of the costs and benefits facing that entrepreneur. The business community can directly reduce the costs of entrepreneurship, by providing resources the entrepreneur needs to pursue a vision of the future. And the business community can help provide the organizational core for the entrepreneur, subsidizing the costs of collective action.

Not only can the business community reduce the costs of progrowth entrepreneurship, it can also influence its benefits. Most local politicians, including the entrepreneurs we identified, are themselves members of the business community, with backgrounds in law, insurance, or real estate. By advocating progrowth policies, probusiness political entrepreneurs may be trying to create an economic environment they believe will benefit not only their community but their own business prospects as well. Moreover, by maintaining good relations with the business community, progrowth entrepreneurs may expect future rewards from other members of that community.

The progrowth entrepreneur proposes policies to encourage economic development. These progrowth entrepreneurs take advantage of the current distribution of property rights and the ideology that "growth is good." And they profit from the resources made available by local business interests. However, there are problems with the growth machine that are undermining its appeal, giving rise to political opportunities for a new generation of entrepreneurs to challenge the politics of growth. We turn to a study of these individuals in the next chapter.

CHAPTER 7.

Entrepreneurial Challenges to the Status Quo: The Case of the Growth Machine

WHILE POLITICS supporting growth is perhaps the dominant pattern throughout the United States, in many communities residential support for progrowth policies has been replaced by growing opposition to further development. Such opposition can be widespread, transcending socioeconomic lines (e.g., Protash and Baldassare 1983; Fainstein and Fainstein 1983; Bollens 1990). Opposition is often organized around neighborhood groups seeking to protect their communities from the deleterious effects of continued growth. These groups then provide fertile ground for a new class of politicians who challenge the policies of the growth machine. We believe that these politicians demonstrate many dimensions of our theory of public entrepreneurship.

We identify two different types of entrepreneurs who contest the established policies of the growth machine. Ultimately, we argue that these entrepreneurs are proposing a redefinition of the property rights to growth, transferring these rights away from the traditional downtown interests that presently dominate the politics of growth.

The first type of entrepreneur we study has been identified by Peter Eisinger, and emphasizes new "demand-side" policies. This entrepreneur uses rhetoric to change people's attitudes toward growth (that is, the demand-side entrepreneur tries to move people's ideas within the existing policy domain favoring growth policies). In contrast, the second type, the antigrowth entrepreneur, seeks to introduce a new policy dimension to the politics of growth, and thereby shift the terms and outcome of the policy debate using the tools of heresthetics.

EISINGER'S DEMAND-SIDE ENTREPRENEUR

The case of Sonya Cranshaw (see box) provides a good illustration of the more proactive economic development efforts that have become increasingly common in recent years. Eisinger (1988) presents a comprehensive review of the "modern" tools of economic development offered by state and local governments. Eisinger argues that traditionally subnational governments concentrated on "supply-side" policies. The strategic

SONYA CRANSHAW:
A DEMAND-SIDE PROGROWTH ENTREPRENEUR

Sonya Cranshaw was a progressive village president in Hanover Park, a northwestern suburb of Chicago, who advocated balanced growth. In 1987, she brokered an impressive deal that should pay off well for the community.

One real estate development firm owned a large parcel of land upon which it sought to construct more single-family residences. The village preferred moderate-scale commercial development in that area. *The Chicago Tribune* quoted Cranshaw: "We felt we had an overabundance of residential development and decided to diversify our development . . . primarily to broaden our tax base, and to create some job opportunities for residents."

Rather than passively waiting for private market forces to structure patterns of growth for Hanover Park, Cranshaw led the village into playing an entrepreneurial role. The village purchased a large parcel of land from the residential developer, who then returned the $650,000 purchase price to the village to pay for infrastructure investments that the developer needed to build residences on a portion of the land he retained. The village then sold pieces of the land parcel they had purchased to a commercial developer to construct a business park. In this commercial deal, the village was able to get the industrial park to pay for its own infrastructure.

Because of Cranshaw's entrepreneurial activities, the village got the business park where and when it wanted it, with attendant tax revenues and local job opportunities. The two developers were able to build the commercial and residential projects they wanted to build, and the village did not pay for expensive infrastructure.

underpinning of the supply-side approach is for communities to maximize their comparative locational advantage, mostly by lowering the capital costs for businesses choosing to locate in a community. The ideological underpinnings of this approach are consistent with a capitalist system and local supply-side policies defer to the prerogatives of capital, relegating governments to a subsidiary and responsive role. The emblematic policy of this approach is tax abatements, which are offered to induce a firm to locate in a community by reducing the capital costs of building in the community.[1]

Demand Side   Supply Side

Fig. 7.1. The Single Dimension of the Supply versus Demand Argument

Eisinger (1988: 73–74) enumerates the specific assumptions of the supply-side approach: First is the idea that "private business possesses a special claim to efficiency, effectiveness, and vision. . . . A second is the proposition that it is optimally efficient for the private sector, acting without government direction or constraint, to allocate resources functionally and geographically. . . . A third is the conviction that the marketplace is a valid testing and winnowing process for firms and entrepreneurs which will in the long run produce economic growth. This competition should, therefore, be allowed to run its course."

The demand-side entrepreneur challenges this ideology, but does not challenge the fundamental assumption that growth is good for local communities. As portrayed in figure 7.1, the strategic objective of the challenge for Eisinger's demand-side entrepreneur is to shift public opinion on the single dimension of proeconomic development from favoring supply-side policies to favoring demand-side policies.

What "profit" does the demand-side entrepreneur seek in shifting opinions within the terms of the economic development debate? First, there may be legitimate policy reasons for advocating the use of new economic development policies. Many supply-side policies are at the end of their product lives and have declining payoffs (see Schneider 1992). But more important from the viewpoint of the entrepreneurial politician, traditional supply-side policies are now standardized techniques that are found in the "tool box" of almost all local governments—they are more like commodities than they are specialized products. As standard policies, these tools are now in the domain of a cadre of professional managers (Blair, Fichtenbaum, and Swaney 1984), reducing the profits available to political entrepreneurs. By introducing new demand-side policies, entrepreneurs can (or at least they promise they can) produce higher benefits for their community. And if these new demand-side policies are at the beginning of the product life, extraordinary profits for the entrepreneur and the community are indeed possible.

The strategic task for the demand-side entrepreneur is to find the appropriate rhetoric to move people's opinions on the single progrowth dimension. This requires promoting a new idea of government-business relations and the capacity of government to "grow" the economy. Eisinger argues that the demand-side policies have a fundamentally different ideological position on the relationship between capital and government.

For Eisinger, the "demand-side model stresses the need to attract or develop industries that export beyond local borders. . . . The policy implications of the demand-side export-base model require that planners encourage the development of only certain selected industries" (1988: 76). The demand-side entrepreneur argues that government must become a more active partner with private enterprise and that it uses its resources to help local industries develop new markets and develop and test new technologies. This is an ideological challenge to the passive government role. The entrepreneur must persuade people to believe in a new, more expansive governmental role. The ideology is technocratic and expansive, the policies are new, and the rewards for success are high.

Demand-side entrepreneurs who try to shift people's opinions can present a reconceptualization of the strategies and outcomes of intercommunity competition. We draw on game theoretic terms to highlight the strategy that underlies traditional supply-side policies and then to develop the strategies used by the demand-side entrepreneur.

THE SUPPLY-SIDE VERSUS THE DEMAND-SIDE ECONOMIC DEVELOPMENT "GAME"

Consider the case of two communities choosing whether or not to offer tax abatements. We portray this as a simple two by two game—each community can choose to offer an abatement or not to abate. While there are multiple outcomes, the supply-side politician stresses only the two highlighted boxes on the diagonal in panel 1 of figure 7.2. That is, the choice the supply-side politician presents is simple: if our community gives tax abatements, then we will win. If we don't give tax abatements, some other community will give them, and we will lose. The two other outcomes of the choice situation are not presented.

Politician's Community

		Don't Abate	Abate
Other	Don't Abate	0, 0	− , +
Communities	Abate	+ , −	− , −

Fig. 7.2. Hypothetical Payoffs for Use of Standard Supply-side Policies from the Perspective of a Traditional Progrowth Politician: The Case of Tax Abatements

There is considerable empirical evidence that the outcome of this game is for all communities to offer tax abatements. This of course resembles the outcome of a prisoner's dilemma game: individual communities hoping to profit by offering abatements instead find themselves at the lower right corner of the game—a suboptimal result in which communities offer tax abatements that are not profitable and may actually cost them more than they get in return.

There are many theoretical solutions to the prisoner's dilemma game, some of which have real counterparts in choices over growth policy. One solution to this suboptimal outcome would be to find a way to move all communities jointly out of the tax abatement game, shifting the outcome to the northwest corner of figure 7.2. Regional pacts between state governors are common, in which they swear that they will not raid neighboring states for businesses. However, even with limited numbers of actors (that is, governors) who interact frequently, defections are common. At the local level the task of solving this dilemma is even harder, if for no other reason than that larger numbers of actors are involved, and it is almost impossible for a politician to unilaterally declare the end of tax abatements hoping that other cities will cooperate in moving to a more efficient outcome.

Demand-side entrepreneurs try to solve this dilemma by proposing a new economic development game. The demand-side entrepreneur rephrases the choice as follows: communities can continue to offer traditional supply-side policies or they can offer new demand-side policies. We depict the new demand-side game in figure 7.3. To the extent that the entrepreneur persuades people to accept this conceptualization, they will obviously choose the demand-side policies the entrepreneur is "selling." In this new game, demand-side policies are the dominant strategy since a community choosing demand-side policies playing against a community offering supply-side policies always wins. And even if all communities choose demand-side policies, the expanding economic pie still produces net gains for the community choosing demand-side policies.

In short, the demand-side entrepreneur uses rhetoric to persuade local citizens to reconceptualize the economic development game and to shift the terms of the debate to favor the entrepreneur's preferred policies. To the extent that this occurs, the property rights to growth are shifted away from the existing growth machine in which local politicians are subservient to traditional downtown business interests and in which growth policies are institutionalized in the hands of bureaucrats. By using a new ideological conceptualization of the role of government vis-a-vis business, the demand-side entrepreneur stands to garner extraordinary profits in the growth game.

Eisingerian Entrepreneur's Community

	Use Supply-Side Policies	Use Demand-Side Policies
Use Supply Side	$-$, $-$	$-$, $+$
Use Demand Side	$+$, $-$	$+$, $+$

Other Communities

Fig. 7.3. Hypothetical Payoffs for Use of Supply- and Demand-side Policies from the Perspective of an "Eisingerian" Progrowth Entrepreneur

EMPIRICAL EVIDENCE ON SUPPLY- VERSUS DEMAND-SIDE POLICIES

To gather information about the specific policy tools used by demand-side entrepreneurs, we mailed a detailed follow-up questionnaire to communities in which a political entrepreneur was reported in our first survey. Among other items, this questionnaire contained a battery of questions about the specific growth policies the entrepreneur advo-cated.[2] These questions were designed to distinguish between entrepre-neurs who relied on the traditional tools of economic development[3] and those who advocated the use of demand-side growth policies. Figure 7.4 lists the ten progrowth policies about which we queried clerks. Following Eisinger, we divided these policies into demand- and supply-side ap-proaches to economic development.

Supply-Side Policies
　　tax abatements for firms
　　city programs for industrial site development
　　tax increment financing
　　loan guarantees
　　industrial revenue bonds

Demand-Side Policies
　　city venture capital funds for starting up companies
　　city financed incubator projects
　　encouraging foreign investments in the city
　　expanding foreign trade by local firms
　　stricter laws regulating plant closings

Fig. 7.4. Demand-side and Supply-side Progrowth Policies (Based on Eisinger 1988)

TABLE 7.1

Selected Characteristics of Communities without Progrowth
Entrepreneurs and with Demand-side and Supply-side
Progrowth Entrepreneurs

	Suburbs w/o Progrowth Entrepreneur	Demand-side Entrepreneur	Supply-side Entrepreneur
Full-time mayor	.13	.33[a]	.16
Manager	.59	.66	.73[a]
Business groups	2.57	2.83	2.76
Taxpayer groups	2.97	2.77	3.02
Tax rate 1982	0.00	.33	.44[a]
Growth 1970s	−0.02	.01	.02
Median income	0.00	−.19	−.22
Population 1980	0.08	.72[a]	.33
Northeast	.38	.33	.11[a]
North Central	.35	.38	.70[a]
West	.14	.16	.14
South	.13	.11	.05

Notes: Number of observations: Suburbs without progrowth entrepreneur 800;
Demand-side entrepreneurs 18; Supply-side entrepreneurs: 37.

For variables Full-time mayor, Manager, and Northeast through South, entries
are the percent of communities with each type of entrepreneur that has the particular characteristic. That is, of the communities with demand-side entrepreneurs, one-
third had full-time mayors, while only 16 percent of communities with supply-side
entrepreneurs had full-time mayors. For the group variables, the entry is the average
score on a scale of 1 to 5 of the reported political importance of the group (with
higher numbers indicating greater importance). Tax rate through Median income
are the average z-scores: for example, the population in communities with demand-
side entrepreneurs is .7 standard deviations higher than its metropolitan regional
average, while communities with supply-side entrepreneurs are only .33 standard
deviations above average.

[a] Difference between the reported mean in cell and mean for suburbs without
progrowth entrepreneur significant at $p < .05$.

We define a "demand-side" progrowth entrepreneur as someone who
advocated two or more demand-side economic development policies.
Similarly, a "supply-side" progrowth entrepreneur was defined as someone who advocated three or more traditional tools.[4] Among all the
progrowth policies we asked about, the most common were site development, tax abatements, industrial revenue bonds—all "supply-side" policies. In contrast, many fewer entrepreneurs used demand-side policies:
14 percent used venture capital funds; 15 percent advocated incubators;
8 percent encouraged foreign trade or foreign investment; and only 7
percent are trying to impose limits on plant closings.

Unfortunately, given the small sample size of 117 communities that
responded to our second wave questionnaire, rigorous tests of the fac-

tors affecting the emergence of these specific types of entrepreneurs are not possible. However, comparative data does illustrate some patterns in the distribution of demand-side entrepreneurship. Table 7.1 presents the mean values of selected variables for communities with supply-side and demand-side entrepreneurs.[5] We also present the mean values for these variables for the 800 communities that did not have progrowth entrepreneurs. These results highlight some systematic differences between the types of communities supporting different forms of entrepreneurship and they indicate some patterns for further research.

The Life Cycle of Growth Policies

One role of entrepreneurs is to introduce established products into new markets. Another and riskier role for entrepreneurs is to push truly innovative products or policies. Our data suggest that it is more common for progrowth entrepreneurs to advocate the use of the more established tools of economic development than it is for them to advocate more radical ones. While the payoffs for more innovative tools can be greater, so are the risks. Nonetheless, some entrepreneurs are pushing more radical programs and some of these entrepreneurs will succeed, garnering large gains in their visibility and in their reputations.

Assuming that the number of demand-side entrepreneurs grows (especially as the rewards of traditional supply-side policies are bid away) and as their policies prove successful, the downside risks will become better understood and reduced. A winnowing out process will occur in which the best policies will be "certified" and the knowledge of how to enact and manage these policies will diffuse. Over time, a body of these (presently) innovative demand-side policies will become part of the standard tool kit of local politicians. Ultimately, they will be assigned to bureaucratic managers who have learned the techniques and methods of demand-side growth policies. This replicates the process by which the previously "innovative" supply-side economic development policies, such as tax abatements, became standard tools of local government.

The Regional Pattern

Among the patterns that stand out is a distinct regional pattern in the distribution of the two types of progrowth entrepreneurs: supply-side progrowth entrepreneurs are disproportionately found in the North Central region. While only 35 percent of all the suburbs in the sample are in this region, twice that proportion of supply-side entrepreneurs are found there. Again, this may reflect the more conservative attitudes of the region.

Political Incentives for Demand-side Entrepreneurship

Demand-side entrepreneurs are more likely to be found in communities with full-time mayors (one-third of the cities with demand-side entrepreneurs had full-time mayors, while only 16 percent of cities with supply-side entrepreneurs had full-time mayors). We think there may be two related reasons for this. First, full-time mayors may possess the political capital and prestige to embark on more radical entrepreneurial policies. Second, many students of entrepreneurship argue that the most innovative entrepreneurs are likely to have personalities that allow them to believe fervently in a specific vision of the future and allow them vigorously to pursue that vision. Entrepreneurs seeking the more demanding job of full-time mayor may be more likely to have the personality characteristics and commitments that make them willing to embark on the innovative and risky policy paths outlined by Eisinger. Note, too, that communities with demand-side entrepreneurs are relatively larger than those with supply-side progrowth entrepreneurs. The successful pursuit of office in the more intense political environment of larger cities may increase the likelihood of finding an entrepreneur with the personality strengths to pursue more innovative policies.

While these factors are consistent with a theoretical approach to political entrepreneurship, given our limited empirical base, we present these findings as illustrative and as outlining areas for future research.

THE ANTIGROWTH ENTREPRENEUR: INTRODUCING NEW DIMENSIONS INTO LOCAL GROWTH POLITICS

The demand-side entrepreneur seeks to change the outcome of the policy debate by shifting people's preferences within an established progrowth policy dimension. The job of the antigrowth entrepreneur is more challenging. The antigrowth entrepreneur seeks to more thoroughly disrupt the existing progrowth equilibrium by alerting people to a new dimension of debate that differs from the existing conceptual framework of progrowth policies. In this, the antigrowth entrepreneur relies on the tools of the heresthetic.

Our present understanding of the origins and the successes of the antigrowth movement is limited. Research into the antigrowth movement has proceeded along a fairly narrow line with most studies predicated on the assumption that successful opposition to the demands of the growth machine rests on the mobilization of citizen groups. The usual mode of analysis of antigrowth movements relates some general measures of local political, economic, or social conditions to the extent of antigrowth attitudes and antigrowth policies. However, studies along these lines have reported decidedly mixed results (compare, e.g., Gottdeiner and Neiman 1981; Baldasarre and Protash 1982; Albrecht, Bultena, and Hoiberg 1986; Bollens 1990; Logan and Zhou 1990; Donovan and Neiman 1992).

We argue that, fundamentally, this approach is flawed: it is not enough that the objective conditions in a given community may support an antigrowth movement—an antigrowth entrepreneur may be a necessary catalyst for change.

THE ROLE OF THE ANTIGROWTH ENTREPRENEUR

The antigrowth entrepreneur presents an alternative policy dimension that can split the existing progrowth coalition. In order to win elections and justify their policies, progrowth politicians focus on the importance of economic development and the creation of new jobs. In contrast, existing case studies, mostly of large cities, show that the antigrowth entrepreneur stresses different values to mobilize opposition to "downtown," probusiness growth policies. Terms describing this alternative emphasis include Swanstrom's (1985) "urban populism," Clavel's (1986) "progressive city," and Stone and Sanders's (1987) "progressive regimes." The underlying similarity of these disparate analyses is their agreement on how an alternative value, usually equality or the value of neighborhood preservation, can undermine the appeal of the progrowth coalition. Based on studies such as these and on empirical data we present below, we argue that the antigrowth entrepreneur introduces a new dimension to local political debates, fracturing the existing and apparently stable progrowth "equilibrium" and creating a new and more profitable outcome.[6] Figure 7.5 illustrates this process.

Introducing a different dimension into local debate is just one part of the antigrowth entrepreneur's problem. In order to capitalize on any shifts in the terms of local policy debate, the antigrowth entrepreneur is faced with a critical political problem: the entrepreneur must overcome the difficulty of mobilizing residential groups to compensate for the relative ease with which local business groups can organize. Antigrowth coalitions are often based on a diffuse set of interests. Thus, a latent antigrowth coalition faces difficult collective action problems, problems that

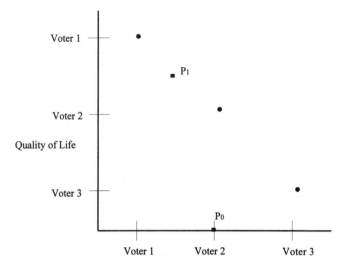

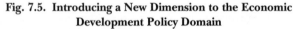

**Fig. 7.5. Introducing a New Dimension to the Economic
Development Policy Domain**

An entrepreneur can introduce a new dimension, e.g., the
quality of life, into the debate about growth. The entrepreneur
now offers policy P_1. This policy is closer in Euclidean space to
both Voter 1 and Voter 2, who now combine to overturn the
previous outcome P_0.

the antigrowth entrepreneur can help solve.[7] This perspective helps explain why so many antigrowth movements have their roots in neighborhood organizations (see the box on the antigrowth entrepreneur; also
Logan and Rabrenovic 1990).

The Neighborhood Basis for Antigrowth Activity

It is easier to solve collective action problems in neighborhoods than in
larger spatial units, and it may be easier to solve these problems in suburbs than in large central cities. The homogeneity of interests, the lower
transaction costs when social status is shared, and the frequency with
which neighbors interact, especially when faced with a proposed development that threatens the character of a neighborhood, all ease the task
of organizing a political base. To the extent that the antigrowth entrepreneur can mobilize a local community and successfully ameliorate or
defuse a threat to a neighborhood, the entrepreneur establishes a reputation and a political base for further challenges to the growth machine.

THOMAS PELLEGRINO:
AN ANTIGROWTH ENTREPRENEUR

Thomas Pellegrino is the full-time mayor of the village of Port Washington North on Long Island, one of the most affluent suburbs in the New York region. Pellegrino developed an antigrowth strategy to deal with the continuing pressure of growth. Port Washington North was incorporated in 1932, with 681 people, but grew to over 3,150 by the mid-1980s. Like so many other suburbs around the country, the village expanded from a mere hamlet into a community of single-family homes, garden apartments, shopping centers, industrial parks, and the home of the world's largest magazine subscription services, Publisher's Clearing House.

Pellegrino earned his entrepreneurial designation by successfully limiting growth pressure, particularly by opposing proposed large-scale condominium projects, new commercial developments, and the expansion of the Publisher's Clearing House facilities. He argued that this commercial growth needed to be balanced by concern for the residential character of the village, the limited capacity of both the area sewer district and the railroad station parking lot, and the need for a strong tax base. As is common with antigrowth entrepreneurs, Mayor Pellegrino found support in neighborhood organizations. In 1982 and 1983, he worked with two newly formed neighborhood groups, the Residents for a More Beautiful Port Washington and the Port Washington North Homeowners Association, to reduce the scale of the expansion of Publisher's Clearing House. This struggle resulted in fierce political and legal battles, in which Pelligrino stood on the side of residents against his village's largest employer. After losing court challenges, he supported a new ordinance to limit the height of future commercial construction in the village: "The intent of this legislation is, in my opinion, to protect the residences that abut these [industrial/commercial] areas." While fighting these battles over growth, Pellegrino managed to keep property taxes stable, while maintaining a high level of local services.

In 1993, Pellegrino was still the mayor of Port Washington North. Growth has continued to be a contentious issue, including a recent proposed shopping center that includes a fast food restaurant, the type of which has become increasingly unpopular in affluent New York City suburbs. Again, Pellegrino forced compromises on the part of the new businesses to meet the concerns of residents and their neighborhood groups. In his pursuit of a slow and balanced approach to local growth, Pellegrino has mobilized policy input through frequent public hearings, and has used this as a basis for developing a cooperative approach with the Board of Trustees.

In turn, these neighborhood organizations provide the functional equivalent of "screening" by which the quality and sincerity of a potential antigrowth entrepreneur is established. Most markets rely on intermediation to facilitate adjustment and to screen for quality—but screening for the quality of an entrepreneur is difficult (Casson 1982). Given the uncertainty and complexity of challenges to the growth machine and the potential profits of successful challenges to the established progrowth elite, many people who would not qualify as "true" antigrowth entrepreneurs may be tempted to offer antigrowth policies, engaging in "opportunistic behavior" (Williamson 1985).

Reputation is perhaps the most important screen by which to limit such opportunism. As shown in transaction cost economics, reputation is most directly and reliably built on a history of successful trades that produces confidence in the reliability of future transactions (Shapiro 1983; Bull 1983). We believe that service in local neighborhood and civic associations screens for quality, by testing for entrepreneurial ability and by allowing an individual to build a reputation for valued leadership traits such as reliability and honesty.

Our emphasis on the role of entrepreneurs leads to a less deterministic view of politics than embodied in most studies of antigrowth politics. Entrepreneurship by its very nature is not a routine, predictable part of the political scene. Thus, the failure of existing studies adequately to explain or predict antigrowth policies is not surprising. Without an understanding of the presently nonroutinized nature of antigrowth politics, the standard approach of linking objective indicators of local conditions to policy outcomes simply will not work. Instead of looking at factors that may affect the adoption of local antigrowth *policies*, we look at the factors that affect the probable emergence of an antigrowth *entrepreneur*.

THE LOCAL BASIS FOR THE ANTIGROWTH ENTREPRENEUR

For purposes of this empirical analysis, we classify an antigrowth entre-preneur as an individual (a) who was identified by the clerk in our sam-ple cities as an entrepreneur and (b) who advocated capping residential, commercial, or industrial growth.[8] As noted earlier, about 27 percent of the clerks identified an entrepreneur in their community. Using our definition, the antigrowth entrepreneur is relatively rare: only about 6 percent of the communities we surveyed had an antigrowth entre-preneur. In contrast, recall that progrowth entrepreneurs were more than twice as likely to be found.

In the following empirical analysis, we analyze the emergence of a local antigrowth entrepreneur as a dichotomous (0,1) variable (with 1 meaning an antigrowth entrepreneur was reported in the community) and use probit analysis to identify local conditions affecting the probabil-ity that an entrepreneur was found in a given community.[9]

LOCAL FACTORS AFFECTING THE EMERGENCE OF THE ANTIGROWTH ENTREPRENEUR

Previous work has shown a clear regional pattern to the distribution of antigrowth entrepreneurs—they are disproportionately found in the West. Donovan and Neiman (1992) argue that this regional pattern rests on the distribution of political factors—the participatory political struc-tures of the West make local governments more open to challenges to the status quo.

Not surprisingly, we find that the probability of finding an antigrowth entrepreneur is a function of theoretically interesting political condi-tions (see table 7.2.1). Note that the probability of finding an antigrowth entrepreneur increases when the representation system is based on dis-tricts rather than at-large and when the office of mayor is full time.[10] Even more important, note that the strength of neighborhood groups does increase the likelihood of finding an antigrowth entrepreneur in at-large cities but not in cities with district elections.[11]

Table 7.2.2 reports in more detail the changes in the actual probability of finding an antigrowth entrepreneur as a function of changes in the most important conditions identified in table 7.2.1. The effects of a full-time mayor (regardless of the form of election) is striking: changing from no mayor to a full-time mayor increases the probability of finding an antigrowth entrepreneur from 1 percent to 20 percent in at-large

TABLE 7.2.1

The Effects of Political Conditions on the
Probable Emergence of an Antigrowth
Entrepreneur

	Coefficient	Std. Error	p > t
Full-time mayor	.78	.19	.00
Turnover	.04	.14	.76
Term length	−.12	.15	.41
Manager	.36	.18	.05
At-large	−1.01	.42	.01
Nonpartisan	.15	.21	.45
Parties	.05	.05	.36
Business groups	.01	.06	.83
Taxpayer groups	.02	.06	.74
Neighbor groups	−.08	.09	.40
Interaction	.24	.12	.04
West	.61	.26	.02
North Central	.33	.20	.12
South	.46	.25	.06
Constant	−1.98	.39	.00

Source: Survey of city clerks. West, North Central, South: four main geographic regions delineated by U.S. Bureau of the Census (Northeast is the omitted category).

Notes: Number of observations: 788. Chi square: 35.11 (14 degrees of freedom). Prob > chi square: .081. Full-time mayor: 1 = full-time mayor; 0 = part-time mayor. Manager: 1 = city manager; 0 = no city manager. At-large: 1 = at-large elections; 0 = district elections. Nonpartisan: 1 = nonpartisan elections; 0 = partisan. Term length: 0 = 2-year term; 1 = 4-year term. Turnover: the number of different mayors in the last 10 years. Business groups: reported strength of business groups such as the chamber of commerce: 1 = not very important; 5 = very important. Taxpayer groups, Neighborhood groups, Parties: same as Business groups. Interaction: = 0 in district cities; = value of neighborhood group in at-large cities.

cities and from 5 percent to 37 percent in cities with district elections. The role of small-scale organization in encouraging antigrowth entrepreneurship (district representation or neighborhood groups in at-large systems) is also clearly evident: for every condition shown in table 7.2.1, the probability of finding an antigrowth entrepreneur is considerably higher in cities with district elections compared to cities using at-large elections. The only condition in which the probability of finding an

TABLE 7.2.2

Sensitivity Analysis: The Effects of Political Variables on the Probability of
Finding an Antigrowth Entrepreneur

	No Mayor	Mayor	Full-time Mayor	−1 s.d. Interact	+1 s.d. Interact
At-large	.01	.06	.20	.12	.41
District	.05	.15	.37	.43	.43

Note: In this set of communities, the mean probability is .07. Interact is set at its mean and the dichotomous variables are set at their modal value while the conditions in the table are changed. Interact measures the interaction of the form of representation (district or at-large) and the strength of neighborhood groups. Since Interact assumes a value of 0 in district systems, the probability reported in the last two columns of the District row do not change. In the At-large row, its effects are estimated setting the mayor variable equal to "Full-time."

antigrowth entrepreneur in at-large cities approaches that in cities using district elections is the final cell in table 7.2.2—that is, when neighborhood groups are extremely strong. We believe this clearly shows the relationship between spatial decentralization, the size of constituencies, and the intensity of the collective action problem facing political entrepreneurs.

In contrast, note that the effects of demographic variables on the emergence of the antigrowth entrepreneur are weak (see tables 7.3.1 and 7.3.2) and that the fiscal and expenditure patterns reported in table 7.4.1 have no effect. In many previous studies, demographic variables have not been found to affect antigrowth activity. Our results are similar: with one important exception—the relative rate of growth during the 1980s—the probability with which an antigrowth entrepreneur emerges is not affected by local demographic or fiscal conditions.[12]

ENTREPRENEURIAL PROFITS AND THE POLITICS OF GROWTH

The progrowth entrepreneur we discussed in the previous chapter seeks to take advantage of the prevailing link between the ideology of growth and the privileged position of local business interests. These progrowth entrepreneurs may represent the last wave of the diffusion of what are now well developed tools of local development. The risks here are low— the policy products have been well-identified and used in a variety of circumstances. Moreover, by building on a core of established local interests, the costs of this type of entrepreneurship are also low. But we believe that the benefits of this type of entrepreneurship are correspondingly low. Since the "market for jobs" is now so fully developed, most

TABLE 7.3.1

The Effects of Demographic Conditions on the
Probable Emergence of an Antigrowth
Entrepreneur

	Coefficient	Std. Error	$p > t$
Median income	−.02	.09	.83
Renter percent	−.00	.08	.92
Distance	−.02	.07	.69
Growth 1980s	.17	.06	.01
Black percent	.13	.07	.07
West	.49	.20	.01
North Central	.25	.20	.14
South	.47	.20	.02
Constant	−1.77	.13	.00

Source: Renter percent, Black percent, population 1980: 1980 Census of Population and Housing. Population 1990: counts generated by PL 94-171. West, North Central, South: four main geographic regions delineated by U.S. Bureau of the Census (Northeast is the omitted category). Distance: maps.

Notes: Number of observations: 829. Chi square: 17.09 (8 degrees of freedom). Prob > chi square: .04. All variables are z-scores standardized by MSA means and standard deviations, that is, they are measures of the position of a community on that condition relative to its neighbors. Median income: relative community income 1980. Growth 1980: z-score of population 1990/population 1980.

TABLE 7.3.2

Sensitivity Analysis: The Effects of Demographic Variables on
the Probability of Finding an Antigrowth Entrepreneur

	Black percent	Growth	Joint Probability
Maximum effect	.08	.09	.11
Minimum effect	.05	.05	.03

Note: In the set of communities for which this particular probit was estimated, the mean probability is .17. To estimate the maximum effect we set the variables at either + or −1 (since these are z-scores the mean = 0, the standard deviation = 1).

TABLE 7.4.1

The Effects of Fiscal and Budgetary Conditions on the
Probable Emergence of an Antigrowth Entrepreneur

	Coefficient	Std. Error	$p > t$
Allocational expenditures	.07	.09	.43
Developmental expenditures	.03	.08	.66
Redistributive expenditures	−.15	.11	.16
Tax rate	−.08	.08	.33
True value	.01	.09	.83
West	.35	.22	.11
North Central	−.01	.20	.95
South	.26	.24	.28
Constant	−1.62	.15	.00

Source: True value, tax rate: state and local sources, adjusted for differences in assessment practices. Expenditures: 1982 Census of Governments, Finance, File A. West, North Central, South: four main geographic regions delineated by U.S. Bureau of the Census (Northeast is the omitted category).

Notes: Number of observations: 659. Chi square: 8.94 (8 degrees of freedom). Prob > chi square: .02. All variables are z-scores standardized by MSA means and standard deviations, that is, they are measures of the position of a community on that condition relative to its neighbors.

political opportunities for progrowth entrepreneurs using traditional supply-side policies have been identified and bid away in a highly competitive market for economic development. In a process replicating private markets where entrepreneurial leadership is replaced by bureaucratic processes handled by managers, many traditional progrowth policy tools have been routinized and are now handled by a cadre of bureaucrats (e.g., Blair, Fichtenbaum, and Swaney 1984; Eisinger 1988).

As policy tools become standard procedures, entrepreneurs must seek innovative policies to appeal to local citizens. Not surprisingly, a new class of entrepreneurs is now emerging, as political leaders in a number of state and local governments experiment with a range of "demand-side" policies to promote economic development. This is to be expected: as the payoffs (or "profits") for traditional economic development policies have dwindled, political entrepreneurs create and experiment with new policies with potentially higher rewards. In the domain of growth policies, demand-side policies represent a new set of tools that may produce high profits for their entrepreneurial proponents. However, to the extent that these innovative policies are successful, over time more and more politicians will advocate them. Ultimately these new (and presently) entrepreneurial tools will themselves become standardized and transformed into bureaucratic standard operating procedures. Following Schumpeter, as this occurs, the next generation of entrepreneurs will emerge advocating yet another set of economic development tools and policies.

Demand-side entrepreneurs are seeking to reorient the debate about the right mix of tools to attract the right mix of businesses. The antigrowth entrepreneur's task is different, and more challenging. In attacking the growth machine, the antigrowth entrepreneur seeks to overturn the core arrangements of the growth machine and deflate the ideology that growth is good. These entrepreneurs must change people's ideas about growth, and they often do this through heresthetics. And compared to the traditional progrowth entrepreneur who can build on the privileged position of business groups, entrepreneurs challenging these entrenched interests face more severe collective action problems—they must often seek dynamically new political bases in neighborhoods and community organizations.

While antigrowth entrepreneurship is more radical than other forms of growth politics, the emergence of antigrowth entrepreneurs is nonetheless structured by a calculation of the benefits and costs of entrepreneurship. The antigrowth entrepreneur is more likely to appear in a political environment in which the rewards for entrepreneurship are higher (e.g., a full-time office of the mayor) and in which the obstacles to successful collective action are reduced (e.g., district elections or strong neighborhood groups). We showed that the incentives and obstacles inherent in the local political structure are more important than economic and demographic factors in explaining the emergence of entrepreneurial political leaders who launch challenges to progrowth policies.

Neither demand-side nor antigrowth entrepreneurship are unique political phenomena. Rather, these forms of entrepreneurship are just recent forms of a never-ending series of dynamic political challenges to prevailing practices in local governments. Over time, local governments have experienced waves of entrepreneurs who have seized opportunities to create new coalitions, using innovative ideas in the pursuit of local political office and preferred public policies. Right now, many local entrepreneurs are seizing on the politics of growth as a domain in which to gain high profits by pushing new policy products. But other issues, such as taxes, privatization, race, or environmental policies, also provide opportunities. We have focused on the issue of growth because it is central to contemporary local politics and because the life cycle of entrepreneurial profits in this policy domain is so clear. But in local politics, many policy domains are generating opportunities for entrepreneurs to seize.

CHAPTER 8

Bureaucratic Entrepreneurs:
The Case of City Managers

So FAR IN this book we have focused on political entrepreneurs—individuals who seek elective office to pursue their vision of change. Almost all the other entrepreneurs we identified in our field work held bureaucratic positions. In this chapter, we refine our theory of the public entrepreneur and apply it to bureaucrats. Our goal here is to understand the behavior of what we call *bureaucratic entrepreneurs* and study the ways in which they interact with politicians. We argue that bureaucratic entrepreneurs, like their political counterparts, want to make a difference in their community's policies. Given their expertise and the domains in which they operate, bureaucratic entrepreneurs engage in the act of "creative discovery" by exploiting new policy and management opportunities to advance their ideas.

Political scientists have long recognized that unelected bureaucrats influence the implementation of public policies and they have demonstrated that bureaucrats can sometimes play an even more important role, by actually shaping policy agendas and formulating new policies. Despite an accumulating body of work, studies of entrepreneurial bureaucrats, like most studies of entrepreneurs in general, have relied mostly on biographical studies of individuals whose actions produced innovative or unexpected policy changes (see, e.g., Lewis 1980; Doig and Hargrove 1987; Kirchheimer 1989; Weissert 1991). According to Wilson, such studies show that the personalities and actions of individual executives are critical to explaining innovative bureaucratic change. Not surprisingly, Wilson then concludes that: "It is not easy to build a useful social science theory out of 'chance appearances'" (1989: 227). However, throughout this book we have argued that the emergence of entrepreneurs in the American system of local government is in fact systematically related to definable and measurable characteristics of local communities.

Our task in this chapter is to identify the local conditions that affect the emergence of bureaucratic entrepreneurs. More exactly, since the overwhelming majority (85 percent) of the bureaucratic entrepreneurs identified in our study were city managers, we focus on the factors that affect the emergence of this particular set of bureaucrat entrepreneurs.

Opportunities for Bureaucratic Entrepreneurship in Local Government

Suburban governments were buffeted by major changes in the last two decades, including sharp reductions in intergovernmental aid, intense citizen demands for new services and lower taxes, increasing concerns about the value of growth, and rapidly escalating costs of basic service delivery. For public entrepreneurs, these changes presented opportunities to be seized.

Empirically, we found that entrepreneurial leadership in local government came mostly from elected politicians, especially mayors. However, bureaucratic employees, in particular city managers, constituted another significant source of entrepreneurial talent. As the chief operating officers of their communities, city managers are a well-defined professional group who share similar training in public administration and are linked together by professional organizations and overlapping career paths (Kammerer 1964; Ammons and Newell 1989). Their training and their strategic position in government presents city managers opportunities to act entrepreneurially, and defined career paths give them the incentives to seize those opportunities. In response to the growing challenges facing local communities, a number of entrepreneurial city managers emerged in the communities we studied.

While entrepreneurial managers are an important source of entrepreneurial policies, we believe that they represent a secondary source of innovation—entrepreneurial city managers are more likely to emerge when politicians do not play an entrepreneurial role in communities that demand change. Moreover, we will show that the reasons behind the emergence of bureaucratic entrepreneurs are different than those driving political entrepreneurs. And we will show that the interaction between entrepreneurial managers and politicians is important: bureaucratic entrepreneurs may make explicit or implicit deals with their elected political "sovereigns" that differ from the types of deals that political entrepreneurs must make with their constituents in their own approach to policy change.

TOWARD A THEORY OF ENTREPRENEURIAL CITY MANAGERS

Policy innovation in the United States is often a "bottom-up" process driven by political and managerial entrepreneurship in local governments (see especially Osborne and Gaebler 1990; also see Eisinger 1988; Altshuler and Zegans 1990; Golden 1991; Sanger and Levin 1992). The city managers that help propel this process operate in a complex and difficult environment. Local economic and fiscal conditions are constantly changing and the preferences and policy demands of politicians and citizens can be unstable. Local agency heads and politicians may present roadblocks to city managers trying to change policy directions and city employees may have vested interests in the status quo.

In trying to exercise innovative leadership, entrepreneurial bureaucrats face two worlds: an internal world defined by the demands of managing the local bureaucracy, and a complex external world defined by the political, legal, and economic milieu in which cities exist.

Internal issues relate largely to the ability of managers to motivate public sector employees to perform more efficiently and to comply with organizational goals. Solving these types of problems is a task facing every government manager—but for entrepreneurial managers seeking change, the need to motivate workers to be more productive and conform to new styles of service delivery is even greater.

External issues are defined by the constraints and opportunities presented by the changing environment managers face and by their need to interact with local politicians, interest groups, actors in higher levels of government, and the media to create coalitions supporting new policies. The goals, strategies, and constraints entrepreneurial managers face differ across these two domains. In the following sections, we develop our theoretical approach to bureaucratic entrepreneurship in local government, focusing on the internal and external world these entrepreneurs face.

THE GOALS OF CITY MANAGERS

We have shown that most economic theories of entrepreneurship argue that the pursuit of profits drives the entrepreneurial process. In turn, the supply of entrepreneurs increases with the potential for "entrepreneurial profits." City managers may in fact be motivated by the pursuit of individual monetary rewards. Compared to entrepreneurial politicians, who are more anchored to a specific geographic base where their supporters (most importantly voters) reside, entrepreneurial managers operate in a national job market. In this market, city managers who are interested in advancing their careers do so by moving up to a position in a larger city with a higher salary, more resources to control, more autonomy, and greater prestige within the profession (Kammerer 1964; Barber 1988). This means that monetary profits can actually accrue to successful entrepreneurial managers—to the extent that they succeed in advocating and implementing new policies, they can be rewarded by career advancement.

But such advancement and attendant higher salaries alone are not sufficient to understand why some city managers are more entrepreneurial than others: managers are also motivated by the desire to achieve specific policy goals, by the desire to solve problems, and by the desire to serve the public. (Evidence of the importance of these alternate incentives is found in Kingdon 1984 and Walker 1981; also see Downs 1967; Wilson 1989; DeSantis, Glass, and Newell 1992.) City managers are also motivated by their desire to maintain a positive relationship to professional policy communities, which help define the ideas that are in "good currency." Studies show that local managers are involved in professional networks from which they learn about new policy ideas and to which their professional egos are tied (Walker 1981; also see Oakerson and Parks 1988; Ammons and Newell 1989). While such studies produce insights into the source of ideas and the strategies of entrepreneurs, they do not identify systematically the conditions under which bureaucratic entrepreneurs are likely to emerge and the constraints these entrepreneurs face—the task to which we now turn.

The Internal World of the Entrepreneurial Manager

Whatever their specific goals, entrepreneurial managers face constraints from the organizational environment in which they operate, particularly in getting subordinates to implement new policies successfully. While bureaucratic entrepreneurs play a critical role importing and formulating new policies, ultimately their success is tied to how well policies are carried out. Mazmanian and Sabatier (1983) argue that leadership is the *only* bureaucratic variable crucial to successful policy implementation. But how do managers lead?

According to Miller (1992), all managers, regardless of whether they are in the private or the public sector, have available two basic approaches to persuade and motivate workers to implement their policies. The first approach, tracing back to Max Weber and Frederick Winslow Taylor and related to today's principal/agent models, emphasizes control and hierarchy to achieve an optimal mix of incentives and monitoring techniques to influence subordinates (see Moe 1984). However, even the most clever employment contract cannot overcome the problems of shirking in bureaucratic structures, problems which are far more severe in the public sector than in private firms (Wilson 1989; Miller 1992).

An alternate approach, harkening back to Chester Barnard and Philip Selznick, argues that control mechanisms are not enough to guarantee achievement of the leader's goals. From this perspective, leaders must master motivational and rhetorical skills to inspire workers to work toward organizational goals. Ouchi (1980) argues, for example, that the problem of "performance ambiguity" (which is endemic to the delivery of almost all local public goods) is best managed by transforming the operating units of an organization into the equivalent of a "clan" united by "organic solidarity." Similarly, for Wilson (1989: 156), the best solution to shirking is to inculcate in workers a shared sense of mission, even if there are no financial payoffs. Both Kreps (1990) and Miller (1992) stress the importance of corporate culture in motivating workers. In suburban governments, city managers usually cannot motivate workers with financial rewards and they do not have large personal staffs to monitor bureaucratic behavior closely. Consequently, entrepreneurial managers may have to rely on their interpersonal skills to motivate their subordinates.

The External World of the Entrepreneurial Manager

City managers face multiple external constraints, including economic conditions that limit their options (Peterson 1981; Schneider 1989). Reduced intergovernmental aid, stagnating property tax revenues, and mandates imposed by higher levels of government (e.g., Lovell et al. 1979; ACIR 1985) further constrain entrepreneurial opportunities. Managers also face political limits imposed by the actions of politicians and interest groups (Svara 1990). Many scholars of bureaucratic leadership argue that external relations may be even more important than internal implementation strategies.

Lynn (1990) notes that entrepreneurial managers are more likely to focus on external agency issues, while non-entrepreneurial "administrators" focus mostly inward. Wilson (1989: 203) summarizes studies of successful executives saying "all had one thing in common: They found or maintained the support of key external constituencies." Managerial entrepreneurs often try to develop technical expertise within their organization as a resource to use in bargaining with external constituents and their elected sovereigns (see, e.g., Miller and Moe 1983; Niskanen 1975). As reform ideas and professionalization have become more widespread, city managers have gained power and autonomy, which has not been countered by a professionalization of city council or mayoral staff support (Ammons and Newell 1989; Nalbandian 1989; Protasel 1988). The relative lack of full-time potential political overseers supported by large staffs may give local bureaucrats more discretion to use expertise as a "cover" for entrepreneurial behavior.

This discretion is far from complete. Politically, bureaucratic entrepreneurship may be constrained because the range, complexity, and size of local programs are more limited than at higher levels of government, reducing the information asymmetry that is the source of much bureaucratic power. The relatively small size of the voting public may also encourage more direct bureaucratic accountability to voters in local jurisdictions. Local interest groups can also restrict entrepreneurial managers by ringing "fire alarms" to which politicians attend (McCubbins and Schwartz 1984), and the openness of local governments allows individual citizen demands to constrain bureaucratic autonomy (Sharp 1986). This combination of economic, financial, and political constraints limits entrepreneurial behavior by managers.

But successful entrepreneurial managers learn to overcome these limits and they often consciously underestimate external obstacles (Sanger and Levin 1992; see also Hirschman 1967). Moreover, while the economic approach to human behavior assumes fixed preferences, a crucial feature of politics is that preferences can be changed (Wilson 1980; Jones 1989). Entrepreneurial managers may be able to change the preferences of other actors who otherwise might constrain them and they may be able to manipulate policy agendas to achieve their goals (Hammond 1986; Hammond, Hill, and Miller 1986; Riker 1986).

Clearly, scholars need to synthesize many disparate themes to develop a more systematic theory of bureaucratic entrepreneurship. As we have argued throughout this book, we believe that the development of better theory must take place in conjunction with concrete empirical evidence about where entrepreneurs are found and what they do. In the following pages, we identify the local conditions that increase the likelihood of finding an entrepreneurial city manager. To understand how and when city managers can emerge as entrepreneurs, we compare these conditions to the factors associated with the absence of entrepreneurial leadership and with the emergence of entrepreneurs in elected offices.

WHERE DO ENTREPRENEURIAL CITY MANAGERS EMERGE?

The suburbs in our sample hosted a number of entrepreneurial city managers: almost 20 percent of the entrepreneurs named by our respondents were city managers. Our first goal is to identify the conditions associated with the emergence of entrepreneurial city managers. As in most of our empirical work, one of our first concerns here is to identify the possible effects of region. This is especially important since municipalities in the South and West are so much more likely to have a city manager than are cities in other parts of the country.[1] However, entrepreneurial city managers are *not* regionally distributed: once the regional distribution of city managers is controlled, entrepreneurial city managers are not more likely to be found in any given geographic region. Absent a regional pattern of emergence, we turn to the effects of other local conditions.

Conditions in some communities create the demand for dynamic political or policy change. In some of these communities, entrepreneurial politicians emerge to seize the opportunities created by this demand. However, if politicians do not step forward, entrepreneurial managers are more likely to be found. Thus, while our specific interest here is in bureaucratic entrepreneurs, they cannot be studied in isolation: we identify the factors associated with the emergence of bureaucratic entrepreneurs and compare these directly to those affecting the emergence of political entrepreneurs.[2]

Mayors and Managers as Policy Leaders

Mayors and managers assume many different patterns of policy leadership. In some cities, managers are the dominant policymakers; in other cities, mayors take the lead; in still others, neither the mayor nor the manager is particularly active (see especially Morgan and Watson 1992; Svara 1990; Protasel 1988). Patterns of cooperation also differ. Since politicians generally hire (and can and do fire) the city manager, it is not surprising that in many cities managers cooperate closely with mayors. However, mayors and managers can be highly competitive. This is especially so when the mayor is a full-time elected official. As Whitaker and DeHoog (1991: 162) note: "elected mayors may be more likely to oppose the manager (to see him or her as a rival leader) and elected mayors may be more able to build popular support for their opposition to the manager."

The most fundamental difference between mayors and managers is obvious: managers do not face the need to be elected to office directly by the voters of their city. In turn, the basis of their political support differs from that of politicians and their allegiance may be as much to professional norms of performance as it is to elected officials (Gormley 1989). Thus, political conditions will affect the emergence of a city manager as a bureaucratic entrepreneur. However, we will show that the relationship between the effects of political conditions and the emergence of managerial entrepreneurs, on one hand, and political entrepreneurs, on the other, differs in theoretically important ways.

The Effects of Political Conditions

In table 8.1 we present a multinomial logit analysis jointly identifying and comparing the political structural conditions under which entrepreneurial managers and entrepreneurial politicians are likely to emerge, controlling for the four major geographic regions as defined by the U.S.

TABLE 8.1
Multinomial Logit Analysis: The Impact of Political Structure on the
Emergence of Entrepreneurs

	Entrepreneurial Managers			Entrepreneurial Politicians		
	Coeff.	Std. Er.	P > t	Coeff.	Std. Er.	P > t
City manager	3.07	.75	.00	−.08	.18	.63
Mayor	−.95	.56	.09	.82	.40	.04
Mayor competitive	−.16	.11	.15	.13	.06	.02
Mayor term	.34	.38	.36	−.34	.19	.07
Council competitive	−.01	.13	.93	.01	.07	.91
Northeast	−.20	.54	.71	−.10	.29	.72
North Central	.28	.49	.57	.08	.27	.77
South	.39	.53	.47	−.27	.32	.42
Constant	−4.21	.94	.00	−2.23	.45	.00

Source: The dependent variable and first five independent variables come from survey of city clerks. The regional variables are defined by the U.S. Bureau of the Census.

Notes: Chi square = 68 with 894 degrees of freedom. p. < .01. Total N = 903. N of entrepreneurial managers = 49. Mean predicted value = .052. N of entrepreneurial politicians = 201. Mean predicted value = .216. City manager and mayor = 1 if city has office; 0 otherwise. The competitiveness of the mayoral and council races is measured on a 1-5 scale, with 5 most competitive. Mayor's term = 1 if >2 years; 0 if < or = 2 years.

Bureau of the Census.[3] Multinomial logit goes a step beyond the probit technique we employed in previous chapters: using this multinomial approach we compare the relative probabilities of multiple outcomes rather than just two. In this multinomial analysis, our dependent variable takes on three values: 0 when no entrepreneur was identified in a community (true in the majority of communities, n = 699), 1 when an entrepreneurial politician was cited (n = 208), and 2 when an entrepreneurial manager was named by the clerk (n = 49).[4]

Following our previous analysis identifying the effects of political conditions on the benefits and costs of political entrepreneurship, in this analysis we include several variables assessing the structure of local government. These measures include whether or not the suburban community has an office of city manager and whether or not it has a mayor's office. We also measure the length of the mayor's term and the degree of competitiveness in mayoral and council elections.[5] In table 8.1, we present the effects of these structural variables. In table 8.2 we present the effects of another set of political conditions by measuring the effects of the local interest group environment on the emergence of entrepreneurs.

We begin with an obvious fact: a community must have an office of city manager for an entrepreneurial manager to emerge. Not surprisingly

TABLE 8.2

Multinomial Logit Analysis: The Impact of External Group Strength and
Fiscal Conditions on the Emergence of Entrepreneurs

	Entrepreneurial Managers			Entrepreneurial Politicians		
	Coeff.	Std. Er.	P > t	Coeff.	Std. Er.	P > t
Chamber	.15	.16	.35	.08	.09	.34
Taxpayer	−.48	.16	.00	−.11	.09	.21
Neighborhood	.02	.16	.89	.16	.09	.08
Pay ratio	.45	.19	.02	.05	.11	.66
Union	−.33	.18	.07	−.06	.11	.59
Debt/PC	.18	.17	.28	.20	.11	.05
Northeast	−.47	.57	.41	−.42	.30	.16
North Central	−.03	.52	.95	−.01	.28	.98
South	.45	.58	.43	−.20	.34	.56
Constant	−1.72	.73	.02	−1.42	.42	.00

Sources: Union, Debt/PC, and the nominator of Pay ratio are from 1982 Census of Governments. The denominator of Pay ratio is from the Bureau of Labor Statistics. Each of these three measures is converted into a z-score based on the MSA pattern. The variable has a regional mean of zero and standard deviation of one, and measures the condition in a specific community relative to the metropolitan area average.

Notes: Chi square = 37 with 675 degrees of freedom. p < .01. Total N = 685 (less than in table 8.1 because data for some communities was missing). N of entrepreneurial managers = 49. Mean predicted value = .060. N of entrepreneurial politicians = 201. Mean predicted value = .228.

The Chamber, Taxpayer, and Neighborhood variables are the reported strength of local chamber of commerce, taxpayer, and neighborhood groups with a range of 1 to 5, with 5 the strongest value. Pay ratio = the ratio of the average public sector wage to the average Metropolitan Statistical Area manufacturing wage. Union = the percentage of municipal workers that are unionized. Debt/PC = the total debt of the community per capita.

that variable is extremely important in predicting the emergence of a bureaucratic entrepreneur.[6] Using a sensitivity analysis, the results of which are presented in table 8.3, we found that if all communities had city managers, ceteris paribus, the average likelihood of an entrepreneurial manager emerging would almost double from .052, the sample mean, to .091. Mayors also matter greatly in predicting the emergence of entrepreneurial city managers: cities with mayors are significantly less likely to house an entrepreneurial city manager. Table 8.3 shows that if no communities had mayors, the average likelihood of an entrepreneurial manager emerging would more than double, from .052 to .123.

We turn in more detail to the balance between mayors and managers. As the right-hand portion of table 8.1 shows, *political* entrepreneurs are *more* likely to emerge when a community has a mayor's office, when the

TABLE 8.3

Sensitivity Analysis: The Impact of Changing Significant
Variables from Tables 8.1 and 8.2 on the Probability of
an Entrepreneurial Manager Emerging

	Predictions At		
	Mean	High Extreme	Low Extreme
From Table 8.1:			
Mayor	.052	.123	.048
City Manager	.052	.091	.005
From Table 8.2:			
Taxpayer	.060	.117	.022
Pay ratio	.060	.170	.016
Union	.060	.129	.013
Taxpayer, Pay ratio,			
and Union jointly	.060	.505	.001

Notes: The mean prediction on an entrepreneurial manager emerging is .052 in table 8.1 and .059 in table 8.2. In this sensitivity analysis,
we vary the significant independent variables to their extreme values
above and below their own means, and let the other variables assume
their values.

From table 8.1, if there were no mayor in any community (mayor
set to 0), the likelihood of an entrepreneurial manager emerging
would increase to .123, while if every community had a mayor (mayor
set to 1), the likelihood would fall to .048. Similarly, if all communities
had a city manager, the likelihood would increase to .091, while if no
community had a city manager, the likelihood would fall to nearly
zero (which is true by definition).

From table 8.2, taxpayer group strength, the public/private pay
ratio, and union percentage are varied to their extremes to determine
the impact on the emergence of entrepreneurial managers with the
impact of other variables held constant. In the last row, all three of
these variables are set to their extreme values at the same time.

mayoral races are relatively competitive, and when the mayor's term is
shorter. We believe that all of these factors increase the opportunities for
political entrepreneurs to capture the office of mayor and increase the
payoff for entrepreneurial actions in the political sphere. Note that if a
community has a city manager, the probability of finding a political entrepreneur does *not* significantly change. On the other hand, if a city has
a mayor, an entrepreneurial manager is less likely to be found. To us,
this suggests that citizens seek political entrepreneurship first, regardless
of whether or not the community has a city manager. Indeed, even most
city managers prefer that mayors take an active policy leadership role
(Wikstrom 1979; Morgan and Watson 1992).

The Effects of Other Local Conditions

In earlier chapters, we showed that local demographic factors, such as race and growth, significantly affected the probability that an entrepreneurial politician will emerge. These demographic changes create new dimensions of policy debate and new cleavages upon which to organize political and electoral alliances. In contrast, these same demographic characteristics do not affect the probability with which an entrepreneurial city manager emerges.[7] Entrepreneurial managers head existing organizations with resources and technical expertise and they do not usually need to create new citizen-based political alliances to support their policy innovations.

However, other factors that do not affect the emergence of political entrepreneurs affect the emergence of entrepreneurial managers. Most notably, entrepreneurial city managers are more likely to be found in municipalities in which local public sector workers are highly paid relative to the prevailing private sector manufacturing wages in that region.[8] In contrast, a more heavily unionized local municipal work force reduces the probable emergence of an entrepreneurial manager. We believe that strong unions may oppose entrepreneurial managers who focus on cutting costs—one of the strategies entrepreneurial city managers frequently advocate.

Municipal unions are an important internal group with which managers must negotiate, but entrepreneurial managers also need political support from external interest groups. In local politics some groups represent concentrated interests, such as the chamber of commerce, some represent dispersed citizens, such as taxpayer groups, while others represent citizens in specific geographic areas, such as neighborhood groups. Empirically, when taxpayer groups in a community are relatively *weak*, and thus unlikely to represent citizen interest in constraining taxes, an entrepreneurial city manager is more likely to emerge, often linking efficiency in government service provision to lower or stable taxes. In contrast, entrepreneurial politicians are more likely to emerge when neighborhood groups are important, reflecting their need for geographic electoral support and the important role that neighborhood organizations play as launching pads for entrepreneurial politicians.

In short, entrepreneurial city managers are more likely to emerge to address efficiency issues, such as pay scales for government workers and high taxes, particularly when local interest groups have not been able to address these issues effectively through elected politicians. To make this argument more concrete, the sensitivity analysis in table 8.3 shows that,

USING USER FEES:
PAUL LEONARD OF PERKASIE, PENNSLYVANIA

An innovative local manager identified in our survey of entre-preneurs is Paul Leonard of Perkasie, Pennsylvania, a rapidly growing borough of 6,200 people, twenty-five miles north of Philadelphia. Perkasie faced a major solid waste disposal prob-lem in the late 1980s. Leonard's solutions were innovative enough to be reported on the front page of the June 21, 1989 *Wall Street Journal* in a story by Bill Paul: "Pollution Solution: Pennsylvania Town Finds a Way to Get Locals to Recycle Trash."

As in many other jurisdictions, waste disposal was a growing problem as the borough's cost per ton skyrocketed 900 percent from 1981 to 1987. According to the *Journal:* "When town lead-ers proposed an incinerator, public opposition killed the idea."

Given this manifestation of the "not in my backyard (NIMBY)" syndrome, Perkasie needed a solution. But as the *Journal* noted: "federal and most state environmental officials haven't yet found a way to reduce the waste stream. Perkasie, it seems, is ahead of them."

As Leonard said: "We've let Adam Smith lead the way." Perkasie experimented with market incentives. According to the *Journal:* "Despairing of getting federal or state help, Mr. Leon-ard, the borough manager, decided to experiment. Although it wasn't the first community to try per-bag fees, Perkasie appar-ently is the first to have linked such fees with the threat of fines, a powerful incentive to recycle."

Leonard's innovation proved successful. After implementa-tion of the program, the amount of garbage that needed to be disposed by Perkasie dropped by more than 50 percent, as peo-ple recycled as much as possible. Leonard acted as a "cheer-leader" to develop a positive attitude about recycling in Perkasie: "We're not going to let the big guys dump on us any-more. Why should we pay to dispose of trash that companies needlessly produce?"

As is the case with many successful entrepreneurs, Leonard is not yet satisfied. According to the *Journal:* "Leonard says he doesn't even want plastic garbage bags. He is considering switch-ing to a heavy duty paper bag." While recycling is not his only area of responsibility, manager Leonard addressed the commu-nity's most pressing problem with an innovative solution that has earned him national attention.

ceteris paribus, very weak taxpayer groups or weak municipal unions can more than double the likelihood of finding an entrepreneurial manager. In contrast, very high public pay ratios can triple that probability.[9] Moreover, when these three factors are combined at their extreme values, the likelihood of an entrepreneurial manager emerging changes from virtually zero (.001) to more than 50 percent (.505).

The importance of efficiency issues in the emergence of entrepreneurial city managers may also help explain the policies these managers pursue. Entrepreneurial managers are significantly more likely than entrepreneurial politicians to support new user fees and development impact fees, and to contract out for services.[10] (See the box on City Manager Leonard of Perkasie, Pennsylvania for an example of an innovative use of fees.) But it is important to remember that entrepreneurial bureaucrats must always interact with their local political leadership—and many make deals with politicians about how any cost savings from innovative policies will be allocated (see Stein 1990: chapter 7).

THE ACTIONS OF ENTREPRENEURIAL MANAGERS

To gather more detailed information on the personalities, strategies, and ideas of the entrepreneurial managers, we sent a follow-up survey to the forty-nine city clerks who named an entrepreneurial city manager in our first survey. We asked for more detailed information on the career lines, personality traits, and strategic choices of the entrepreneur. We received thirty-one usable responses, providing us with detailed information on 63 percent of the city managers named as entrepreneurs. Although this is not a large sample, our entrepreneurial managers match closely the demographic information reported by ICMA for a much larger sample of the nation's city managers. We present the following descriptive information as suggestive of patterns of local bureaucratic entrepreneurship.

The Motivation for Introducing New Ideas

Existing theories argue that entrepreneurs are motivated by strong needs to achieve. Hargrove and Glidewell (1990) also cite the importance of strong personal incentives and a strong belief in specific policies, but add other factors: wide-ranging government experience, an open-minded evaluation process, an attraction to experimentation, and a willingness to risk failure. Similarly, Sanger and Levin (1992) find that entrepreneurs create personal missions, take risks, have a bias toward action and purposely underestimate constraints.

To assess the importance of these factors as motivation for the entrepreneurial city manager to introduce new ideas/policies, we asked clerks to identify the forces to which these entrepreneurs were responding. The single most common reason given was the city manager's own desire for a leadership role (60 percent). But managerial entrepreneurship is not totally self-motivated. City managers respond to demands from local politicians (43 percent) and demands from citizens (40 percent). Thus, entrepreneurial managers get their ideas mainly from professional organizations, newspapers, and other communities, but the force that pushes them to introduce the ideas is most often their own leadership needs, buttressed by demands from politicians and citizens.

City managers are more likely to be innovative when they previously worked in another city and if they have a broader professional orientation (Wilson 1989; Carlson 1961; Rosenthal and Crain 1968). Of the entrepreneurial managers in our sample, 67 percent played important roles in professional organizations. In their prior employment, 62 percent had been city managers in another town (while only 20 percent had moved up within their town's government, and 10 percent came from the private sector). Thus, nearly two-thirds of these entrepreneurs followed a city manager career track and a similar percentage were active in professional organizations.

What was the origin of their new policy ideas? As suggested by Oakerson and Parks (1988), professional organizations are among the most important sources of new managerial ideas (about 75 percent of the clerks suggested that the entrepreneurial city manager got his/her ideas from such organizations). This was followed by newspapers (69 percent) and by other communities (64 percent). Local politicians and entrepreneurial city managers engage in only limited cross-fertilization—only 21 percent of the clerks named local politicians as an ideas source, a result supported by Morgan and Watson's (1992) findings on the limited frequency of mayor/manager team leadership.

Compared to entrepreneurial politicians, entrepreneurial managers are much less likely (3 percent versus 21 percent) to introduce policy ideas that are very different from ideas in circulation in their metropolitan region. Many of the innovations managers introduce are defined by their professional networks and guided by prevailing norms. In contrast, political entrepreneurs are much more likely to argue for more radical changes to create a winning electoral coalition, proposals that need not stand rigorous tests of professional scrutiny.

Constraints on Entrepreneurial Managers

Entrepreneurial city managers face constraints. Congruent with arguments presented by Peterson (1981) and Schneider (1989), the most binding constraints on the innovative behavior of managers are fiscal ones. Fully 78 percent of our respondents cited both tax limitations and growing fiscal problems as constraints on city managers (also see DeSantis, Glass, and Newell 1992: 449). (See the box on Manager Healy of Cambridge for innovative action under severe fiscal constraints.) The intergovernmental system imposed further limits on the behavior of managers: 54 percent of our respondents cited intergovernmental mandates and 46 percent cited changing intergovernmental aid as constraining factors. Local politicians (cited by 53 percent) are also important constraints on the freedom of city managers since they ultimately hire and fire managers.

In both the political and managerial domains, entrepreneurs need to create and maintain a coalition to support their policies. Entrepreneurial managers are more likely to work within the existing political power structure than are entrepreneurial politicians. Most entrepreneurial managers head existing organizations and, unlike many entrepreneurial politicians, do not have to build or maintain new organizations. Thus, entrepreneurial managers are less likely than their political counterparts to be the catalysts behind the formation of new neighborhood or taxpayer groups. But entrepreneurial managers are as likely as entrepreneurial politicians to rely on new business groups, a traditional component of the power elite in most communities.

Entrepreneurial Strategies

To overcome constraints, city managers need effective strategies. Motivating subordinates to higher levels of performance is the most important internal task facing an entrepreneur (Miller 1992). Entrepreneurial city managers seem to rise to the task—the ability to inspire or motivate workers was rated "much better" or "better than the average city manager or similar local official" for 84 percent of the entrepreneurs, while the ability to monitor and control workers was similarly rated for 65 percent. In facing this task, entrepreneurial city managers rely on teamwork. We asked the clerks whether the entrepreneur stressed a teamwork strategy or hierarchy, or some mix: 6 percent cited all teamwork, 58 percent cited mainly teamwork, 33 percent cited an even mix of the two

FACING FISCAL CONSTRAINTS:
ROBERT HEALY OF CAMBRIDGE, MASSACHUSETTS

The case of Robert Healy, the city manager of Cambridge, Massachusetts, a large suburban city just across the Charles River from Boston, illustrates several of the themes of our research. Healy was hired as city manager in 1982. Perhaps Healy's most important challenge was dealing with the fiscal environment, specifically cuts in property tax revenue mandated by Massachusetts' Proposition 2½.

According to the *Boston Globe* (February 13, 1990): "In 1981, after passage of Proposition 2½, the city's bond rating was suspended by rating services that believed the measure to limit property taxes would make it difficult for Cambridge to make bond payments. The city rebounded, however, and its bond rating rose several times." Healy was a major force behind the rebound. In the first year of mandated cuts in 1982, Healy was able to juggle the budget and find a few sources of surplus from previous years, allowing budget cuts to be made without too much pain for most of Cambridge's citizens. In 1983, Proposition 2½ mandated a 15 percent cut in property tax revenue. With a preliminary budget proposal to the city council and community, Healy showed the extreme budget cuts that would be necessary to achieve this reduction: "The fat that people talk about does not exist in the city's budget. Next year, the public works department will barely be able to collect the rubbish."

This bleak vision of the future pushed the Cambridge city council toward action and also led to the formation of a citizen's initiative designed to force a referendum vote, which, under the rules of Proposition 2½ could postpone the 15 percent cut for one year if two-thirds of the community voters voted twice to do so. Healy supported this referendum and it indeed met the stringent requirements for enactment. Thus, the 1983 budget was funded at the level of the previous year and cuts were put off until more fundamental changes could be made. With this success and others, the *Boston Globe* notes about Healy: "The walls outside his office are decorated with awards from professional groups such as the Governmental Finance Officers Association of the United States and Canada."

Healy, a Cambridge resident since birth, first came to work for the former city manager in 1974. With two decades of expe-

HEALY (cont.)

rience, he has also been able to innovate in other areas. He was a leading player in attracting commercial growth in the 1980s, which led to some antigrowth opposition. Healy argues that growth is linked to services and taxes: "I think balanced and controlled development have been important to the financial health of this city."

As an entrepreneur with innovative ideas, Healy attracts controversy. One councilor notes: "His power under the charter is immense. He can set policy in areas that never reach the council. So, it is extremely important that he be held accountable." But another councilor notes that Healy can be a team player: "He tends to carry out policy that he believes is supported by the majority of the council."

Healy recognizes that he is controversial: "This is a complicated, diverse city and any decision you make is going to have 50 percent against and 50 percent for." The *Globe* notes that Healy "says he has had to make unpopular decisions that have not endeared him to neighborhoods, but believes this is the nature of the job."

Thus, Healy's case illustrates some of the constraints and opportunities that entrepreneurial managers faced in the 1980s. By going well beyond their simple job description, they were able to motivate change, when politicians could not or would not do so.

approaches, 3 percent cited mainly hierarchy, and no one suggested all hierarchy. Rather than relying only on monitoring and control, entrepreneurial city managers try to inculcate a sense of mission through teamwork.

Without the need to run for office, much of the work of entrepreneurial managers is not subject to rigorous public examination: by defining issues as technical, managers can often limit the scope of political debate (see, e.g., Baumgartner 1989). On the other hand, some policies *require* an expansion of debate, especially when key politicians are opposed to an issue and an entrepreneurial manager believes there is broader political support. The main strategy of entrepreneurial managers is to handle issues behind the scenes (true for 70 percent). Only 22 percent of respondents said that the entrepreneur's main strategy for handling issues was to go public. This provides further support for the picture of entrepreneurial city managers working with existing power structures rather than trying to overturn them.

In building support, entrepreneurial city managers call on a range of the tools. Of our respondents, 86 percent rated the entrepreneur's use of strategic information as "substantial" or "very substantial," 77 percent rated similarly the use of bureaucratic or technical expertise, 54 percent rated the use of local media, and 40 percent rated the use of rhetoric. Theoretically, we know that entrepreneurs can inject a new dimension into political debates in order to create new coalitions; empirically, 90 percent of the entrepreneurial managers introduced new ideas or issues to create support across groups; and 66 percent linked two seemingly unrelated issues to create broader support.

Entrepreneurial managers need to sell new policies not only to the citizenry but also to elected politicians. We found that 42 percent of the entrepreneurial managers took political heat to shield politicians very or fairly often, 33 percent did so sometimes, while only 25 percent rarely or never did so. Entrepreneurial managers were generous in sharing credit for policy innovations: 66 percent shared credit very or fairly often, while 24 percent shared credit only sometimes, and 10 percent rarely or never shared credit. By helping politicians look good, entrepreneurial managers may build political capital in their efforts to implement innovative policies. Similarly, the bureaucratic entrepreneur may receive budgetary rewards from politicians in return for innovative policies (see Stein 1990: chapter 7).

We recognize that we are studying a relatively small number of entrepreneurial city managers. Thus, the information presented in this section of the chapter should be taken as suggestive, especially since we can not compare some of it to managers in communities without an entrepreneurial city manager. Still, these thirty-one responses represent 63 percent of all of the entrepreneurial managers named from a nationwide sample of nearly 1,000 suburban clerks. Their actions document dimensions of entrepreneurial bureaucratic behavior that are congruent with existing studies of city managers who take an active lead in policy development.

THE ENTREPRENEURIAL CITY MANAGER

How do these disparate patterns integrate into a coherent picture of bureaucratic entrepreneurship in local government? In approaching this question, it is important to remember that American cities are part of a varied and open system of government filled with opportunities for entrepreneurial behavior and that different types of actors can emerge as entrepreneurs seeking to motivate dynamic change in local policies. The mayor's office was the most common focal point for the entrepreneurs we found, but fully 20 percent of the entrepreneurs we found were city managers. This represents a significant proportion of innovative leaders. Yet, only a small proportion of city managers were entrepreneurs: about 1 in 11 of the city managers in our sample of communities was named as an entrepreneur.

Like their political counterparts, entrepreneurial city managers are most likely to seize the opportunity to motivate dynamic change when the benefit/cost ratio shifts in favor of entrepreneurial profits. However, we believe that the demand for bureaucratic entrepreneurship is a "derived demand." The path of local entrepreneurship runs first through the mayor's office. In turn, bureaucratic entrepreneurs are more likely to emerge when the local political climate does not breed entrepreneurial politicians.

Furthermore, the balance between entrepreneurial mayors and entrepreneurial managers is structured by the different incentive structures they face. Unlike elected officials, city managers have a national market for their services. By some accounts, city managers have an average tenure of less than five years, frequently changing jobs and moving to larger cities, where they are paid higher wages and gain greater visibility in their profession. Given an organized and mobile labor market, monetary incentives may in fact propel the emergence of entrepreneurial city managers. In somewhat more cumbersome language, entrepreneurial actions by city managers can be driven by a "residual claimancy" that arises in the management of localities—that is, a manager may innovate with the expectation of the rewards (or "profit") that comes in the form of promotion to a larger, more visible, and better paying municipality.

In contrast, it is extremely difficult for an elected mayor of one community to move to another locale or state to run for a comparable or higher elected position (charges of "carpet bagging" are usually fatal in such situations). Thus, elected politicians are predominantly vertically mobile—their career advancement is defined by their ability to run for higher offices with larger constituencies and more political visibility (for example, mayors run for the state legislature, for Congress, or for a statewide office such as governor or attorney general). To succeed in this "vertical market," elected officials need to maximize votes.

At the local level of government we study, vote maximization can probably be best achieved through the provision of particularistic benefits delivered via the services the city provides. More exactly, politicians can succeed through the provision of high-quality services at a given tax rate (Schneider 1989). In contrast, bureaucrats are more concerned with maximizing their own agency budgets, in part to prove that they are ready for advancement to larger and better paying positions and in part to satisfy professional norms (see Niskanen 1971; Dunleavey 1991). The major variable the manager has to pursue these goals is the mix of employees in his or her agency, for example, balancing production workers with supervisory personnel and unionized with nonunionized workers.[11] However, the mix that is ideal for the manager is not necessarily the mix that delivers the services at the cost structure the politician desires. This divergence in incentives creates a classic principal/agent problem between elected politicians and city managers.

Since the politician can monitor the behavior of the bureaucrat (and the politician can fire city managers), the bureaucrat has incentives to conform to the wishes of the politician. However, politicians confront an upper limit to the effectiveness of their monitoring activities; each additional unit of monitoring nets a smaller marginal return in savings (Moe 1984). One solution is for the politician to somehow motivate the city manager with rhetoric and appeals to teamwork—creating a "culture" of cooperation and innovation (Kreps 1990).

The other solution is for the politician to find a means by which bureaucrats can be induced to innovate while not threatening the manager's interests. Stein (1990) outlines a simple but effective exchange agreement politicians can use to ensure the manager's claims on the profits of innovation and hence, to induce managers to innovate. Essentially, according to Stein, the politician proposes a deal along the following lines: If an innovation succeeds, both the manager and the politician share the profits. Given success, the manager gains in budgetary authority and in professional stature, while the politician claims credit for more cost-effective services, increasing future voter support. As insurance, the politician agrees to hold harmless the manager against any policy failure. Thus, if an innovation fails, the manager gets the *present* level of budgetary resources.

In this deal, in exchange for the potential of higher budgets contingent on policy success, managers accept a lower guaranteed yearly budget *increment*. In turn, the politician uses the money that would have gone for a budgetary increase to keep taxes down. An additional element in this negotiation is an agreement in which the city manager is willing to give credit to the politician for the innovation (helping the politician's search for electoral success and higher office) while ensuring that the bureaucrat's budget has the opportunity to grow (thus helping the bureaucrat in search of career advancement).

This deal is obviously strongly affected by the different incentives these two sets of actors face. Sometimes there is incentive compatibility between managers and politicians. For example, the growing fiscal problems of local government and an increasingly harsh intergovernmental milieu present constraints on the freedom of city managers to implement any new policies. Given these limits, entrepreneurial city managers can try to increase the efficiency of local service delivery by adopting approaches that are in good currency, such as user fees and privatization. Entrepreneurial city managers can also turn inward, trying to improve the efficiency of their work force by promoting teamwork and inspiring their workers to implement more efficient policies. In each of these examples, the managerial drive to efficiency may help entrepreneurial politicians seeking their own success.

However, sometimes politicians and managers can be at odds over innovation. Given the professional and political differences between entrepreneurial city managers and local politicians, it is not surprising that the specific policies they advocate and the coalitions they build differ. Entrepreneurial city managers are relatively more cautious in their policy proposals. They are likely to advocate ideas that have been "vetted" by their professional associations and that can increase their professional reputation (and their upward career mobility). In contrast, political entrepreneurs are more likely to advocate more untried ideas and to create a broader mass political base in the community that can serve as a springboard for upward electoral mobility. The propensity of entrepreneurial politicians to engage in riskier behavior may put them in conflict with city managers pursuing different types of innovations. How these conflicts play out is a function of the personalities of the actors, their ability to mobilize the different constituencies that represent their different bases of power, and the structural factors that define the relative strength of each office. However, while we have a theoretical "outline" defining the incentives and strategies that structure the relationship between innovative city managers and their elected sovereigns, specifying the details of the relationship and more fully specifying the conditions affecting the outcome of their conflicting needs remain critical issues for research in local government.

While much is left for future research, we do know that the world of bureaucratic innovation and entrepreneurship is complex—but not beyond systematic study. We have shown that the emergence of managerial entrepreneurs and the behavior they adopt are not "random" events. Bureaucratic entrepreneurs, while responding to a different set of incentives and constraints than political entrepreneurs, use a rational benefit/ cost expectation in designing and pursuing their innovations and strategies. And their relationship with elected political leaders is structured by identifiable aspects of the incentives that managers and politicians face. As such, the tools of social science can be employed to study the emergence and the policy behavior of these actors in local government.

Part Three

THE MILIEUX OF THE PUBLIC
ENTREPRENEUR

IN THIS PART, we turn to an investigation of the broader social and political milieu in which public entrepreneurs must operate. Even more than most economic and political actors, the successful public entrepreneur can not be a solitary "Robinson Crusoe," but must constantly be interacting with others in the community. Political entrepreneurs are likely to learn some of the requisite skills in the business sector and can build up important contacts through business networks. To develop innovative ideas, to see a demand for new services, and to build a political coalition upon which to succeed, a political entrepreneur must have political interaction and connections.

In chapter 9, we analyze the business sector and consider the emergence of entrepreneurs as a function of the local and metropolitan environment. In essence, this chapter focuses on the larger issue of the supply of entrepreneurs. Entrepreneurs engaged in deal making and brokering activities in the private sector may be able to carry over those same skills into the public sector. If they are local businesspeople, they may also benefit themselves from improved economic development or quality of life in the community. On the other hand, if entrepreneurial opportunities in the larger metropolitan region or in the local private sector are substantial, then the opportunity costs of pursuing political entrepreneurial opportunities will be substantial. Thus, we analyze in particular those sectors most closely related to private sector entrepreneurship—the high-tech sector and the finance, insurance, and real estate sectors.

In chapter 10, we turn to the issue of the demand for entrepreneurs by local citizens with high levels of information. Here we use a different data set, a survey of both established residents and recent movers to Suffolk County, New York, to understand how citizens gather information, and how accurate is the information they gather. Some of these citizens, many of whom we show to be recent movers to that community, may themselves act as entrepreneurs by providing benefits for others in that community through their entry choice. As a group, they combine their exit, entry, and voice powers to influence local politics. Informed citizens like the subset of the community that we identify are most likely to provide support for entrepreneurs and for change.

CHAPTER 9

The Business-Government Nexus in the
Local Market for Entrepreneurs

WE HAVE RELIED heavily on economic concepts to develop a model of
the market for local public entrepreneurs. In this chapter, building on
the concept of the reservation wage for entrepreneurs discussed earlier
in the book and the decision calculus underlying it, we show an interrela-
tionship between the private sector and public sector entrepreneurship.
We demonstrate how opportunities in the private sector, especially in
high-technology manufacturing and finance, affect the frequency of
public entrepreneurship. In so doing, we modify the simple economic
decision process underlying the concept of the reservation wage by considering how entrepreneurs are "embedded" in social networks.

In developing the concept of embeddedness, we combine insights
from sociology and anthropology with more orthodox economic notions
drawn from the study of labor markets and explore more fully the supply
function for entrepreneurs. We also review evidence from a variety of
fields to show how entrepreneurs use these networks to achieve their
goals, drawing on their social contacts for support and in discovering
opportunities. This leads us to explore the extent to which the supply of
entrepreneurial talent is affected by differences in organizational structure (Mohr 1969; Walker 1981), social milieux (Berger 1991; Maillat and
Lecoq 1992), and the social and economic networks that define relationships across interdependent activities in regions (Granovetter 1985). We
then return to the question of the demand for entrepreneurship and
show how demand may be affected by the networks in which potential
entrepreneurs are embedded. In so doing, we show parallels between
the concerns of those scholars (mostly in such disciplines as sociology
and anthropology) who focus on the entrepreneur as a socially embedded actor and the concerns of neoinstitutional economists, who acknowledge the critical role broader social institutions play in economic
development.

This parallelism is especially evident in the work of Douglass North
(1990), who characterizes institutions as social arrangements that "reduce uncertainty by providing a structure to everyday life." These institutions include "any form of constraint that human beings devise to

shape human interaction . . . both in formal constraints—such as rules that human beings devise—and in informal constraints—such as conventions and codes of behavior" (pp. 3–4).

For North, society's institutional arrangements have consequences for economic development:

> Incremental change comes from the perceptions of the entrepreneurs in political and economic organizations that they could do better by altering the existing institutional framework at some margin. But the perceptions critically depend on both the information that the entrepreneurs receive and the way they process that information. . . . The actors must frequently act on incomplete information and process the information that they do receive through mental constructs that can result in persistently inefficient paths. Transaction costs in political and economic markets make for inefficient property rights, but the imperfect subjective models of the players as they attempt to understand the complexities of the problems they confront can lead to the persistence of such property rights. (pp. 8–9)

In North's view, the growth of the U.S. economy in the nineteenth century is clearly a success story. The basic institutional framework that evolved by the beginning of that century (especially the Constitution and the Northwest Ordinance, as well as norms of behavior rewarding hard work) induced the development of economic and political organizations that provided incentives for increased productivity and economic growth. Much of this growth was sparked by a wave of entrepreneurial activity. In contrast, North identifies other times and other countries where institutional frameworks have emerged embodying a set of incentives that foster organizations that are themselves unproductive and block others from undertaking productive activity. Such a path to inefficiency can persist because the transaction costs of the political and economic markets together with the subjective models actors carry prevent moves toward more efficient outcomes.

North's work is exciting. But the empirical work of neoinstitutionalists often does not adequately document the processes by which social arrangements and interactions may aid or hinder the entrepreneur. In developing the argument in this chapter, we cast our net broadly across several of the social sciences. By widening our focus to consider entrepreneurs within their broader social context, like North, we are led to see a causal arrow that runs from the broader social arrangements (both formal and informal institutions and organizations) to the emergence and activities of entrepreneurs themselves. This widened analytical focus leads us to augment the model of public entrepreneurship that we have developed to this point.

ENTREPRENEURS AS EMBEDDED
SOCIAL ACTORS

Granovetter pioneered the development of the concepts of embeddedness and social contacts as modifiers of purely economic transactions. For Granovetter, social actors "do not behave or decide as atoms outside a social context. . . . Their attempts at purposive action are instead embedded in concrete, ongoing systems of social relations" (1985: 487). Aldrich and Zimmer (1986) explicitly use Granovetter's concept of networks to explain patterns of entrepreneurship, arguing that "entrepreneurship is a social role, embedded in a social context. Investigators cannot treat entrepreneurs in isolation as autonomous decisionmakers or lump them together with others with similar social characteristics, without regard to context." Instead, Aldrich and Zimmer argue that researchers should be concerned with "the effects of social networks in facilitating or inhibiting the activities of potential entrepreneurs" (p. 20; also see Lavoie 1991).

The importance of social embeddedness to entrepreneurs is supported by studies of the origins of business entrepreneurs. Birley (1985: 109) argues that contacts are usually the main source of new ideas that entrepreneurs see and exploit. Entrepreneurs tend to form smaller, for-profit organizations, and they tend to start businesses similar to those in which they were previously employed, in the same location, and with previous colleagues as partners. That is, entrepreneurs situate their new firms in the networks in which they previously operated. For these private sector entrepreneurs, clearly a local network is in place that eases the burdens of entrepreneurship: "Informal contacts, mainly business contacts, are seen overall to be the most helpful in assembling the elements of the business" (Birley 1985: 113; also see Young and Frances 1991). Like their private sector counterparts, public sector entrepreneurs also rely on networks, making repeated use of contacts they have established over the course of years of professional and political activities (King 1988: 78–79, 277; Kingdon 1984: 189–190; Heclo 1978; Smith 1991).

Studies demonstrating the importance of the geographical milieu and social networks to the nurturing of entrepreneurial behavior are complemented by studies that show the importance of organizational form and culture (e.g., Becker 1970; Mohr 1969; Walker 1981) and the climate of innovation within states (e.g., Walker 1969) for entrepreneurial action. The relationship between these conditions and entrepreneurship can be analyzed from a transaction costs perspective.

The Importance of Networks in Reducing Transaction Costs

Networks matter because they create efficiencies in assembling the resources necessary in production processes. In networks, transactions occur neither through discrete exchanges nor by administrative fiat; rather, they are built on the repeated interactions of actors engaged in reciprocal, preferential, and mutually supportive actions. The efficiency of contracting is increased by a shared orientation—knowledge that the parties assume each has about the other and that they use in communication and problem solving. Insights into the relationship between shared orientation and efficiency are built, directly or indirectly, on findings of ethnomethodologists (e.g., Garfinkel 1967), who argue that expressions and actions cannot be fully understood without an understanding of the background and "culture" of which the speaker is part. Repeated interactions, shared training, and socialization all increase the efficiency of communications by reducing cultural barriers to transactions.

While anthropologists were particularly quick to build on this insight and to emphasize the role of networks, the importance of shared orientation between individuals entering into agreements is clear to social scientists from a variety of disciplines who study contracts and other economic activities. Nelson and Winter (1982: 99–107) recognize the importance of shared orientation when they argue that repeated, complex interactions require a specialized language that transcends "plain English." They describe this specialized language as a local "dialect" filled with shared words, concepts, and short-hand terms referring to particular processes, products, and concepts. The concept of corporate culture, which acts as a guide to what behavior is permissible, what norms are valued, and what meanings are assigned to terms used in organizations, places networks directly in the context of transaction cost economics (Kreps 1990; Miller 1992; Brehm and Gates 1993).

The importance of networks within organizations and across interdependent firms is the core of Granovetter's concept of structural embeddedness. The focus on networks of interrelationships has more recently been used in studies that show how local regional economies can create a culture of entrepreneurship and act as incubators of innovation. Echoing Granovetter, Maillat and Lecoq (1992: 2) argue that entrepreneurial enterprises are not "isolated innovative agents calculating where [they] can find the best location." Rather, these enterprises are generated in a supportive *regional milieu*, which is defined by geographical conditions favorable to the emergence of new production activities and capable of sustaining the development of firms in the early stages of growth. Thus, the regional milieu generates "specific skills and solidarity among local firms and socio-economic characteristics. Innovation capability depends on the specific nature and intensity of territorial relations in generating a localized dynamic process of collective learning through informal networks and mutual long-term relationships" (Maillat and Lecoq 1992: 14).

In a further extension of Granovetter's argument, Romo and Schwartz (n.d.: 9–10) argue that "regional economies are stable social structures comprised of an intricate web of routinized material and informational transactions, most of which *do not* operate through markets. These relationships ultimately congeal into long-term dependencies and they therefore act as relational 'glue.'" While many economists have sought to explain the agglomerations that are observed among interdependent sectors in the same region in terms of external economies of scale, Romo and Schwartz argue that the value of regional proximity can be better understood in terms of the broad set of relationships in which economic production is embedded. They argue that efficiencies are maximized by repeated face-to-face interactions—and that these efficiencies become part of a locality-specific "production culture" that provide the rationale for locational proximity (also see Markusen 1987). Thus, the value of social interactions highlighted in these works parallels Williamson's perspective on repeated trades, that is, long-term networks built on a shared language, trust, and reputation reduce transaction costs and increase efficiency.

Because networks embody greater flexibility and lower transaction costs, they may be "lighter on their feet" than hierarchies (Powell 1991: 271). But like any productive relationship, networks take considerable effort to establish and sustain. Networks are particularly appropriate in circumstances where there is a need for efficient, reliable information. This makes them particularly useful to entrepreneurs, who must make rapid use of available information if they are to achieve high profits. But given the loose nature of the relationships established in networks, trust is vital.

For public entrepreneurs, developing trust in relationships and in support networks is vital to the pursuit of their goals. For example, King (1988: 461) found that the ability of public entrepreneurs to develop a policy network "magnified the individual's influence, pooled resources, and created synergism." Similarly, Kingdon (1984: 189–190) found that successful policy entrepreneurs establish and maintain networks within their particular policy communities (also see Heclo 1978 and Smith 1991). While there are clear payoffs for these actions, they are not simply taken for purely instrumental reasons. Kingdon (1984: 130) suggests that much of the reward of public entrepreneurship comes from "solidary" incentives, and from simply playing the policy game: entrepreneurs "enjoy advocacy, they enjoy being at or near the set of power, they enjoy being part of the action. They make calls, they have lunch, write memos, and draft proposals, probably for the other [e.g., instrumental] reasons we have discussed . . . but in combination with the simple pleasure they take in participating." Thus, there are many rewards, both pecuniary and nonpecuniary, for entrepreneurs who are adept at assembling and coordinating teams, or who are skilled in constructing and manipulating networks, no matter what their locus of activities.

NETWORKS AND THE SUPPLY OF ENTREPRENEURS

We expect that the supply of entrepreneurs conforms to regularities observed in any other labor market. But we also believe that the organization and institutional arrangements of the local milieu will influence the supply of entrepreneurs in any given sector of the economy (private or public). From a labor market perspective, entrepreneurs will appear in any sector of the economy to the extent that the estimated returns from entering that sector are at least as high as those of the best foregone opportunity available in other sectors. Following Casson (1982: 335–336), the supply of entrepreneurs can be thought of as infinitely elastic at "the prevailing real wage"—the opportunity cost of entrepreneurship. But once the expected returns from entrepreneurship rise above this level, the supply of entrepreneurs will be similar to the supply of any other factor of production. That is, entrepreneurship will positively increase with the expected rate of return.[1]

However, we argue that this simple labor market model of the supply of entrepreneurs must be modified to account for the effects of networks on the behavior of entrepreneurs. And the model must also be modified to allow for the effects that developments in one sector of the economy (for instance high-technology manufacturing, finance, or government) have in reallocating entrepreneurial opportunities across sectors.

Networks can increase the supply of entrepreneurs by reducing the costs of entrepreneurship. For example, an established network of private sector entrepreneurs can provide the psychological and emotional support for further entrepreneurship in both the private *and* the public sector. Moreover, an established network reduces the organizational costs facing an entrepreneur. That is, an individual who is tied into a network of entrepreneurs has access to relevant experts that may ease the cost of assembling the necessary teams to pursue entrepreneurial activities. Networks also make available new models of programs, policies, and organizations. An individual exposed to an entrepreneurial private sector network could then engage in arbitrage by proposing the adaptation of private sector entrepreneurial ideas into the public sector. Being a member of a private sector entrepreneurial network therefore reduces the costs of idea generation and reduces the costs of assembling a team to develop and implement those ideas.

NETWORKS AND THE DEMAND FOR ENTREPRENEURS

We have rooted the demand for entrepreneurs in a function of two factors: (1) the rate of change in the technologies of production and (2) the rate of change in the preferences of consumers. More rapid change in either factor leads to a greater demand for entrepreneurs to present new alternatives in their pursuit of entrepreneurial profits. Entrepreneurs are able to correctly discover and/or diagnose the shortcomings or gaps in the status quo and select an appropriate prescription for how those problems may be remedied. Furthermore, many entrepreneurs seek to generate demand by contributing to discussions or debates and "framing" problems in ways that make them amenable to solution using his or her chosen approach. Second, the uncertainty inherent in entrepreneurial changes makes them risky investments. What makes entrepreneurs a unique class of social actors is that they, unlike many others, are sufficiently willing to believe in their vision of change to take entrepreneurial risks.

Networks affect these demand-side conditions. An individual tied into an entrepreneurial private sector network is more likely to discover opportunities in the public sector, especially in times of discontent with public sector activities when businesslike reforms are often presented as panaceas for the problems of government. Thus, in an environment where such reforms are supported, opportunities for arbitrage increase and individuals tied into a private sector entrepreneurial network can seize these opportunities. Moreover, being tied into such a network reduces the risks of advocating such reforms: that is, the network has "vetted" ideas and certified some set of them as worthwhile—some ideas are in "good currency" (Schon 1971: 123).

LOCAL BUSINESS CONDITIONS AND THE EMERGENCE OF
PUBLIC ENTREPRENEURS

Our task in this chapter is to identify the effects of theoretically important aspects of the local business environment on the emergence of public entrepreneurs. Specifically, we argue that a higher density of private sector entrepreneurs increases both the supply of and demand for public sector entrepreneurs. We use measures of the composition of the regional and the local economy as surrogate measures of the number of entrepreneurs in a local milieu and of the density of entrepreneurial networks.

Identifying the Density of Private Entrepreneurs

Many analysts argue that during the 1980s, the two most dynamically changing sectors of the economy were high-technology manufacturing (for example, Markusen, Hall, and Glasmeier 1986) and the FIRE (finance, insurance, and real estate) sector of the service economy (Stanback 1991). Moreover, most analysts believe that entrepreneurial activity is more likely to be found in small firms than in large ones (e.g., Birch 1987). Therefore, we assume that, ceteris paribus, a greater number of workers or firms in high-tech manufacturing and in the FIRE sector at the community and at the regional level can be used as indicators of a more intense entrepreneurial milieu. This is especially so when the firms in these sectors are small and therefore more likely to be start-up enterprises exploiting the vision of an emerging private sector entrepreneur.

THE EFFECTS OF COUNTY BUSINESS PATTERNS

The communities for which we have data on public entrepreneurship are located in 184 counties located throughout the country. We used data from the census report, *County Business Patterns,* to measure the concentration of high-tech manufacturing and FIRE activities in each of these counties. We use the number of employees in each of these sectors in 1982 and 1987 to reflect the density of entrepreneurial activity, assuming that density increases with the size of the sector. Methodologically, we "attach" these contextual variables measured at the county level to each of the individual communities in the county.[2]

In table 9.1, controlling for geographic location, we report the results of a cross-sectional probit analysis to measure the effect of the size of these two sectors on the likelihood of finding a public sector entrepreneur in 1982 and again in 1987. In table 9.2, we show how *changes* in the size of each sector between 1982 and 1987 affected the probability of finding a public entrepreneur.

In each of our estimates, we include a measure of the ratio of the public sector wage in a community to the prevailing manufacturing wage in the region.[3] We use this ratio to measure the alternative wage rate for

TABLE 9.1

The Effects of County Employment in FIRE and High Tech
on the Likelihood of Finding a Public Entrepreneur,
1982 and 1987

Explanatory Variables	1982		1987	
	Coefficient (Std. Error)	P > t	Coefficient (Std. Error)	P > t
County FIRE	.045	.01	.033	.02
employment (in 000s)	(.019)		(.012)	
County high-tech	−.053	.01	−.048	.02
employment (in 000s)	(.023)		(.021)	
Pay ratio	.004	.08	.004	.13
	(.002)		(.002)	
North Central	.232	.05	.231	.05
	(.121)		(.122)	
West	.333	.07	.366	.03
	(.184)		(.174)	
South	.187	.25	.133	.40
	(.164)		(.159)	
Constant	−1.268	.00	−1.195	.00
	(.269)		(.265)	

Notes: The Northeast is the excluded region. Summary statistics 1982: Chi square = 17.89 with 6 degrees of freedom. $P = .007$. Total N = 762. Summary statistics 1987: Chi square = 15.08 with 6 degrees of freedom. $P = .02$. Total $N = 782$.

public entrepreneurship: the higher the wage ratio, the lower the opportunity costs for operating in the public sector rather than the private one. This measure allows us to control for the individual monetary benefit/cost calculus of allocating entrepreneurial activity.

In the cross-sectional probit estimates reported in table 9.1, we show that the probability of finding a public entrepreneur does increase as the number of county-level employees in the FIRE sector grows. As in previous chapters, we use sensitivity analysis to show how changes in environmental variables affect the probability of finding a public entrepreneur.

Among all our communities, the predicted mean probability of finding a public entrepreneur is 0.28, but this probability varies significantly with the size of the regional FIRE sector. With county-level employment set at one standard deviation above the mean, the probability of finding a public entrepreneur rises from .28 to .37 in 1982 and .35 in 1987. In contrast, if we set county-level employment in the FIRE sector to zero, the probability of finding a public entrepreneur drops to .21 in 1982 and .22 in 1987.[4]

TABLE 9.2

The Effects of Change in County Employment in FIRE
and High Tech on the Likelihood of Finding a Public
Entrepreneur, 1982–1987

	Coefficient	Std. Error	$p > t$
County FIRE employment	−.494	.249	.04
County high-tech employment	−.001	.004	.71
Pay ratio	.004	.002	.09
North Central	.274	.112	.01
West	.187	.162	.23
South	.238	.163	.14
Constant	−.540	.419	.19

Notes: Parameters estimated using probit analysis. Number of observations = 751. Chi square with 6 degrees of freedom = 16.21. Prob = 0.01.

Also consistent with our expectations, as the public/private wage ratio increases, the likelihood of finding a public sector entrepreneur also increases. Thus, when public sector wages approach or exceed the prevailing private sector wages, the opportunity costs for entrepreneurial activity in the public sector drop. However, the probability of finding a public entrepreneur actually decreases as county high-tech employment increases—a point we return to below.

In table 9.2 we present patterns over time. Longitudinally, growth in employment in the FIRE sector actually *reduces* the probability of finding a public sector entrepreneur. We believe the explanation for this negative relationship is straightforward: when opportunities are rapidly increasing in the FIRE sector, the relatively fixed supply of entrepreneurs is diverted away from public sector entrepreneurship to pursue private opportunities. Repeating the results of the cross-sectional analysis, the probability of finding a public entrepreneur rises with a higher public/private wage ratio.

THE EFFECTS OF LOCAL BUSINESS PATTERNS

These county-level patterns confirm a link between entrepreneurial activity in the private sector and entrepreneurship in the public sector. Next, we test the link at the community level, using a unique set of data prepared by the Missouri Data Center that merges ZIP codes with three- and four-digit Standard Industry Codes (SIC) based on 1990 data. For each combination of ZIP/SI Codes, the distribution of firms in each of nine size categories was reported. We matched our communities with their ZIP codes and created a highly detailed description of the composition of the local employment base. Specifically, we used the ZIP/SIC data to identify the number of small high-tech firms and the number of small FIRE firms in each community in our sample.[5]

We use the number of small firms in each of these two sectors as estimators for the likelihood of finding a public entrepreneur. We recognize that these data come from 1990, while our data track the emergence of public sector entrepreneurs during the 1980s. However, since the 1990 data set is unique and local economic conditions usually change slowly (see Schneider 1989; Schneider 1992), we believe the benefits of this analysis far exceed the costs imposed by measurement error. As in all our empirical work, we control for region.

Paralleling the county-level results, the effects of a concentration of FIRE firms on the emergence of public entrepreneurs are compelling. As evident in table 9.3, the number of small FIRE firms directly increases the probability of finding a public entrepreneur. We use sensitivity analyses to show the range of effects.

For the entire set of communities for which we have complete data, the predicted mean probability of finding a public entrepreneur is .29. However, if we set local employment in the FIRE sector to zero, the probability of finding a public entrepreneur drops to .23.[6] But setting local FIRE employment at one standard deviation above the mean level, the probability of finding a public entrepreneur rises 5 percent—to .34. In contrast, the number of small high-tech firms in a community does not affect the probability of finding a public entrepreneur.

TABLE 9.3

The Effects of Local Small FIRE and High-Tech Firms on the
Likelihood of Finding a Public Entrepreneur, 1982–1987

	Coefficient	Std. Error	$p > t$
Local small FIRE establishments	.003	.001	.01
Local small high-tech establishments	−.022	.022	.31
Pay ratio	.003	.003	.34
North Central	.367	.145	.01
West	.069	.206	.73
South	.061	.202	.76
Constant	−1.129	.329	.00

Notes: Parameters estimated using probit analysis. Number of observations = 468. Chi square with 6 degrees of freedom = 15.75. Prob = 0.01.

RETHINKING THE BUSINESS-GOVERNMENT NEXUS

We believe that public entrepreneurs are "embedded" social actors and that local institutional and organizational arrangements alter the likelihood of finding public entrepreneurs. By widening our focus to consider the economic and social milieux in which public entrepreneurs operate, and thereby recognizing the importance of social networks for supporting entrepreneurship, it is possible to significantly improve our ability to predict their emergence under given conditions.

Our data show that a concentration of activity in the local and regional finance, insurance, and real estate sector supports the emergence of local public entrepreneurs. In contrast, the number of high-technology manufacturing firms either has no effect or a negative effect on the likelihood of finding public entrepreneurs. As is evident in our data and in the box on the "embedded entrepreneur," the link between the FIRE sector and public entrepreneurship is particularly important.

Robert Reich (1991) describes an emerging class of "symbolic analysts." These workers are the new elite in the nation's work force, poised to capture the greatest profits from the emerging information-based economy: "Symbolic analysts solve, identify and broker problems by manipulating symbols. They simplify reality into abstract images that can be rearranged, juggled, experimented with, communicated to other specialists and then, eventually, transformed back into reality. The manipulations are done with analytic tools, sharpened by experience." Actors in the FIRE sector typically make their living from interacting closely with others, often forming transitory relationships for business expediency.

The FIRE sector provides a training ground for deal makers. But these creative and innovative thinkers can also use their skills in the political realm. That is, their human capital is a valuable commodity in the public sector. Furthermore, for "symbolic analysts," a tour of duty as an elected official is likely to add to their stock of human capital—a stock that is directly built on such skills as team building, networking, and influencing the conceptual thinking of others (King 1988). Thus, the transition from the private FIRE sector to the public domain is relatively easy and in fact can be profitable in the long run.

The high-technology sector is identified as the sector most likely to provide the engine for America's continued role as a leader in the global economy (Feller 1992). We believe that entrepreneurs in communities or regions with a greater number of high-technology firms are more likely to enter those firms than to become public entrepreneurs. In part, the reservation price in such a milieu is likely to be higher.

ALAN GUSSACK:
AN EMBEDDED ENTREPRENEUR

Alan Gussack was a dynamic five-term mayor of the affluent, close-in New York City suburb of Great Neck Plaza. Until his untimely death in office at age forty-nine in 1992, he typified an entrepreneur embedded in the service sector of his community.

Gussack was an active businessman and he used his career and his contacts to help define his political career. He spent most of his life in Great Neck Plaza, in New York, and worked as a consultant for Volkswagen and other major corporations helping them identify sites for business expansion. His first political office was as deputy mayor at age twenty-nine. When he became mayor, he sought to make Great Neck Plaza attractive to desirable white-collar service employers. He pioneered the idea of local business improvement districts and he had a statewide impact by spearheading a movement to amend New York State's General Business Law in 1989 to allow local jurisdictions to establish such districts. His activities linking government to the business environment also included a downtown improvement program and other tools to recruit new businesses. In a classic example of networking, Gussack also served on the board of the Nassau County Community Economic Corporation. Thus, as with many other entrepreneurs we studied, Gussack's impact went beyond his own city. State Assemblyman Thomas DiNapoli noted that Gussack "established a statewide reputation as a leading voice for strengthening and improving the role of local municipalities in the betterment of our communities."

In addition, the skills useful in high-tech manufacturing do not fit as tightly with the skills useful in public entrepreneurship. For professionals in the high-tech sector, a tour of duty in government could have significant opportunity costs and high-tech entrepreneurs may not be able to capitalize on public sector experience to the same degree as can professionals in the FIRE sector. For a professional in the high-tech sector, a stint in government may, in fact, reduce human capital. Given rapid technological changes, someone returning to the high-tech sector may find that their previous manufacturing-related skills have been overtaken by new developments and that the skills picked up in government are of little use.

What do these findings tell us about the organizational and institutional arrangements supportive of entrepreneurship? Our findings indicate that the FIRE sector can be a fountainhead of entrepreneurship in the local market for public goods. Further, entrepreneurs who move from the FIRE sector into positions in the public sector may be able to use their office in local government as a position from which to act as "brokers," using networks and their ties to other entrepreneurs to bring energy and innovation to places in which entrepreneurial skills and reforms are badly needed.

Our data suggest that the regions most likely to gain from Eisingerian demand-side entrepreneurial policies and other innovative actions to stimulate the local economy through incubators, high-tech parks, and university-industry relationships will be those that already have a well-developed FIRE sector talent pool and networks from which to draw the requisite entrepreneurial actors. There is an irony here in that the actions of "the entrepreneurial state," by assisting in the development of high-technology industries, may ultimately bid up the reservation wage for entrepreneurship or lead to rapid growth in FIRE activities. This growth may inadvertently reduce the potential for government to tap the pool of entrepreneurial talent to fill key positions in its own elected, managerial, and high-level advisory ranks. Ironically, then, success in fostering private sector growth may ultimately lead to stagnation in the public sector.

CHAPTER 10

Entry, Voice, and Support for Entrepreneurs

IN THE LOCAL market for public goods, entrepreneurs perceive a demand for political change and act upon their discovery of the opportunities rooted in that demand. To capitalize on these opportunities, entrepreneurs seek elected or appointed office, and then use the powers of their office to try to redirect local politics and policies. But, to be successful, entrepreneurs need to solve difficult collective action problems—a task we argue can be eased by building coalitions for change built on a set of informed and active citizens who favor new policy directions. In this chapter, we identify those citizens who have the greatest incentives to become informed and active in local politics and how they can form a core of support for political entrepreneurs. In addition, we show how some citizens can inject change into local politics by their mobility choices.

For nearly four decades, many social scientists studying urban politics have relied on Tiebout's (1956) concepts of exit and "voting with one's feet" to explain how the local market for public goods operates (also see Ostrom, Tiebout, and Warren 1961). Extending Tiebout's focus, Hirschman (1970) identified exit as only one option consumers have in dealing with suppliers. Developing a broader range of strategic options available to consumers, Hirschman argued that organizations and institutions are driven by the "exit, voice, and loyalty" of their customers. Sharp (1984), Lowery and Lyons (1989), and others used Hirschman's extended set of options to study citizen/consumer choices in local government. In this chapter, we extend even further the options. Here, we develop a focus on the *entry* decisions of a subset of ordinary citizen/consumers—movers—and show how their entry decisions help drive the local market for public goods.

Movers make self-interested choices about where to live. This is evident as they shop around to choose a house that fits their personal needs within their budget constraints. However, we will show that, at the margin, many locational choices are affected by the information movers gather about local public services and taxes. As they gather this information and as they compare the bundles of goods and services made available by different communities in the local market for public goods,

This chapter is written with Sam Best.

movers play a role supporting entrepreneurship in the local public marketplace.[1]

This supporting role comes from several sources. First, informed movers affect the goods and services offered to other citizen/consumers who have fewer incentives to gather information about local public goods and services. Second, by not entering communities that they do not see as competitive, informed movers provide a different kind of demand for policy change than is provided by direct political voice.

Informed movers can also provide a basis for political challenges mounted by entrepreneurs in communities whose policies are not competitive with neighboring communities or whose policies are not responsive to changing tastes. For example, since even well-informed movers are constrained in their choices of homes and communities, they may be forced to live in a community that is not delivering local services in an efficient manner. These well-informed in-movers may then join with established residents to support a public entrepreneur who promises dynamic improvements in the service/tax realm. Alternatively, if well-informed movers locate in a community that is already relatively efficient in providing local public services, they may have little interest in supporting an entrepreneur who advocates a major change in the way in which local public goods are produced. However, these movers may support an antigrowth entrepreneur, who promises to maintain the quality of life in the community that attracted the movers in the first place.

In short, there are links between the processes identified in the Tiebout model and the processes producing entrepreneurial politics. To examine these links, we first address a current theoretically critical debate on the role of information in making a Tiebout-like market actually work. Then we come back to the impact that informed entry decisions can have on local politics and on political entrepreneurs.

ADDING COMPLEXITY TO THE TIEBOUT MODEL

As is well known, Tiebout argued that by shopping around across communities, mobile citizen/consumers increase the efficiency and the responsiveness of local governments. In this marketlike approach to local public goods, citizens choose to locate in a community whose taxes and services most closely match their own individual tastes and "mobility provides the local public goods counterpart to the private market's shopping trip" (Tiebout 1956: 422). Although there are many differences between a pure market for private goods and a local market for public goods that limit the effects of competition,[2] a substantial body of research based on the Tiebout model has shown that allocative efficiency is increased through the spatial sorting process and that local governments in polycentric regions deliver services more efficiently and responsively than do monocentric local governments (Ostrom, Tiebout, and Warren 1961; Parks and Ostrom 1981; Sjoquist 1982; Ostrom 1972; DiLorenzo 1983; Schneider 1986b, 1989; Zax 1989).

While these aggregate level findings are compelling, scholars have attacked the Tiebout model from a variety of perspectives. At its very core, like many models in neoclassical economics, the Tiebout model is a model of "pure" competition based on a set of highly abstract principles (perfect mobility, an urban area built on a featureless plane, perfect information, etc.). In the almost four decades since its publication, researchers have attacked the extreme conditions detailed in these principles. However, one very common approach to testing the robustness of abstract models (and the approach we used in the first section of this book) is through the progressive relaxation of the highly restrictive assumptions built into the original model. In this manner, models are made more complex, more nuanced, and more congruent with empirical realities.

Oakerson and Parks (1988), for example, questioned the exclusive reliance on mobility underlying the Tiebout model. They argue that political activity, or "voice," is at least as important as mobility (exit) in determining local government service/tax decisions. Others argue that the role of local governments in the Tiebout model is too passive. In the Tiebout model, government policies are "more or less set," but governments actually engage in strategic behavior in determining their services and taxes. In addition to our work here on political entrepreneurs, Ostrom, Tiebout, and Warren (1961), Peterson (1981), Schneider (1989), and Stein (1990) among others, all introduce a more active government dimension to the Tiebout model.[3]

While these debates continue, it is Tiebout's notion that citizen/consumers "vote with their feet," the central theoretical construct in the model, that has recently attracted the most attention. Critics have raised questions about several aspects of this individual-level focus of the model. First, the Tiebout model assumes that citizens are perfectly mobile—that they can easily exit a community that does not satisfy their preferences and that they can enter a new community that offers a service/tax package they prefer. Rather than the frictionless plane of the Tiebout model, as Orbell and Uno (1972) argued long ago, numerous real world constraints on the mobility of individuals limit exit. But it is what Lowery and Lyons (1989) call the "information assumption" of the model that has attracted the most recent attention (also see Sharp 1984; Lyons and Lowery 1989; Lowery, Lyons, and DeHoog 1990). Lowery and Lyons argue that the Tiebout exit/entry process requires high levels of information on the part of individual citizen/consumers—that for the Tiebout model to work citizen/consumers must have accurate knowledge of the alternative local public service/tax packages being offered elsewhere in their region.

Using a carefully matched sample of residents in a polycentric and a monocentric metropolitan region, Lowery and Lyons investigated several of the individual-level information assumptions they believe underlie the Tiebout model. Specifically, they question whether individuals are aware of alternative service/tax packages in other local governments; whether they are motivated to exit a jurisdiction if its service/tax package does not align with their preferences; and whether they make their relocation decisions based on the alternative service/tax packages offered by municipalities.

Lowery and Lyons find little empirical evidence that any of these assumptions hold.[4] They conclude (1989: 94–95) that the organization of local government and the range of services offered in a metropolitan region "just do not seem to influence attitudes and behaviors in the gross manner suggested by the Tiebout model . . . [and] many of the aggregate-level findings on service delivery may have to be rethought."

THE MACRO-MICRO DISPARITY

Lowery and Lyons pose a fundamental theoretical question: Is it possible to reconcile macro-level evidence that illustrates the effects of Tiebout mechanisms on local government efficiency with evidence that at the micro-level key assumptions are violated? Although macro-micro level disparities are not uncommon in social science, this matter is probably most familiar to those who have followed recent debates in macroeconomics between Keynesians and the micro-level advocates of rational expectations models. On one hand, we could argue that as long as macro-level models predict well, then nothing is to be gained by comparing their underlying assumptions to micro-level evidence. This position is illustrated in the famous "as if" dictum credited to Milton Friedman (1953). On the other hand, others argue that since science is concerned with accurate explanation, the "as if" dictum is simply not acceptable.

In reviewing the conflict in economics, Blinder (1989: 123–124) notes that "neither side is hostile either to first principles or to factual accuracy. We all agree that the ideal macro theory would be built up logically from first principles and would explain the data well. But we also agree that such a theory is a long way off." Blinder goes on to note that good science is not always built on solid micro foundations. For example, scientific breakthroughs in thermodynamics, chemistry, and medicine have all been accomplished without strong micro-level theory. On the strength of this conclusion, Blinder argues that empirical regularities formulated and tested directly at only the macro level clearly have a place in science.

Despite Blinder's argument, social scientists interested in the underlying social and political processes that give rise to observed data no doubt feel frustrated with theory that cannot reconcile macro- and micro-level evidence. In the research reported here, we place the aggregate-level data that supports the Tiebout model on a micro-level foundation that is built on a better understanding of markets and the role of consumers than evident in most political science. We believe that the current debate over the micro-level assumptions of the Tiebout model is built on a faulty understanding of how markets work. In particular, research on the "information assumption" has not focused on how markets can be driven by a subset of actors and by the information search processes in which they engage.

We believe that a fundamental source of problems in correctly specifying the Tiebout model is the belief that *all* movers must hold information about comparative service/tax packages. Indeed, Lowery and Lyons go even further and imply that all *citizens* must have accurate information about local goods and services. In fact, studies of private sector markets show that only a subset of consumers, especially those with high incomes, are likely to gather information about their purchases (Katona and Mueller 1955; Newman and Staelin 1972; Claxton, Fry, and Portis 1974; Thorelli and Engledow 1980). More important, these studies show that even a small percentage of buyers can effectively drive a market toward a competitive outcome.[5] That a local market for public goods can be driven toward a competitive outcome by a subset of informed citizen/consumers thus parallels empirical findings for competitive private sector markets. In other words, for the local market for public goods to be competitive, only a small proportion of movers need to have information on the various packages of goods and services local governments offer. This is particularly true if these knowledgeable movers are high income. In the next sections, we refine the Tiebout model by relaxing the implicit assumption that competition is driven by the actions of all movers and concentrate on the effects that can be produced by a small number of more highly informed actors.

The Role of Consumers

There is a critical difference between the role of the average consumer (whose level of information may be low) and the informed (or "marginal") consumer. The failure to understand the importance of marginal consumers and the costs that different classes of citizen/consumers face has fundamentally flawed research into the information individuals need to drive a Tiebout-like market. Much of the recent research on movers and the Tiebout model is overly focused on the threat of *exit*.[6] We believe that it is the *entry* decisions of movers, not their exit decisions, that are more theoretically attuned to Tiebout's description of mobile citizen/consumers. Most residential moves are motivated by factors that have nothing to do with public services; rather, they are motivated by changes in employment, or changes in life circumstances. But once forced to shop around for a new house, a new community, and an attendant new local government, the *marginal* costs of gathering information about local public services are low. Thus, actual movers, as they choose among their entry options, may be as close to Tiebout's "frictionless mover" as we will find in the real world. But no search process can reveal all aspects of the package of taxes and services municipalities offer in the local market for public goods. In turn, we discuss the "search" and "experience" aspects of local public goods, and these characteristics affect the micro- and macro-level outcomes in the local market.

Pressure toward Competitive Equilibria

Our empirical focus is at the individual microlevel, establishing the comparative levels of knowledge recent movers and more established residents actually have about local government service/tax packages. But our theoretical focus is on the link between these results and other market processes, including the behavior of entrepreneurs. We seek to identify why municipalities respond to consumer search and how the behavior of citizen/consumers can produce macro-level forces that push the local market for public goods toward competitive outcomes.

We discuss these issues in detail below, concentrating on the difference between marginal and average consumers. We then develop the outlines of a more rigorous theoretical approach to the study of the individual-level assumptions underlying the Tiebout model of the local market for public goods and discuss how the particular nature of this market affects competitive outcomes. In the development of our argument, we update the Tiebout model to respond to many of the criticisms that have subsequently been leveled at it, incorporating the costs of information gathering, the costs of mobility, and the strategic interests of municipal governments. With this theoretical structure in place, we use data from a survey of over 500 recent movers and established residents in Suffolk County, New York, to present evidence on how a class of informed citizen/consumers may satisfy some of the individual-level assumptions that *actually* underlie the role of citizen/consumers in the local market for public goods.

THE ROLE OF THE MARGINAL CONSUMER

By analyzing the responses of a sample of *all* individuals in two metropolitan areas, Lowery and Lyons have de facto based their criticism of the Tiebout model on the behavior of the "average consumer." Since according to Lowery and Lyons the average citizen does not know much about local services and taxes, they conclude that the Tiebout model of the local market for public goods cannot be operative. But the focus on the average consumer as the driving force in markets is misplaced: Economists recognize that both theory and empirical research should focus on the marginal consumer.

Rhoads (1985: 144) argues that in many markets the marginal consumers are the most careful and well-informed shoppers, whose actions generate "competitive pressures that help keep prices reasonable for less-informed, non-searching consumers as well" (also see Thorelli and Engledow 1980 on "information seekers" and Feick and Price 1987 on "market mavens"). This set of informed consumers acting in their own self-interest help create an efficient market. Schwartz and Wilde (1979: 638) specify the argument further. For them, "the presence of at least some consumer search in a market creates the possibility of a 'pecuniary externality': persons who search sometimes protect nonsearchers from overreaching firms." More to the point, they argue, *"the conventional analysis asks the wrong question.* Rather than asking whether an idealized individual is sufficiently informed to maximize his own utility, the appropriate normative inquiry is whether competition among firms for *particular groups of searchers* is, in any given market, sufficient to generate optimal prices and terms for *all consumers*" (p. 638; emphasis added). In applying this argument to the Tiebout market, replace the term "firms" with "municipalities."[7]

To illustrate this point in the context of a private good, consider the decision to buy a car. Most cars last several years. For much of the time between car purchases, a consumer need not know anything about the costs or benefits of different models of new cars—the consumer is not looking to buy a car and there would be no benefit in expending resources to gather information. However, when consumers enter the car market, they engage in an extensive search about the cost and quality of various car models. A survey of *all* consumers would show that despite the millions of dollars spent by car companies advertising their products, the *average* consumer has little accurate information about different car models. Yet, the car market is highly competitive, because it is driven by the marginal consumer—the relatively small proportion of the population that is "in the market" at any given time and for whom the benefits of search outweigh the costs of gathering information.

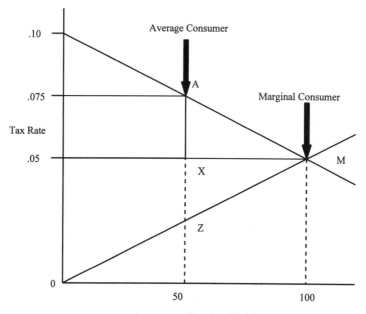

Fig. 10.1. The Effects of the Marginal Consumer on Efficiency in the Local Market for Public Goods

While the "average consumer" is willing to pay a tax rate of $.075, the well-informed "marginal consumer" drives the market tax price to $.05. The triangle, MAX, represents the surplus citizen/consumers gain from the pressure toward a more efficient competitive equilibrium. The triangle MZX also represents an efficiency gain, but one that accrues more directly to producers. The degree to which this producer surplus is transferred back to citizen/consumers is a function of the exactive capacity of local bureaucrats (see Niskanen 1971; Schneider 1989). The rectangle A-X-.05-.075 represents an additional transfer from municipalities to citizen/consumers. The pecuniary advantage generated by the marginal citizen/consumer is the sum of MAX plus whatever part of the triangle MXZ is returned to consumers. If there is no price discrimination, the gain is divided among all citizen/consumers.

This argument can be made graphically. Figure 10.1 shows a typical supply and demand curve. We assume that price discrimination is not feasible in the depicted market, as is usually the case by law for the service/tax packages cities offer to their residents. The market clearing tax price for the package of public goods is $.05 per $1,000 of home value and 100 units will be purchased. But the average consumer in this market is actually willing to pay a tax rate of $.075 for the public goods.[8] In contrast, the marginal consumer will not purchase the good at this higher tax price (perhaps because this consumer is better informed about the real worth of public goods).

In a fully competitive market, the marginal consumer will drive the tax price down to $.05 per unit, which is what *every* consumer, including the average consumer, will pay. This is the source of the pecuniary externality that the marginal consumer generates but accrues to all citizen/consumers. We recognize that the local market for public goods is not fully competitive, so that there is variation in the tax prices local governments charge and the services they provide. But in either the public or the private market, the pressure toward competitive pricing is driven by the same mechanism: By having more accurate information about prices, the marginal consumer drives the market toward a competitive level.

THE SEARCH FOR INFORMATION

As economists have recognized that few markets fulfill assumptions of complete information and perfect competition, they have studied the role of information in markets and patterns of consumer search. Complete information is too costly to generate in most transactions and no party ever has fully complete information about a product or service (Stigler 1961; Nelson 1970; and Akerlof 1970 are the seminal works in the area of information economics). Subsequent to these explorations, economists have done theoretical work on price-quality relationships, on the elements of search and experience that allow consumers to learn about purchases, and on how competitive markets can act in the absence of full information by all consumers. They have identified two basic types of search: sequential and fixed sample (Cave 1985). While there are important differences in the equilibria expected from either of these broad search processes, under either approach, more extensive search and greater numbers of informed consumers in any market produce stronger pressure toward competitive outcomes.

Bucklin (1969: 416) summarizes the critical processes: "Fundamental to the efficient operation of a competitively organized market economy is the function of consumer search. If buyers fail to seek out alternative prices and qualities and thereby become ill informed, markets become segmented, prices rise, and consumer surpluses are transferred to the entrepreneurial sector."

Unfortunately, economists have done little empirical work on these questions. However, their colleagues in the more applied fields of business, marketing, and consumer research have provided some evidence in real private sector markets, which we summarize here.

In the American economy, where many markets are competitive, much of the research into private goods markets shows that many or most consumers do not comparison shop very much. For example, Claxton, Fry, and Portis (1974) found only 5 percent of furniture buyers and 8 percent of appliance buyers to be store-intensive, thorough shoppers, with an average of twenty store visits for furniture shoppers, compared to eight or less for other shoppers. They found that these informed subsets of shoppers utilized more sources of information and had higher incomes. For the other buyers, Claxton, Fry, and Portis (1974: 35) conclude: "A basic conclusion from available studies is that pre-purchase search is a relatively limited activity, even in the case of major durables." Earlier, Katona and Mueller (1955) found that 47 percent of those purchasing durables bought at the only store they visited, a percentage that jumps to 70 percent for nondurables. Thus, most consumers do not do a lot of comparative shopping for these products that are sold in what we would consider to be competitive markets.

Other studies also find a group of consumers that search more than others. These consumers are more interested in and "involved with" the product and also usually have higher incomes (Katona and Mueller 1955; Newman and Staelin 1972; Claxton, Fry, and Portis 1974).

Two sets of studies in particular have focused on the critical importance of consumers who search more (and presumably are therefore better informed about comparative price and quality information). Feick and Price (1987) labeled the upper third of information seekers "market mavens," who are likely to be opinion leaders and to share comparative information with other, less informed consumers. Slama and Williams (1990) generalize Feick and Price's findings to more markets and confirm that market mavens provide comparative product information to others for many products and services, including real estate.

In a second line of research, based on a major cross-national study over many years and focusing on users of consumer information (such as *Consumer Reports* subscribers in the United States), Thorelli and Engledow (1980) identify a category of "Information Seekers" (IS) who are significantly more interested and more knowledgeable than the average consumer (AC in their parlance). They argue that these "ISs," who make up 10–20 percent of the population and are higher income than ACs, help to police the market by comparative shopping and by complaining more (e.g., voice in our parlance) if products and services are not adequate:

> [T]he test reports magazine subscribers represent a fairly homogeneous and cosmopolitan group of information-sensitive consumers, which may be

found in all industrially advanced countries, and which is significantly different from the average consumer group. We . . . estimate that from 10 percent to 20 percent of the consumers in a high consumption economy may be [Information Seekers]. . . . They are both affluent and consumption-oriented, so that they account for a large number of total purchases and a large dollar volume . . . in their role of opinion-leaders and vigilantes of the marketplace, the IS constitute a public good. (Thorelli and Engledow 1980: 12–14)

Thus, economic and consumer evidence supports the notion of a cadre of high-income consumers helping to make markets more efficient, even in the face of large numbers of nonsearching consumers.

Movers as Marginal Consumers

The low level of information held by the "average consumer" is the strongest criticism leveled against the Tiebout model. How, critics ask, can a Tiebout market work when the vast majority of citizens do not possess information about the services and taxes that local governments offer? As with other kinds of political activity, many citizens may be "rationally ignorant" (Downs 1957). But given the role of marginal consumers highlighted in our theory and in these studies of private markets, we do not need to demonstrate that large numbers of people have high levels of information, we need only identify specific classes of individuals who know more about services and taxes.

One class of individuals who may help drive the Tiebout market are actual movers. Most citizens do not exit their community because of dissatisfaction with the quality of the local service/tax package. Rather, moves are overwhelmingly driven by employment considerations or changes in family status—in short, the decision to move is largely exogenous to the local market for public goods (Long 1974; Fields 1979; but see Blank 1985; Gramlich and Laren 1984; Peterson and Rom 1989; Percy and Hawkins 1992). However, once an individual, driven by personal or employment reasons, is facing the high transaction costs of moving, the incremental costs of gathering information on local services and taxes are low.

The marginal cost of gathering information is reduced by the role of intermediaries who provide information to consumers at a low cost (Rhoads 1985; Friedman 1962). For example, the costs movers face for gathering information about alternative communities may be reduced by real estate agents, who provide information about schools, local services, and taxes in addition to information about specific houses. Citizens also utilize information gathered by others. According to Kozol

(1991: 120) the New York State publication *Statistical Profiles of Public School Districts* became "a small best-seller."

Moreover, at the time of major real estate transactions, movers are also most sensitive to the future capitalization of housing value and will resist purchasing housing in a community that does not offer a competitive stream of capitalization because of poor services and high taxes. Thus, entry decisions are more likely to be driven by local services and taxes, and, in turn, it is at the point of *entry* not of *exit* that the Tiebout mechanisms are most likely to come into play.

Search and Experience

But even if movers have incentives to search, they face limits in their ability to gather accurate information. Economists distinguish between search goods, the quality of which can largely be determined prior to purchase, and experience goods, which must be consumed in order to learn their quality (Nelson 1970; Weimer and Vining 1992). Markets for experience goods can be inefficient, as consumers either cannot verify product quality at the time of purchase or they must expend relatively large resources (compared to the price of the good) to do so.

Wilde (1981: 1123) shows that even relatively simple private goods possess some "search characteristics" and some "experience characteristics." For the complicated package of local public goods that Tiebout's shoppers purchase along with their residential location, we expect to find some characteristics best ascertained through search and others that require experience. For example, the local tax rate, the student/ faculty ratio in local schools, and the number of parks in a community may be easily assessed at low search costs. Far greater search costs are required to determine the stability of the local budget and the likelihood of future tax increases, the ability of local schools to place students in quality colleges, and the safety of the parks at night. These aspects of local public goods may be best learned through experience. Given relatively lower search costs for movers, we expect movers to gather much of their information about public services and taxes through search. Given the role of experience in assessing elements of the local service/tax package, we expect that established residents will increase their accurate knowledge of local public goods over time.

Search Processes and Market Equilibria

What type of search processes are mobile entrants likely to pursue and how will that affect the relationship between communities? The two types of search that citizens can utilize, sequential and fixed sample, will affect intermunicipal equilibria differently. Using sequential search, a citizen acquires information on each community's service/tax package in sequence until the marginal costs of additional search exceed the marginal benefits of finding the most preferred service/tax package. This strategy assumes that the citizen has some prior notion of the distribution of service/tax packages available, even though they may not know the particulars of any given package. Without this prior information, the mover would be unable to recognize the potential benefits of additional search.

If citizens engage in sequential search, economists identify two possible equilibria (Cave 1985; Schwartz and Wilde 1979; Rothschild 1973). First, if the search costs for citizens are significantly high, then the public goods market equilibria would settle at the monopoly price. In contrast, if a significant number of citizens can search for service/tax packages at low cost, then municipalities may be forced to compete to increase their tax base by producing public services more efficiently. Hence, the public goods market would approach the competitive price. While Schwartz and Wilde (1979), Gatswirth (1976), and others note significant problems with assuming this search pattern, the importance of the marginal consumer for whom search costs are lower is obvious.

It is more likely that many citizen/consumers will utilize fixed sample searches, in which they decide how many service/tax packages to learn about before making a decision. A fixed sample search also makes more sense when the greatest portion of the search cost is in locating a source where information on a number of jurisdictions is available (see Stigler 1961 for the seminal discussion of fixed search strategies). This is clearly the case when a mobile resident contacts a realtor before making the locational decision.

If most individuals use a fixed sample search strategy where some limit their sample to only one community and others compare more than one, economists have identified three possible market equilibria (Cave 1985; Schwartz and Wilde 1979; and Rothschild 1973). First, when a significant number of citizens compare more than one service/tax package, market equilibrium will be closer to the competitive price. Second, at the other extreme, if there are no consumers searching more than one community service/tax package, the market equilibrium will be near the monopoly price (as it would also be in the case of a consolidated metropolitan government with no competitive alternatives).[9] In between these two alternatives, if the number of citizens who conduct searches is too small to support a competitive price, but it is still a significant number, then a mass of prices will occur at the competitive price with the rest dispersed up to the monopoly price. This occurs because a large portion of individuals are not shopping, making it profitable for some communities to provide public services at supracompetitive prices. However, there are still enough searchers to prevent too many communities from engaging in this practice, thus resulting in a "mass point" near the competitive price.

The Nature of Search in the Market for Local Public Goods

How likely is it that movers will engage in search for public service/tax packages that they prefer? As noted above, consumers utilize cost-benefit calculations in their search processes (e.g., Lanzetta and Kanareff 1962; Stigler 1961) and as the value of a good increases so does the number of individuals who engage in comparative shopping (Bucklin 1966; Udell 1966; Bucklin 1969; Newman and Staelin 1972; Punj and Staelin 1983; Beatty and Smith 1987). Houses are the most expensive purchases most individuals ever make, and they have correspondingly strong incentives to gather information. And as we will see, more expensive house prices seem to be associated with movers gathering more accurate information.

Second, search costs can be reduced by factors including positive and negative advertising, and supplier reputation. Advertising reduces search costs by making information on service/tax packages more accessible to more people at a lower cost. Advertising is not as prevalent in the market for public goods as it is in the market for private goods, but it is not unknown (e.g., advertisements for attractive places to retire to) and information does circulate through newspapers and local television newscasts reporting on service/tax packages. Communities often advertise to attract businesses, and in that process often highlight their community as a desirable place to live for employees of those businesses. Reputation can also provide information to consumers, especially for public goods. Consider the regionwide reputation some municipalities acquire for their schools, taxes, roads, parks, or libraries. A poor reputation is difficult to shed.

Finally, the fact that citizen relocation choices are more "mass" than "individual" means that communities can not easily discriminate between consumers on relevant criteria. In an individual transaction, for example, used car sellers can usually distinguish between sophisticated and unsophisticated purchasers and can offer alternative prices to each. On the other hand, mass transactions make price discrimination impossible because of the cost of obtaining information that differentiates consumers. While they often can do so for large and unique businesses, municipalities are unable (often by law) to offer different service/tax packages to different citizens. Therefore, if communities want to attract mobile residents with a competitive package, they must offer the same package to permanent residents. Thus, consumers face different configurations of producers in private markets and in the local market for public goods. These configurations affect the incentives individuals have to engage in search and the effects search will have on the competitiveness and responsiveness of producers.

In a market characterized by a single provider, consumers have no incentives to engage in search because there are no choices among goods. And the provider has little or no incentive to be efficient or responsive in its behavior. As is well known, the outcome is a monopoly price higher than the competitive equilibrium. Consider next a market that is characterized by multiple producers but one in which consumers are all ignorant of the quality of goods or the prices that alternate producers charge: that is, consumers are engaging in either no search or low-quality search. As in the monopoly market, producers have few incentives to charge anything less than the monopoly price: the presence of multiple producers *alone* does not produce efficiency gains over the monopoly market. However, more efficient outcomes begin to emerge as soon as some consumers engage in search and gather information about the quality and prices of goods provided by alternate producers. Wilde and Schwartz (1979: 551) note: "the likelihood of competitive equilibria obtaining varies directly with the number of consumers who visit more than one firm [local governments] and with the number of firms such 'comparison shoppers' visit." And even a little comparative information can go a long way. As Bucklin (1969: 416) notes: "The value to the buyer of even a little information is striking."

THE INCENTIVES OF MUNICIPAL GOVERNMENTS IN THE LOCAL MARKET FOR PUBLIC GOODS

To earn profits, business firms respond to informed consumers of private goods. We argue that there is similar pressure for local governments to respond to informed consumers of local public goods. But there are distinctive characteristics of the local market for public goods that affect how these market mechanisms come into play. While models of markets for private goods alert us to important underlying mechanisms of competition and efficiency, they must be modified in order to help us understand processes in the provision of public goods, especially local public goods.

Tiebout's original formulation relegated municipal governments to a secondary role, portraying them as inactive agents. This simplifying assumption may have resulted because of his concern for a "pure" theory of competition in metropolitan regions. In the case of pure competition for private goods, the strategies and actions of suppliers are irrelevant to understanding market outcomes. By analogy, in a purely competitive public market, the actions of government need not be modeled. But as Tiebout himself recognized (in Ostrom, Tiebout, and Warren 1961), for many reasons, especially since the local market for public goods is not purely competitive, municipal governments are not passive actors in the local market for public goods. In fact, many local governments are led by political entrepreneurs who act strategically to advance their own community's interests in the context of multiple competitive municipalities.

From the perspective of local public finance, not all citizen/consumers are equally valuable to communities, and municipalities have incentives to fashion service/tax packages to appeal to certain individuals, and not others. In fact, the "average consumer" may be of no particular interest to competitive cities. Rather, current community residents have incentives to use the tools of their local government to maximize the level of local wealth in their community. Present members of a community are interested in making their community more attractive to an individual with above-average wealth. Given a fixed tax rate and legal constraints on limiting access to local public services, individuals buying above-average cost housing in a community pay what Buchanan has called a "net fiscal dividend" to present residents (Buchanan 1981). According to Peterson (1981) and Schneider (1989), one of the most effective ways to attract such residents is by offering an efficient mix of services (and related taxes) important to above-average income individuals.

In turn, even if only these above-average income individuals make their entry decisions based on service/tax packages, the Tiebout model could still operate as predicted. That is, given the structure of the local market for public goods, if only relatively wealthy individuals shop around, their actions may be sufficient to drive the services and tax decisions of local government and the process illustrated in figure 10.1 can be extended to the local market for public goods.

Obviously, we cannot gather all the information to fully analyze equilibria in different metropolitan market settings. However, we take an important first step by focusing on the search processes of the citizen/consumer in the local market for public goods. Specifically, we use empirical survey data to understand how movers and nonmovers gather comparative information about local government services in a polycentric market setting.

MOVERS, SEARCH, AND EFFICIENCY IN THE LOCAL MARKET FOR PUBLIC GOODS

To address some of the issues raised by our theoretical perspective, we conducted two telephone surveys of households in Suffolk County, New York. This county, with a population of approximately 1.3 million, has a polycentric structure of government, consisting of ten towns, twenty-four incorporated villages, seventy-one school districts, and innumerable special districts.

The first survey was designed to test the knowledge established (nonmoving) householders had of local government services. The second survey tested the knowledge of householders who had recently bought houses in Suffolk County. Appendix 10.1 describes in detail the methods used and the demographic profile of these surveys.

In this chapter, we focus on the results for school district expenditures and taxes.[10] We consider respondents to be "informed" if they accurately ranked their own district on both expenditures and tax rates relative to other school districts in Suffolk County.[11] We first compare the accuracy of the information held by movers categorized by their level of wealth and interest in local schools. We then present a multivariate probit analysis of the influence of these characteristics of movers on their accuracy. In a second probit analysis, we pool recent movers and established residents to examine the search and experience aspects of accurate information about local services. Then, we present data on the quality and sources of information search used by movers. Finally, we relate accurate knowledge to the use of political voice within a community.

Not surprisingly, our data show that the level of accurate information held by all citizens is low. Overall, 21 percent of our respondents accurately evaluated the ranking of their schools—about 50 percent higher than what would be expected by chance. Recent movers taken as a whole actually had less accurate information about their schools than did nonmovers: 19 percent of movers accurately judged the expenditures and taxes of their school district, compared to 24 percent of established residents. But the accuracy of information increases with theoretically important characteristics of movers.

Local governments have strategic interests in attending to the interests of high-wealth individuals. Thus, if these individuals seek out and hold more accurate information about services and taxes then pressure for efficiency may result, regardless of the "average" level of information held by all citizen/consumers. To examine differences in information, we divided our sample of movers and nonmovers into two categories: those with household incomes above the average for the sample ($50,000) and those with incomes below the average.[12] Compared to low-wealth respondents, high-income respondents were significantly more likely to have accurate information about their school districts: While low-income movers proved accurate only 12 percent of the time, high-income movers were accurate 28 percent of the time.[13]

As we noted above, marketing studies shows that certain consumers are more "involved" with some purchases and that it is these individuals who make markets. We assess the relative importance of local govern-

TABLE 10.1

Factors Influencing the Accuracy of Recent Movers Concerning Local
School Expenditures and Tax Rates—Recent Homebuyers

	Coeff.	Std. Error	t	P > t
School important	.426	.244	1.75	.08
Kids in school	.408	.222	1.84	.07
Income	.763	.225	3.40	.00
Constant	−1.818	.270	−6.74	.00

Notes: $N = 224$; chi square = 20.4, $p < .001$. The dependent variable = 1 when respondents correctly identified both their school tax rate and expenditures as average, above average, or below average, 0 otherwise. The dependent variable = 1 for 42 of the cases. The School important variable = 1 if respondents said that local schools were very important to them. The Kids in school variable = 1 if respondents have children of school age, and 0 otherwise. The Income variable = 1 if the household income exceeds the sample median, and 0 otherwise.

ment services to the location decisions of movers using two questions. We asked movers to name the factors that were important to them in choosing the community in which they chose to buy their house. Forty percent of movers volunteered that the quality of schools, parks, and other local services affected their choice of community. We then asked movers directly whether or not the quality of local schools was important to their choice of community. The percentage of respondents who said yes is high: 68 percent of movers said that schools were very important. Movers do attend to information about local services, especially schools, when making their entry decisions.

In table 10.1, we present a probit analysis, testing the influence of attentiveness to schools, the presence of school-age children, and income level on the accuracy of information held by movers. The results confirm that even with other factors included, higher income movers are much more likely to hold accurate information about their local school district. Movers also are more accurate when they report caring about local schools (at $p < .08$) and when they have children in the schools (at $p < .07$).

Probit allows for a sensitivity analysis to determine how changing the values of independent variables affects the probability that an individual held accurate information. For all movers in table 10.1, the probability of having accurate information among all movers is 19 percent. But if all movers had high income, the accuracy would increase to 26 percent. If all movers cared very much about local schools, accuracy would increase to 22 percent, and if all movers had school-age children, accuracy would increase to 27 percent. But if all movers had high income, cared about schools, *and* had school children, the accuracy rate would jump to 41 percent—triple the chance accuracy rate. We take this as evidence of a

TABLE 10.2

Factors Influencing the Accuracy of Respondents Concerning Local
School Expenditures and Tax Rates—All Homeowners

	Coeff.	Std. Error	t	P > t
Time in community	.078	.031	2.55	.01
Kids in school	.295	.144	2.05	.04
Income	.370	.140	2.64	.01
Constant	−1.162	.135	−8.63	.00

Notes: $N = 422$; chi square $= 16.6$; $p < .001$. The dependent variable $= 1$ when respondents correctly identified both their school tax rate and expenditures as average, above average, or below average, 0 otherwise. The dependent variable $= 1$ in 89 of the cases. The Time in community variable is the square root of the number of years of residence in the present community ($= 0$ for recent movers). The Kids in school variable $= 1$ if the family has children of school age. The Income variable $= 1$ if the family income exceeds the sample median, 0 otherwise.

class of mobile and valuable residents who know more about the relative performance of their schools.

We present a second probit analysis in table 10.2 to compare the effects of income and school-age children on accuracy for the entire sample of Long Island residents, including nonmovers. Because local public goods may have a significant experience dimension, we test the effects of length of residence in a community on the probability a respondent has accurate information. As table 10.2 reports, accuracy does increase with time in a community, reflecting an experience goods aspect of local public services (Bledsoe and Stoker 1992 find a similar result for other kinds of information about local politics). For the entire sample, replicating the results for movers alone, respondents are also more accurate when they have children in school and when they have higher incomes.

Repeating the sensitivity analysis, across the entire sample, the probability of having accurate information is 24 percent. But if all respondents had children in schools, accuracy would increase to 30 percent. And if all respondents had high income, accuracy would increase to 29 percent. If respondents had no experience living in the community, accuracy would fall to 19 percent. Combining these two conditions for all respondents increases the accuracy rate to 37 percent—165 percent higher than chance.

To illustrate the search and experience dimensions of local public goods in visual form for both recent movers and established residents, figure 10.2 compares the increasing effect of length of residence on the accuracy of information (the experience dimension) with the accuracy of recent movers divided into those with low incomes and high incomes. The graph illustrates that high-income movers treat local public goods as a search good by gathering accurate comparative information while they

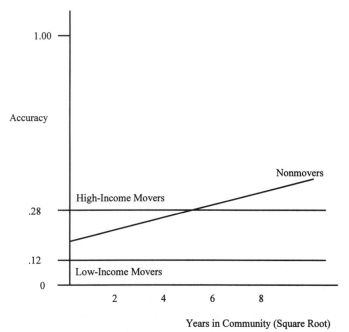

Fig. 10.2. Search, Experience, and Accuracy

are considering a housing purchase. For nonmovers, there is a clear linear trend relating time in a community to accuracy about schools.[14]

Our survey evidence also illuminates the type of search process of movers. Compared to low-income movers, movers with higher resources are significantly more likely to use "institutional sources," such as schools and governments, to provide them with information. People with lower incomes are more likely (at $p < .07$) to rely more on "personal sources," especially friends and family, for information about local services (see Slama and Tashchian 1985: 72 for parallel evidence from private markets). More importantly, movers who report caring more about local government services are more likely to use both kinds of sources to gather information than are other respondents (significant at $p < .06$).

Incorporating the Role of Voice

One important criticism of the Tiebout model is its failure to identify the importance of voice as a driving force in the local market for public goods. We believe that voice reinforces the pivotal role of the high-income marginal consumer. Inman (1978) found that a group virtually identical to our informed consumers—young, high-income households with children—even though making up a small percentage of the population were likely to have their preferences for school budgets met. They achieved their success through active participation in the local political process—that is, through voice.

The knowledgeable mover will be more able to make comparisons between services and taxes in competing jurisdictions and will have solid evidence upon which to base complaints about the services currently provided. Paralleling Inman, we find that better informed movers are also significantly more likely to have engaged in higher levels of political activity.[15] These individuals combine entry and voice to increase their power as consumers over the behavior of municipal agencies. We also find that nonmovers are more likely to use voice by being politically active when they have higher incomes and have been in that community longer. This matches other results related to political participation increasing with length of residence (e.g., Alford and Lee 1968; Bollens and Schmandt 1970) and to increasing dissatisfaction with local services like street maintenance and parks with longer residency (Miller and Miller 1991). Thus, high-income movers and nonmovers form a class of citizens who utilize entry and voice as effective mechanisms to motivate policy changes that can benefit all citizens. Their informed political activity can help provide a group of supporters for political entrepreneurs. By utilizing voice within their community and exit/entry in the intercommunity context, these mobile citizens provide the pressure for change and link the political choices and policies generated in the intra- and intercommunity spheres.

MOVERS, INFORMATION, AND ENTREPRENEURS

Citizens act in their own self-interest when choosing a community in which to live, but in doing so they generate pressure for policy changes that benefit others. In this way, they create the same kinds of positive externalities that any entrepreneur does. The number of "citizen entrepreneurs" is much greater than the number of political or managerial entrepreneurs we discussed earlier. However, these citizen entrepreneurs are a still a small subset of all of the actors in comparable situations who could potentially collect information about local public goods and taxes.

Higher-income movers are more likely to gather comparative information through search, while nonmovers are more likely to rely on experience. Together, using entry and political voice, these citizens can provide support for political and bureaucratic entrepreneurs who wish to change the politics and policies of their community.[16] In part, these groups help provide a demand for change that political entrepreneurs can emerge to fulfill. Given intercommunity competition, the exit and entry decisions of high-income movers provide economic and fiscal pressure to change policies. Within communities, the use of voice by high-income movers and by established residents can provide a core of support upon which an entrepreneur can build a foundation of votes for change. Thus, in local government the "many" citizen entrepreneurs can create a demand-side milieux supportive of policy change led by the "few" political and managerial entrepreneurs.

————————————— **APPENDIX 10.1** —————————————

For the survey of nonmoving householders, we generated a telephone number sampling pool using listed telephone numbers and the "add-a-digit" approach (Lavrakas 1987: 39–41). This survey was conducted in October and November 1991, and the interviewers were undergraduate students participating for class credit. The overall response rate was 49 percent. To obtain this response rate, up to a total of nine call-backs were made to every selected telephone number. All selected individuals who refused on the first call were recontacted by an experienced interviewer, and households with listed telephone numbers received an advanced letter informing them of their selection in the study. The response rate was calculated as the ratio of completions to the sum of completions, refusals, and numbers at which there was no answer. Of the 310 completed interviews, only the 239 cases in which the residents owned and had been living in the present residence for at least a year were included in the subsequent analysis.

For Suffolk residents who had recently bought houses, a more complicated procedure was used to generate the telephone number sampling pool. Lists containing all the names and addresses of recent purchasers (plus the price of the house) as recorded at the Suffolk County Clerk's office during October 1991 were obtained from a local company, Long Island Profiles. Telephone numbers were then matched with the listed names and addresses. The questionnaire contained items with wording identical to that used in the survey of established residents. These questions were augmented with others having to do with matters such as reasons for moving and the nature of the search undertaken. This survey was conducted in January 1992 using the best interviewers from the previous survey. The overall response rate was 54 percent, resulting in 259 completed interviews.

Both samples achieved a fairly even mix of the sexes (the sample of established residents had 44 percent male and 56 percent female respondents, while the sample of recent movers had 53 percent male and 47 percent female). Our sample of established residents had lived in their current homes for an average of eighteen years. Aside from this difference in length of residency, the demographics of the established residents and recent movers were quite similar. The majority of respondents were white (93 percent) and well educated (37 percent had completed some college and 39 percent had completed a college degree). The average household income of established residents was between $35,000 and $40,000, slightly lower than the average for recent movers of between $40,000 and $50,000.

The average age of the established residents was forty-six years; the average for recent movers was thirty-five years. Reflecting this difference, established residents were more likely to have children, and 33 percent of them had children in school, compared with 24 percent for recent movers. However, recent movers were more likely to expect children in the future (88 percent compared with 62 percent).

Going by national figures, the respondents in both samples were better educated and had slightly higher income than the general population. According to the 1991 *Statistical Abstract of the United States,* in 1989, 17 percent of the population had some college and 21 percent had completed a college degree. In the same year, the median household income was $34,000. At $157,000, the average price of the houses purchased by the recent movers was also somewhat higher than the comparable national figure. According to the *Family Economics Review* (vol. 4, no. 1, March 1991), the median sale price in 1989 of a single-family home in the United States was $120,000.

Per-student expenditures in Suffolk County range from $7,107 for the 9,225 students in William Floyd district to $43,048 for the 43 students in Fire Island district. The highest per-student expenditure for districts with over 100 pupils is $16,051 for the 1,940 students in Shoreham-Wading River district.

Average school expenditure per student in Suffolk County were $9,664 in 1990 (the most recently available figures at the time of the survey). This average figure is high even for the northeastern states, and is almost twice the average school expenditure per student for the nation as a whole. The 1992 *Almanac of the 50 States* puts the average per pupil expenditure in the United States in 1990 at $4,890.

APPENDIX 10.2

MOVERS, SEARCH, AND INFORMATION:
ARE THERE ENOUGH MOVERS TO MAKE A MARKET?

Our results show that many established residents are ignorant of local services and taxes. For most of these residents, ignorance is "rational" since they are not making any relevant decisions based upon these issues. Does this mean that there are no competitive forces in the local market for public goods?

Economic theory suggests that it is not necessary for all consumers to be informed about choices in order for a market to move toward a competitive equilibrium. If some subset of consumers make accurate comparisons and act on that knowledge, that may be sufficient to make a market behave competitively. And if these consumers are the most desirable segment of the market, the pressure for competition may be even greater.

High-income movers have more accurate information about local public services and taxes. These important households gather comparative information and they act upon this information when making their entry choice. But even more important for understanding the local market for public goods, these citizens are the very people that communities have the strongest incentives to attract.

Are there enough of these people to make a market? Or in more general terms: How many consumers must have accurate information for a market, particularly a market for local public goods, to be pushed toward a competitive outcome such as Tiebout described? While surprisingly little systematic attention has been devoted to the issue in the economics literature, some observers have offered the view that very few informed consumers can make a market. In a hearing on the Truth-in-Lending Law, Senator Paul Douglas once remarked that a competitive market would exist if "only" 10 percent of the consumers were "cost conscious" (Wilde and Schwartz 1979: 543). Surprisingly, empirical studies have shown that Douglas' impression was really not that far off the mark. Thorelli and Engledow (1980: 14) argue that "information seekers" make up only 10–20 percent of the population. Claxton, Fry, and Portis (1974) showed that only 5–8 percent of furniture and appliance shoppers had extensive information about their purchases. And Inman (1979) showed that a highly informed set of voters, making up about 13 percent of the population, was able to make local school budgets respond to their preferences.

The precise percentage of informed consumers needed is likely to vary according to the price of the good, the ability of suppliers to price discriminate among consumers, the number of alternative suppliers in the market, and the strategic actions available to suppliers. But the purchase of a house and the local public goods that are bundled with that house favor the ability of a subset of consumers to drive a competitive market.

Dagger (1981) estimates conservatively that 20 percent of Americans change their local jurisdictions over a five-year period. Since the upper income half of our mover sample hold much more accurate comparative information, over a five-year period, perhaps 10 percent of the population in an average community will have recently entered the community and have high levels of comparative knowledge of local public goods. We believe that this is enough to put pressure on communities to be competitive in their services, especially since these are the residents most strategically important for the continued fiscal viability of communities.

Clearly, while informed entry helps drive a local market for public goods in something approximating Tiebout's "pure theory," other actions also stimulate competition that forces governments to provide services efficiently. For example, governments try to attract desirable businesses by keeping their taxes low in relation to the services they deliver. Businesses have strong incentives to make well-informed entry choices, reinforcing the concerns of high-income movers.

Largely ignored in the economic literature on Tiebout models is that nonmovers can also use local politics to change service delivery patterns, and, as noted above, they often act as a basis of support for public entrepreneurs who aggregate their collective "voice." As Thorelli and Engledow (1980) noted for information-seeking consumers in the private market, as Sharp (1984; 1986) argued for local public goods, and as Hirschman (1970) noted most generally, mobility and voice are related. Citizens with the most accurate knowledge of local public goods are also more likely to be politically active. This is clearly true for high-income movers. But it is also true for nonmovers: based on the comparative knowledge they acquire over time, they use voice to improve the service/tax package in their community.

While entry pressures communities to be competitive, the combination of entry and voice is likely to provide even more effective pressure on local governments. But it is only by understanding how these micro-level political behaviors interact with macro-level market mechanisms that we can more accurately specify and examine the macro-level Tiebout market.

Part Four

ENTREPRENEURS AND CHANGE IN THE
LOCAL MARKET FOR PUBLIC GOODS

CHAPTER 11.

Entrepreneurs and Change in the
Local Market for Public Goods

ENTREPRENEURS ARE IMPORTANT actors in economic and political markets. In this book, we have examined a large but fragmented literature on entrepreneurship; we have developed a political-economic theory of public entrepreneurs; and we have tested elements of this theory using data from a sample of suburban municipal governments.

Clearly, scholars have used a wide variety of perspectives to explain public entrepreneurship. We have followed closely a paradigm built mostly on economic reasoning. While our approach inevitably led us to consider a market-based model, with particular concern for the supply and demand functions for entrepreneurship, our work diverges significantly from traditional economic models. We have argued that the desire of neoclassical economists for an elegant, tractable, and generalizable theory squeezed the entrepreneurs out of their work. But we demonstrated that once institutions, transaction costs, and dynamic (often endogenous) changes in preferences and technologies are introduced into the neoclassical model, entrepreneurship emerges as a central mechanism driving markets. Compared to traditional microeconomic approaches to modeling supply and demand, we are much more attuned to how institutional constraints, the role of government, and political strategies affect entrepreneurship. Our broader perspective is not surprising since our concern is for *public* entrepreneurship; but our reading of the literature leads us to believe that *all* models of entrepreneurial behavior, regardless of sector, should be informed by such considerations. Thus, components of our model of entrepreneurship transcend the often overdrawn demarcation between public and private markets.

Our investigation has produced important *theoretical* insights into market behavior; however, we have argued repeatedly that the main task of social science is to engage in a dialogue between theory and data. We passionately believe that theoretical advances must be rooted in *empirical* tests of the propositions embodied in that theory. We recognize that this dialogue may be less than totally satisfactory because abstract theories and models can be more elegant and more rigorous than our ability to gather empirical data suitable for testing the propositions of our theories. We know that our empirical work is neither a perfect nor a complete test of the role of entrepreneurs in the local market for public goods. Nonetheless, we have been able to test many elements of our theory with a broad base of empirical data from municipalities located throughout the United States.

While we do not intend to repeat all our findings and their implications, at this point we highlight how our analysis bears on important elements of the supply and demand sides of public entrepreneurship and how these factors affect the local market for public goods.

SUPPLY-SIDE FACTORS

Public entrepreneurs who advocate and propel dynamic changes in policy or politics are not uncommon in the local market for public goods. The image of entrepreneurs as the "dynamic few" is not supported in our research. Clearly, not everyone who influences local policy can be considered a public entrepreneur. But, like the work presented by Osborne and Gaebler, we have documented a relatively open field for actors pushing political, administrative, and policy change in their communities. Empirically, in our sample of 1,000 communities located throughout the country, we discovered hundreds of entrepreneurial actors. Given that there are nearly 100,000 governments or "quasi-governments" in the United States, there may be literally thousands of public entrepreneurs operating in local governments, advocating and propelling political and policy change. The decentralized structure of local government in the United States creates a range of opportunities for dynamic innovation that are often—but not always—seized by entrepreneurs. Our work has identified important aspects of the conversion process that turns potential entrepreneurs into actual ones—that is, we have identified many factors that affect the likelihood that an entrepreneur will emerge.

At the bottom line, we argue that entrepreneurs are rational actors who, explicitly or implicitly, weigh the costs and benefits of entrepreneurial action and pursue innovation when they perceive the ratio of benefits to costs as favorable. Entrepreneurs have talents and energy they can devote to a variety of endeavors. In the private sector, entrepreneurs are usually modeled as pursuing monetary profits. In these models, entrepreneurs are motivated to pursue change in order to earn high rates of return ("entrepreneurial profits"), by seizing or creating opportunities others ignore or don't even see. While this is clearly a simplification of the goals and motivations of private entrepreneurs, the pursuit of monetary profits is a convenient mechanism for reducing the theoretical "clutter" surrounding the motivation of entrepreneurs. However, even simplifying the concept of public entrepreneurial profits as much as possible still yields a complicated objective function.

Public entrepreneurs are motivated by a host of political rewards—power, the ability to influence policy, prestige, and community service. They may also be motivated by the pursuit of private income—and at least one of our entrepreneurs pursuing that goal went too far and landed in jail!

We argue that when the potential rewards for entrepreneurial efforts in the public sector are high, entrepreneurship is more likely to be found. But if potential entrepreneurs can earn higher rewards in another sphere of action, particularly in the private sector, then they are less likely to enter the public sphere. Similarly, when entry barriers or other institutional constraints raise the costs of public entrepreneurship, the supply of entrepreneurs in the public sector will decline.

Public entrepreneurs, then, are not some "supernatural" or extraordinary beings driven by some inner need to create private kingdoms. Rather, they are individuals with particular skills at perceiving opportunities, pursuing risky action, and mobilizing organizations and allies to achieve their goals. This last skill is particularly important in the public sector. While the archetypical image of the private entrepreneur is Stephen Jobs working mostly by himself to put together the first Apple computer in his garage and essentially creating a new industry, even the most innovative public sector entrepreneur faces an environment filled with institutions, bureaucracies, rules and regulations that limit the effects that individuals acting alone can have. Given the world in which they operate, public entrepreneurs must be particularly adept at creating coalitions to support their innovative ideas.

Public entrepreneurs seek support from groups that are most likely to favor their policies and they address the concerns of local voters that might be ignored by the "establishment." The strategies entrepreneurs employ are consistent with many of the theoretical concepts that political scientists have identified in the last decade as important to innovative politicians, including rhetoric, heresthetics, arbitrage, and inspirational leadership to mobilize constituents and workers. Like Moliere's famous M. Jourdain who discovered that he was speaking prose his whole life, our entrepreneurs have been "speaking" contemporary political theory without knowing it.

While the porous nature of local government presents opportunities for entrepreneurs, there is considerable variation in the specific institutional structure of local government across the United States. We have shown systematic relationships between the institutional arrangements of local government and the emergence of entrepreneurs. More specifically, the intensity of collective action problems, the structure of interest groups in local communities, the electoral costs of challenging the status quo, and the opportunities for managerial entrepreneurship all affect the benefits and costs of public entrepreneurship (and hence the likelihood of finding an entrepreneur).

Specific (and measurable) features of local governments influence not only the emergence of public entrepreneurs in a manner consistent with our theory, they also influence the specific types of entrepreneurs that emerge. Using both sophisticated statistical methods and individual case studies, we have related local conditions to the emergence of traditional progrowth entrepreneurs, of demand-side progrowth entrepreneurs, and of antigrowth entrepreneurs. We have also demonstrated how specific structural conditions affect the emergence of city managers, rather than elected officials, as entrepreneurs.

Although public entrepreneurs act as rational individuals as they make their calculations and allocate their resources across sectors, they are not isolated "atomistic" actors. Entrepreneurs are embedded in social networks that help them discover opportunities and help them develop and implement strategies to achieve their goals. These networks affect the benefits and costs that entrepreneurs face. For example, we believe that entrepreneurs embedded in local and regional networks of finance, insurance, and real estate firms face lower costs for public entrepreneurship. These networks produce information and models of innovation that often closely parallel changes in the public sector. Thus, entrepreneurs embedded in these types of networks can more easily spot opportunities for arbitrage between the private and the public sector. Moreover, such embedded entrepreneurs are also more likely to view a sojourn in the public sector as enhancing their human capital (thus increasing the long run rewards for public entrepreneurship). In contrast, being part of a network of high-tech manufacturing firms can impose significant opportunity costs on entrepreneurs considering allocating resources to the public sector.

In short, our supply-side analysis shows that the emergence of public entrepreneurship is not a random occurrence that is immune from statistical modeling. To be sure, the development and emergence of public entrepreneurs is a complicated process. But it is not a process beyond the methods and tools of social science.

DEMAND-SIDE FACTORS

Change occurs in all economic and political institutions. However, social scientists do not yet understand the processes that motivate and propel it. Economists typically approach the demand for change as a function of technological developments or shifts in consumer preferences. That is, change is largely exogenous to their models. However, we believe that entrepreneurial actors *within* social systems motivate change for their own purposes—that is, entrepreneurs play a central role "endogenizing" change in adaptive economic and political systems. In the local market for public goods, change may be even more amenable to manipulation by entrepreneurs because public policies are complex and, most of the time, citizens are rationally ignorant of local policies.

Following Stimson, we believe that there is a zone of acquiescence that places limits on politicians (see Stimson 1991; Simon and March 1958). As long as politicians undertake or propose action within this zone, most citizens will not mobilize in support or in opposition to policy change. However, citizens will not tolerate policies or politicians who move outside the zone. But it is important to always remember that the size and shape of the zone of acquiescence can shift over time.

This zone of acquiescence has important implications for entrepreneurial behavior. Representative democracy puts leaders into a position in which they make policy choices subject to periodic election and other constraints from their constituents (including their entry, exit, and voice decisions). Thus, public entrepreneurs must stay in close touch with changes in the location of the zone and they must adopt new policies to meet changing preferences. Some less venturesome entrepreneurs operate within the zone, "probing" and "experimenting" at the margins. For example, following Eisinger (1988), we demonstrated that some entrepreneurs advocate new demand-side progrowth policies to supplement existing supply-side policies. These entrepreneurial politicians are acting within the broad consensus (or zone) that growth is good and that local government should pursue economic development.

Shifts in the zone may be pushed by exogenous factors, such as the changing composition of the population or changing technologies. In local communities, changing local demographic characteristics may be particularly important and are driven by ever-changing patterns of community development, population change, and economic restructuring that sweep across the United States. In the suburban communities we studied, the changing racial composition of communities has already created opportunities for entrepreneurs and will create many more opportunities in the near future. Similarly, the continuing evolution of the service sector in suburbia may create new networks that can act as springboards for public entrepreneurship. These demographic and economic changes are largely exogenous to local governments—but we can certainly expect the next generation of entrepreneurs to seize the opportunities created by them.

But as political scientists, what we find most interesting is the fact that entrepreneurs can themselves shift the zone of acquiescence. Skillful entrepreneurs can use their strategic skills to exploit the complexity of issues, the vagaries of political decision-making processes, and the considerable uncertainty about the relationship between government actions and societal outcomes to shift the zone to their own advantage. More explicitly, following William Riker, we argue that entrepreneurs can use rhetoric to change public opinion preferences within existing policy space or they can use heresthetics to redefine policy dimensions and thereby radically shift the zone of acquiescence.

Thus, the relationship of the demand for change and the emergence of public entrepreneurs is more complex than is found in most models of entrepreneurship. Entrepreneurs clearly respond to the demand for change, but they also stimulate it. Determining which way the winds of political change are blowing and then leading that shift requires considerable skill; but changing the direction of the winds requires even greater entrepreneurial abilities.

CITIZEN INFORMATION AND PUBLIC ENTREPRENEURSHIP

Public entrepreneurs are not isolated individuals. Rather, they are rooted in networks; they operate in contexts defined by institutional rules and procedures; and they must stand for periodic review by their constituents. Ultimately, the level of information that citizens have about public policies and the distribution of the demand for change in policies are among the most important elements that define the context in which public entrepreneurs operate.

Citizen support of entrepreneurship can be a form of investment in the future. Change is often disruptive and social scientists have observed that people resist it, even when the status quo is not particularly rewarding. Although change may necessitate giving up a more certain present situation for a less certain future one, such a risk is often justified by the promise of a better tomorrow. To economists, change of this nature should be considered an investment in the future.

There are always risks associated with support of entrepreneurial change. Some of these risks are borne by the individual entrepreneur, but others are borne by the citizenry. For example, a demand-side pro-growth entrepreneur is asking the community to divert limited resources and attention to potentially risky growth strategies. These policies may cost the community tax dollars and lost opportunities to lure firms using traditional growth tools such as tax abatements.

When citizens accept changes in policy, they are assuming that the future flow of benefits will exceed the benefits of pursuing present policies. Indeed, our evidence shows that the rhetoric employed by political entrepreneurs is future-oriented, promising better services and a better quality of life in the local community once the entrepreneur's vision of the future is achieved.

Entrepreneurs face citizens with different levels of information and different mechanisms for expressing their support or opposition to public policies. Informed citizens, and particularly movers, affect the entrepreneur's calculations of benefits and costs. Movers are a theoretically central set of actors in understanding the pressure for change. In our work, we looked at the role of movers by presenting a model of the market for local public goods that significantly altered the Tiebout model by incorporating new insights about the number of informed citizens that are necessary to make a market. The processes outlined in Chapter 10 show a dynamic relationship between individual public entrepreneurs and groups of citizens with different levels of concern and information about public services. These processes also led us to discuss the issue of the number of entrepreneurs found in the local market for public goods.

Entrepreneurs: The Few and the Many

Earlier in this book, we noted that the popular perspective on entrepreneurship and the dominant case study approach to entrepreneurs emphasize the importance of the individual entrepreneur. But many scholars, especially those associated with the Austrian School, argue that this approach defines entrepreneurship much too narrowly. In the Austrian approach, entrepreneurship is the product of the action of *all* rational individuals: Austrians view entrepreneurship as a *function*, not a *person*, and they reject the popular concept of entrepreneurs as the "dynamic few." For Mises (1949), in particular, any owner, producer, or consumer who acts in response to change to improve his or her condition and gain profits is to some degree an entrepreneur. Rather than viewing these as opposing arguments, we believe that by combining the *many* informed movers with the *few* public entrepreneurs who help aggregate collective voice, a more satisfactory and richer model of the local market for public goods emerges.

In this book we have shown that there are more public entrepreneurs in local government than one might expect. But in the last decade not every community supported an entrepreneur. Empirically, respondents in only about one in four communities named an entrepreneur. These entrepreneurs are the "few," but they are not so rare as the case study approach to entrepreneurship would lead us to believe.

In our analysis of mobile citizens, the population of individuals acting in the entrepreneurial function is much larger, approaching the broader Austrian conception. These individuals are not self-consciously acting as entrepreneurial leaders; instead, they are making individual market choices that happen to benefit others in the market. In terms of numbers, they are "the many." While the ability of each individual member of the "many" to propel policy change is more limited than that of the public entrepreneurs, the "many" use political voice to support public entrepreneurs and they manipulate their entry decisions to provide support for entrepreneurial policies.

Thus, we believe that the relevant issue for the study of entrepreneurial actors in local politics is not "the few *or* the many" but the relationship between "the few *and* the many." These two sets of actors combine to propel and achieve policy change in local governments. In the democratic and competitive local market for public goods, the few individual political and managerial entrepreneurs must ultimately mobilize the many informed citizens looking to increase their payoffs from the public sector.

ENTREPRENEURS AND SYSTEMIC CHANGE

While we have focused largely on entrepreneurs within individual communities, our discussion of mobility illustrates another critical element of public entrepreneurship in the local market for public goods. Entrepreneurs not only affect internal local political equilibria, they also affect entire systems of cities.

Local communities are in competition with one another to attract resources. As in any competitive markets, responsiveness to changing circumstances is critical. We believe that public entrepreneurs drive responsiveness. In private markets there is intense, continual pressure to innovate and to introduce new products. Falling behind competitors can be disastrous, if not fatal. In the competitive local market for public goods, communities falling behind their competitors will lose desirable citizens and firms, with negative consequences for taxes and the quality of service levels (Schneider 1989).

The way that institutions and organizations respond to change affects how successful they are likely to be over time. When the pace of change is rapid, flexible systems allow innovations to develop and be tested, thereby increasing the likelihood of successful adaptation to changing circumstances. Less flexible systems, whether they are economic systems, individual business firms, or governments, may be rendered ineffective or even obsolete in a rapidly changing environment. The American system of multiple local governments is often criticized as fragmented, but this very system creates multiple opportunities for entrepreneurs who then help local governments develop flexible and innovative responses to the ever-changing environment.

Thus, while our study is based on data drawn from individual cities, our argument is about *systems* and *systemic change*. As evident in our empirical analysis and made explicit in the two previous chapters of the book, we are laying the micro foundation for understanding systemic change. Thus, while we model explicitly the incentive structures of individuals embedded in institutional systems, such micro-based behavior, like ripples created by dropping a stone in a pond, create patterns that move through entire systems. Much of the systemic change brought about by individual behavior is amplified through networks of connections. Based on our analysis, we believe that small numbers of citizens, politicians, and managers can create strong forces for change throughout the system of government in the United States. These networks tie entrepreneurial politicians and managers to one another and they tie these entrepreneurs to other individuals in other cities.

There is also a clear intergovernmental dimension to the diffusion of innovation. Americans have a long-standing propensity to tinker with the way in which public services are delivered. As Hofstadter (1955) and, more recently, Knott and Miller (1987) show, waves of reform have periodically swept across America's state capitals and its myriad local governments, changing patterns of service delivery. Many of these reforms are structured around a dialogue between the national government and local governments, with the federal government endorsing reforms developed in a small number of local areas and then fostering their widespread adoption.

Thus, successful innovative changes in even a single city can be diffused through the entire national *system* of cities. In turn, the systemic effects of innovation are greater than the individual effects of change in any single city. This leads to a paradox facing innovators at the local level: Many of the specific entrepreneurial mayors and managers we talked with and studied were unhappy with the effects their ideas had on their community. They wanted more concrete and more dynamic results in the immediate environment in which they operate. Yet even if their efforts do not accomplish all they hope to achieve in their own individual communities, their innovative ideas and their entrepreneurial energy become part of the dynamic flow of systemic change in the United States. While they may never have heard of Joseph Schumpeter and the idea of "creative destruction," these local public entrepreneurs, like their private sector counterparts, drive the dynamic and ongoing search for improvement and innovation in the American system of public and private markets.

DIRECTIONS FOR FUTURE RESEARCH ON
PUBLIC ENTREPRENEURSHIP

We have developed and tested a theory of the public entrepreneur. But our work does not end the need for research into public entrepreneurship. We believe that future research on public entrepreneurs must be conducted with an appropriate theoretical lens. While entrepreneurial individuals no doubt have high achievement needs and high personal motivation, the broad supply and demand factors that shape their behavior cannot be ignored. Entrepreneurship is embedded in institutional, organizational, and social milieux and can only be understood in terms of the benefits and costs that these milieux present to individuals.

Public entrepreneurs in the local market for public goods occupy a complex position. Opportunities are created by changing policy ideas, changing citizen/consumer preferences, changing technology, and the never-ending changing demography of American cities and suburbs. Entrepreneurs seize the opportunities that emerge when citizen demand for change increases, but entrepreneurs also create *new* opportunities and mobilize citizen demand to support a fresh vision of the future.

Thus, public entrepreneurs are not merely the passive tools of "society"—rather, they are active members of the "state" with their own interests and goals. Entrepreneurs can thus provide a "bridging function" between the theoretical disputes that explore the links between state and society (see, e.g., Almond 1988; Nordlinger 1988). Despite their passionate attachment to their own goals and to their own particular vision of the future, competition between local governments, periodic elections, and the critical role of informed consumers, place limits on the degree to which entrepreneurs can diverge from the underlying preferences and tastes of citizen/consumers. While some entrepreneurs can redefine the zone of acquiescence and create a new set of preferences, consumer sovereignty ultimately reigns. Given the risks that entrepreneurs must take, given the difficult tasks they face in organizing to seize the opportunities they see, and given the power of consumer sovereignty, we suspect that, as in the private market, the rate of entrepreneurial failure in the local market for public goods is high. As Pasour (1989) noted: for the individual entrepreneur, "entrepreneurship may be a game worth winning but it is not always a game worth playing." But to maintain the dynamism of our society as a whole, entrepreneurship is a game we all need played.

Chapter One

1. Building on Kirzner's work, we believe that public entrepreneurs are distinguished by their willingness to present policy proposals and political positions that represent a dynamic change from existing procedures in the policy domain or in the geographic location in which they are operating. We elaborate our theory relying mostly on the economics literature. Roberts (1991) has presented what is perhaps the most recent comprehensive review of the literature on entrepreneurship from a political science perspective.

2. We do not know the actual size of the local population of potential entrepreneurs. Following the recent literature on leadership, we believe the population to be much larger than implied by the biographical case study literature on entrepreneurs that tends to glorify the particular individual who is the subject of the study and implies that the entrepreneur being studied is somehow a "heroic" figure, who by definition is uncommon.

3. At least one of our entrepreneurs has been sent to jail for "appropriating" the profits of his creative financing of development projects in his community.

Chapter Two

1. Coase (1937) notes: "A factor of production . . . does not have to make a series of contracts with the factors with whom he is co-operating within the firm, as would be necessary, of course, if this co-operation were as a direct result of the working of the price mechanism. For this series of contracts is substituted one. . . . The essence of the contract is that it should only state the limits to the powers of the entrepreneur" (p. 75–76). Cheung (1983) notes: "The word 'firm' is simply a shorthand description of a way to organize activities under contractual arrangements that differ from those of ordinary product markets" (p. 3). Demsetz (1988) suggests: "The firm properly viewed is a 'nexus' of contracts" (p. 155).

2. We recognize that patent monopolies can be held for some period of time and that "unnatural monopolies" can be created by political manipulation that creates entry barriers for any other competitors. Thus, while there is no role for entrepreneurs in the case of natural monopolies, entrepreneurs can seek to manipulate government power to create monopolies.

3. See the discussions in Tirole (1989) and Fudenberg and Tirole (1991). Also see some of the most important early studies such as Green and Porter (1984); Radner (1986); Lehrer (1989); Fudenberg and Levine (1990).

4. Surprisingly, the term "entrepreneur" does not appear in the literature with any degree of frequency. In fact, mirroring Baumol's comment about the absence of the term in the index of most standard microeconomics texts, the term also does not appear in the index of many of the standard reference books

on game theory and IO. However, the terms that are used, such as "player" or "actor" and the concern for the strategic choices of firms essentially opens the window for the analysis of entrepreneurs in markets. The absence of the term "entrepreneur" reflects, in part, the lack of consensus in the field of economics about what entrepreneurs do and how to define their activities.

5. The literature on the benefits and costs of polycentricity versus unified government is substantial. Ostrom (1972) lays out the issues in sharp relief, and several works by Lowery and Lyons (1989) or Lyons and Lowery (1989) address these same issues from a much more critical perspective.

6. Again, see Schneider (1989) on how the local market for public goods differs from the fully competitive model.

7. Here the difference between what we call "political entrepreneurs," such as mayors or members of city councils, who create electoral coalitions to support their innovations, and "bureaucratic entrepreneurs," such as city managers or bureau chiefs, is critical. Niskanen (1975) has argued that the control of information is central to the ability of bureau chiefs to achieve their goals—that is, some entrepreneurs may prosper by not disclosing information. Since empirically most of our entrepreneurs operate in the political realm and face periodic elections, we believe that the pressure for greater disclosure of information is greater on most public entrepreneurs than on private sector ones.

8. Information asymmetries and the strategic revelation of information has become an important topic in the study of legislatures (see, e.g., Austen-Smith and Riker 1987, or Gilligan and Krehbiel 1990). The insights contained in such studies of committees and legislatures, set in a particular institutional arena, do not easily carry over to the study of the entrepreneurial process with which we are concerned.

9. Alternatively, many social scientists present case studies that are essentially "biographies" of policies—presenting in great detail the development of policies and/or specific laws.

Chapter Three

1. Kuhn (1963) provides analogous evidence from the natural sciences of how entrepreneurial scholars have successfully framed unsolved problems or "anomalies" in such a way as to place their own preferred set of research questions at the center of the new paradigms in which "normal science" is conducted. McClosky (1983) and Blinder (1989) provide similar evidence regarding the conduct of economic research; Almond (1990) and Lowi (1992) make similar claims about the framing of what constitutes appropriate research problems and methods in the discipline of political science.

2. This result is a demonstration of the efficiency gains from (factor or output) reallocation that are typically discussed by microeconomists with reference to the Edgeworth Box. An Edgeworth Box shows alternative ways of allocating quantities of two outputs (say food and clothing) between two individuals. Each point in the box corresponds to an allocation of the total amount of clothing and food produced between the two consumers. An allocation of resources within the

box is deemed efficient only when a move away from that allocation would not be mutually beneficial to both participants. This is determined with reference to each individual's utility indifference curves. Note that the efficiency criterion used here is that developed by Pareto—a Pareto efficient move will increase at least one individual's utility without reducing anyone else's current utility level. The "contract curve" maps the set of Pareto efficient points within the Edgeworth Box.

3. First, note that while we use the term entrepreneur, there is an evolving political science literature on "leadership" that is quite different from the literature we have used in developing our concept of entrepreneurship. The literature on entrepreneurs is particularly indebted to the Austrian School of Economics, of which the political science literature makes little or no use. Consequently, the points of intersection between the literature on entrepreneurship and the literature on leadership are not as frequent as one would expect.

Additionally (and not surprisingly), much of the political science literature is centered on leadership in Congress and how congressional leaders organize and maintain coalitions. This work is often historical and set within a very specific set of institutional patterns and constraints. There is also a focus on how congressmen use their resources to win reelection. For example, Cain, Ferejohn, and Fiorina's (1987) book, *The Personal Vote*, explores the ways in which a politician can maintain constituency support through a mixture of collective (policy) benefits and selective (constituency service) benefits. There are other studies of the issue of allocating time and resources to win reelection. This work contains many important arguments documenting how congressmen create and maintain collective support for their leadership. However, its context is fairly specific to Congress and the extent to which the arguments developed are directly translatable to the local political milieu with which we are interested is open to question.

4. Later in this book, we explore two distinctly different arenas of local government in which entrepreneurs are found. One arena is bureaucratic: we call entrepreneurs operating in this sphere "managerial entrepreneurs." In chapter 8, we identify a set of individuals who hold bureaucratic positions in local governments and who are dedicated to introducing new management principles to increase the efficiency and productivity of local services. Managerial entrepreneurs can seek, for example, to privatize components of local service delivery or introduce bureaucratic/professional reforms to enhance the quality and reduce the costs of local services by changing established bureaucratic decision rules. Managerial entrepreneurs will face resistance from entrenched interests and must create new constituencies (both within the specific bureaucracy and among external leaders) in order to change these practices.

Managerial entrepreneurs usually do not "deal" in votes and mass organization, and compared to entrepreneurs seeking elective office, they may need to concentrate only on smaller elite-based organizations. There are many biographical studies that focus on the specific problems and strategies of managerial entrepreneurs. In chapter 8, we consider more fully the managerial entrepreneur in the local market for public goods and we develop more fully theoretical propositions and expectations concerning their emergence, strategies, and success.

Right now we are not concerned with this class of entrepreneurs. Instead, we focus on "political entrepreneurs."

5. But see Olson's introduction to Sandler (1992), in which he clearly melds these two different typologies into one.

6. The components of the theory are enumerated by Moe (1980: 74): (a) members of latent groups can only be induced to join through the operation of selective incentives; yet (b) the sale of selective incentives yields a surplus (in successful groups) that can be used by group leaders for lobbying and other expenditures on collective goods; it follows that (c) these political activities are by-products of the operation of selective incentives—they have nothing to do with why members join, but are made possible because members join; therefore (d) the leaders of latent groups may pursue any collective goods they wish without fear of losing member "support," since contributions are independent of political considerations.

7. Of course, these typologies of benefits also include the selective benefits discussed above: those tangible returns with monetary values and are derived from contributions which are at the core of Olson's theory. Note that one could argue that these alternative motivations can still fit into Olson's argument: the decision calculus just requires more input factors.

8. This finding is theoretically grounded in the study of finitely repeated games or repeated games with some uncertainty as to end point. Ostrom and her colleagues have presented some empirical work based on laboratory studies suggesting that this finding might hold for all repeated games; however, at this time, theory is developed only for a subset of all repeated games.

Chapter Four

1. Vernon (1966) is often credited with introducing this idea.

2. There are problems with the simple S-curve of product evolution—for example, not all products follow this cycle and the rate at which different products enter different parts of the curve varies widely (see Scott and Storper 1987 or Maillat and Lecoq 1992). Porter (1980) also notes that industry evolution is affected by long-run changes in growth, demographics, the reduction of uncertainty with time, and the diffusion of proprietary knowledge that all affect the shape of the curve.

3. For critiques and comments on this approach to studying policy diffusion, see Walker (1973) or Berry and Berry (1990).

4. Recent models of the diffusion of innovation across American communities have concentrated on regional issues of geographic proximity, general indicators on policy innovativeness (e.g., Walker 1969), and issue specific factors that are associated with the propensity to adopt a new policy (see Gray 1973; Berry and Berry 1990; Glick and Hays 1991).

5. Sociologists have also adopted a similar position. Witness Granovetter's (1985) concept of "embeddedness." And while Granovetter is not directly concerned with entrepreneurship, his concern for networks and the rooting of economic behavior in ongoing social relations is similar to the argument discussed here.

6. Schumpeter recognized the importance of some of these conditions. In *A Theory of Economic Development* (1961), Schumpeter stressed the importance of the legitimacy of entrepreneurship in driving the conversion of potential entrepreneurs into actual ones (also see Kilby 1971).

Chapter Five

1. For a fuller description of the local market for public goods, see Schneider (1989).

2. In terms of sample construction, we began with all incorporated suburbs with populations greater than 2,500 in 1970 located in the 100 largest metropolitan regions of the United States (with the caveat that not more than three metropolitan areas from any single state be included). This produced a set of over 1,400 suburbs in fifty-five metropolitan regions, of which clerks in 963 communities responded to our survey. However, limits on data availability further reduced the number of cases for analysis. Note that the number of cases in tables will vary because the data missing for each city also varied. We chose to base any given empirical analysis on the maximum number of cities for which we had complete data rather than using a "core" set of communities that had data on all variables.

3. We recognize that this operational definition is broad, encompassing entrepreneurs who change local politics, alter equilibria, develop and implement new ideas or policies, etc. As will become evident as the book develops, we used a combination of follow-up surveys, objective data from various census reports, and selected case studies to explore in more detail what these entrepreneurs have done and how their actions and positions actually differed from previous policies.

4. Since this is the first large-scale survey of suburban municipalities, it is impossible to say whether the 27 percent rate of entrepreneurship is high or low. However, in a comparative study of economic development strategies in close to 200 cities, Clarke (1990) finds "innovative" programs in 5–21 percent of the cities surveyed. Since her numbers are for individual programs, it is not unreasonable to assume that a joint set of programs that might define an entrepreneur will be found in the proportion of cities we report.

In addition to this face validity, we took a sample of cities with entrepreneurs "nominated" by the resident city clerk and mailed a survey to city clerks in neighboring cities asking if in their opinion the nominated individual was indeed entrepreneurial. Our response rates exceeded 50 percent. Of these responses, about half of the city clerks said they did not know enough about the politics of the other city to answer the questions. Of those clerks who did volunteer responses, over 75 percent confirmed the entrepreneurship of the individual we asked about, validating the results we report.

5. Clerks were informed that the survey was part of a large nationwide study of political entrepreneurs. The questionnaire began with a series of questions about the local government structure and local politics. Clerks were then ask to name someone who met our definition of an entrepreneur. Those clerks who "nominated" an entrepreneur were then asked a series of open- and closed-ended questions about the entrepreneur's activities. Clerks could nominate one

or more entrepreneurs in the 1980s. They were also given the opportunity to name any entrepreneurs from the 1970s.

6. We also experimented with a variety of measures of the size, structure, and degree of electoral competition of the city council, but these had no effect on the probability with which an antigrowth entrepreneur emerged.

7. Research into the link between reformed systems of local government and various political/policy outcomes is long-standing. While Donovan and Neiman (1992) show how the initiative and the referendum can further the antigrowth movement, we have no data on the availability of such tools across the suburbs in our sample. We believe that other aspects of local governmental reform can inhibit the rise of antigrowth entrepreneurs, especially by diluting the importance of neighborhood based politics.

8. This measure of group importance, and the ones used in subsequent estimations, are based on the responses of city clerks to a question asking them to evaluate the importance (on a scale of 1 to 5 with 5 being the most important) of a named group in the local political environment. These indicators are standardized to make them similar to the other variables used in the analysis.

9. One could argue that the barriers to entrepreneurship these demographic conditions reflect are absolute, not relative—that is, the relationship between size and the collective action problem is independent of the metropolitan area in which a suburb happens to be located. We thus considered whether or not to standardize these measures. However, we believe that in general it is best to analyze many aspects of politics in suburbs in a regional context, essentially comparing a suburb to its neighbors. In either case, the results using standardized or nonstandardized variables are identical.

10. The tax base is measured as the per capita true value of property in the community. The tax rate is the effective tax rate. These measures are adjusted for differences in assessment practices, using state and county reports.

11. Expenditures on business-related "developmental" services are measured by combining local per capita expenditures on streets and highways, sewers, sanitation, water transport, water supply, gas, electricity, and transit. Redistributive services are defined as health, hospitals, urban renewal, and welfare. Allocational expenditures are for "housekeeping" functions (general administration, general government, financial administration, and buildings) plus public safety (police and fire).

12. Of the variables we use in the following analysis, percent renters and percent black are from the 1980 Census of Population. Population growth is the 1970–1980 rate of growth based on data reported in the 1980 census. Donovan and Neiman (1992) show that the lagged rate of growth is more important than the current rate of growth in determining local growth politics, so we use this measure over growth in the 1980s. Distance is measured as the straight-line linear distance between the outer boundary of the central city and the inner boundary of the suburb.

13. The number of cases in the probit estimate is less than the full number of cases for which we have information on the emergence of a local entrepreneur. Only those cases for which we have information on every independent variable are included in the estimation. Missing data on the fiscal variables, which are not

centrally collected but are gathered from state and county reports, account for the elimination of most cases.

14. Clerks were presented with the type of group and then asked to judge the importance of that group to the career of the entrepreneur using a three-point scale where 1 = not important at all; 2 = somewhat important; and 3 = very important.

15. Here clerks were presented with a list of the eight types of groups and asked to check if that group was part of the coalition the entrepreneur assembled or tried to assemble.

Chapter Six

1. See Iyengar and Kinder (1987) for political and media applications of this insight.

2. Olson's (1982) study of the rise and decline of nations also shows how established groups can maintain control over property rights to the detriment of the society as a whole. The focus of law and the importance of legal precedents also matter. Friedman (1986) and Hughes (1986) provide studies of how the force of law can affect the ability of groups to renegotiate property rights.

3. Libecap's argument is centered on the definition and redefinition of entitlements. Coase's theorem argues that given certain conditions, the initial entitlements established by property rights do not matter, and negotiations and exchanges between involved parties can produce an efficient use of resources. The requirements for Coase's theorem to obtain include (a) the complete specification of entitlements and their exclusive assignment to owners who can protect the use of their property; and (b) the assumption of zero transaction costs—that is, entitlements can be easily transferred from one party to another. The assumption of zero transaction costs further assumes full information. Coase's theorem presents a problem for many social scientists because of its indifference to the wealth effects of initial entitlements. Coase is emphasizing efficiency over equity.

Calabresi and Melamed (1972) document four rules of entitlement that radically affect the distribution of wealth. As made clear in the graphical presentation presented by Fischel (1985: 113), ultimately, in perfect conditions, trade will yield an equilibrium (point E in Fischel's graph). However, depending on who is assigned the initial property rights, Person "A" (Taney in Fischel's example) may have to transfer wealth to Person "B" (Marshall) or B may have to transfer wealth to A. The assignment of initial property rights matters! And entrepreneurs use the equity issue in their fights to assign the property rights of local growth.

4. This is the argument developed by Clarence Stone in his book, *Regime Politics* (1989). See chapter 2 for a more extended discussion of the size principle and the use of selective incentives by business-based interest groups to overcome collective action problems.

5. A "downtown" need not literally be a traditional central business district but could also be a regional shopping mall or office complex in one of Garreau's (1991) "edge cities."

6. For a variety of reasons, the payoffs flowing from the standard tools of economic growth have declined, making the search for new policies by progrowth entrepreneurs understandable. For example, the diffusion of standard probusiness tools across local governments reduces the ability of a politician to claim credit for innovation. Moreover, as the last generation of progrowth tools has become standardized, they are now handled by a cadre of professional managers, rather than political leaders, again reducing the payoffs to entrepreneurial politicians (Blair, Fichtenbaum, and Swaney 1984). The payoff to local communities flowing from the standard tools of growth have declined as competition for jobs has intensified (Milward and Newman 1989) and as the fiscal payoffs for job creation have declined (Schneider 1992).

7. In contrast, and not surprisingly, only 6 percent of the suburbs in our sample had *anti*growth entrepreneurs (individuals who proposed innovative programs to either limit the growth of new firms or cap population growth).

8. It is important to remember that we are identifying those conditions that affect the probability with which a progrowth entrepreneur *emerges*. This is conceptually different from measuring the extent to which progrowth policies are already in place across communities. Here we are examining the conditions that affect the extent to which the economic development policies an entrepreneur advocates represent a "dynamic change" from existing policies. Clearly, communities that have entrepreneurs advocating development policies in a way that represents a dynamic departure from existing practices will be fewer than the number of communities that have already established progrowth policies.

9. This difference was statistically significant at $p < .02$.

Chapter Seven

1. Other policies in the supply-side tradition include tax increment financing, debt financing (through, for example, industrial revenue bonds), and subsidies to other land costs (through, for example, industrial and commercial site development subsidies).

2. We mailed a second questionnaire to all communities in which a political entrepreneur had been identified in the first questionnaire. Political entrepreneurs include mayors, councilpeople, private citizens, and businesspeople named by the city clerks as entrepreneurs. We sent a separate follow-up survey to the clerks who named city managers or bureaucrats as an entrepreneur. Of the 201 communities with political entrepreneurs, we were able to get complete second wave questionnaires from 117.

3. This is not an oxymoron. Remember, the question we asked was whether or not the entrepreneur was espousing policies that represented a dynamic *change* for their particular community. Thus, even though "standard" tools of economic development may be common nationwide, they are not universal. It is possible for a local entrepreneur to espouse these tools as new for a given community.

4. The mean number of traditional policies advocated by progrowth entrepreneurs was 1.7 with a standard deviation of 1.6. We define "standard" supply-side progrowth entrepreneurs as those progrowth entrepreneurs who were about 1

standard deviation or more above the mean in their advocacy of these traditional progrowth policies. The mean number of demand-side policies advocated was .47 with a standard deviation of .94. Eisinger-type entrepreneurs were defined as a progrowth entrepreneur who advocated two or more demand-side policies (this is slightly more than the mean plus one standard deviation, but the distribution of responses made the use of this cutoff more viable than the exact same definition used for the traditional progrowth entrepreneur).

5. In addition to these seven variables, we also report the standardized mean population size of each type of community because there is such a large difference. The means do not differ across types of cities for the other variables used in tables 7.2.1, 7.2.2, 7.3.1, and 7.3.2. A complete table is available from the authors upon request. Note further that this second wave questionnaire upon which this table is built was mailed only to communities with political entrepreneurs. There were a very few progrowth city managers and bureaucrats who were also named as entrepreneurs, but they are not included in this stage of the analysis.

6. What we mean by "profit" for the political entrepreneur is obviously more complex than the monetized concept that underlies economic theory. For the antigrowth entrepreneur, profits can accrue from mounting a successful campaign for political office, such as the office of mayor, or from changing local policies, such as tax abatements or environmental preservation, which affect the rate and composition of local growth.

7. While we have not yet collected the detailed studies of how various antigrowth entrepreneurs actually have overcome such obstacles to create opposing coalitions, the case studies cited earlier provide support for our position. More generally, Moe (1980), Taylor (1982), Doig and Hargrove (1987), Kirchheimer (1989), and others generate a series of observations concerning the strategies and methods of political entrepreneurs—observations that may help inform further research in this area. Also see Schneider and Teske (1992) for a more general theoretical development of the concept of the local political entrepreneur and the collective action problem.

8. Our model of antigrowth entrepreneurship is one of *change* from existing progrowth policies. Hence, we define the antigrowth entrepreneur as someone who is pushing caps on growth in a community where these proposals represent a "dynamic change from existing procedures." To some extent this assumes that progrowth policies are the "default" condition in local communities (an assumption that is rooted in Peterson's explication of the incentives built into competitive cities, studies of the growth machine, and the widespread use of progrowth policies in cities). Further, we recognize that there is a vast variety of different tools that the antigrowth entrepreneur can advocate. Here we do not deal with these differences in policies. However, in ongoing work, we are gathering more data on the specific policies antigrowth entrepreneurs have advocated and the degree to which these do vary from previous policies.

Among antigrowth policies, the most common were the standard tools: review standards, capital improvements, linking traffic and growth. The more radical antigrowth policies are more rare: Only 6 percent have used sewer moratoria, 7 percent population caps, and 8 percent limits on residential rezonings.

9. In this research we are studying the frequency with which political leaders advocate antigrowth policies that represent a departure from the existing norms of the community. We are not studying the extent to which antigrowth policies are already in place. The frequency of dynamic change is probably lower than the frequency with which communities already hold these policies. But since we asked the clerks to name entrepreneurs in the 1980s and the antigrowth movement took root mostly during that decade, the extent to which this is a problem may be minimized.

10. To rule out the possibility that suburban cities with full-time mayors are simply more likely than other cities to have someone whose visibility and policy positions attract the attention of the city clerk (increasing the probability that they will be named as an antigrowth entrepreneur), we tested to see if there were any significant differences in the positions (that is: mayor, city manager, city council member, or private citizen) held by antigrowth entrepreneurs in cities with full-time mayors and cities with part-time mayors. Since there was no significant difference in the distribution of positions across the two types of cities, we believe that the office fundamentally affects the expected benefits and costs of entrepreneurship and the patterns reported in this chapter do not result from clerks simply identifying full-time mayors as antigrowth entrepreneurs because of their higher visibility.

11. That is, the coefficient on the neighborhood group variable is not significant while the coefficient on the interaction term is positive and significant at $p < .05$.

12. We also modeled the effect of changes in the size of local economic base on the emergence of the antigrowth entrepreneur. A large and growing business sector can provide the resources to support the growth machine, but too rapid growth in these sectors may strain the infrastructure of the local community and challenge the quality of life in a community. In results not reported, but available upon request, we found that the relative growth of these business sectors affects the probability of an antigrowth entrepreneur emerging in a town.

Chapter Eight

1. Nearly 60 percent of the communities in our survey had city managers, ranging from almost 90 percent in the western municipalities in our sample to only 25 percent in New England.

2. Although we allowed more than a single entrepreneur to be named, and several clerks did so, most of the respondents named only one entrepreneur in the 1980s. We do not see this as a major problem, however, because a community may not have room for more than one entrepreneur at any given time. For example, Morgan and Watson (1992) found that it was rare for powerful mayors and strong managers to co-exist in the same city.

3. Multinomial logit is an appropriate technique given an unordered dependent variable that takes on more than two values (e.g., 0, 1, 2). See Aldrich and Nelson (1984) or Maddala (1983) for a description of the technique. A positive coefficient on an independent variable indicates an increase in the likelihood that an entrepreneur will emerge in a community with that characteristic, holding all other variables constant.

4. Note that these categories are exclusive—that is, either a city had a managerial entrepreneur or a political entrepreneur or no entrepreneur. In a small handful of cities, our respondents named more than one entrepreneur, but even in these cases it was always the case that the respondent devoted much more attention to one of these individuals than to the others. In this multinomial analysis, we use this person as "the" entrepreneur.

5. These measures of importance are assessed by the responding city clerk on a scale ranging from 1 (not important) to 5 (very important).

6. As noted, about 60 percent of the communities that responded to our survey have city managers. Thus, it is reasonable to include a variable indicating whether or not a community has an office of city manager as an independent variable when explaining the emergence of entrepreneurial politicians. Since we utilized the same set of independent variables in the multinomial probit, this variable is also included in the estimation of the factors that affect the emergence of entrepreneurial managers.

7. We do not report these negative results here, but they are available from the authors upon request. The multinomial equations using the same variables used in chapter 5 are not significant as a whole and virtually none of the individual measures are significant.

8. It is possible that a high pay ratio means that a community has higher quality workers, including the city manager. In this case, one could argue that the higher wages are attracting more talented managers who are more likely to be entrepreneurial. While we cannot yet rule out this possibility, we find the efficiency interpretation more plausible, but recognize that the two factors could be working simultaneously.

9. The average likelihood of an entrepreneurial manager emerging in this analysis is .06. If all communities had very weak taxpayer groups, the average likelihood increases to .117. Similarly, if all communities had municipal labor forces that were not unionized (as is the case in 34 percent of the communities in the sample), the average likelihood would increase to .129. If all communities had public/private pay ratios equal to the largest ratio in the sample, the average likelihood of an entrepreneurial manager emerging increases to .17.

10. Based on a simple chi-squared test, managerial entrepreneurs are significantly more likely than political entrepreneurs to pursue each of these strategies at $p. < .02$.

11. The significant coefficients for the pay ratio and union variables in the estimation of the entrepreneurial manager model are consistent with this position. See McGuire, Ohsfeldt, and van Cott (1987) or Stein (1990).

Chapter Nine

1. Fiorina (1993) uses this approach in a study of relative wages, professionalism, and the supply of state legislators.

2. Unfortunately, the County Business Pattern data do not indicate size of firms. However, in the next stage of analysis conducted at the community level, we do examine the effects of the number of small firms on the emergence of public entrepreneurs.

3. This is defined by the ratio of the average monthly wage of a full-time equiv-

alent local government employee to the average monthly wage of a full-time manufacturing worker in the region. We use this ratio as a proxy for the "reservation wage." See chapter 8, where we link this ratio to the emergence of entrepreneurial managers.

4. We set this to zero for the sensitivity analysis, since a one standard deviation move to below the mean level of FIRE employment results in a negative figure.

5. We define "small" as firms having fewer than twenty employees.

6. We set this to zero for the sensitivity analysis; see note 4.

Chapter Ten

1. The popular perspective on entrepreneurship and the dominant case study approach to entrepreneurs emphasize the importance of the individual entrepreneur. Many scholars, especially those associated with the Austrian School, argue that this approach errs by defining entrepreneurship too narrowly. In the Austrian approach, entrepreneurship is the product of the action of *all* rational individuals. In turn, in Austrian economics, entrepreneurship is a *function*, not an individual *person*, and the popular concept of entrepreneurs as a "dynamic few" is rejected. This position is rooted in the work of the most prominent Austrian economists, including Ludwig von Mises and Frederic von Hayek.

Mises emphasized a very broad notion of purposeful human action which is rooted in individual's efforts to improve their position. For Mises, anyone can be an entrepreneur—any owner, producer, or consumer who acts in response to change to improve his or her condition is to some degree an entrepreneur. As in Kirzner's definition, the singularly most important characteristic of Mises's entrepreneur is alertness to opportunities. And any individual alert to opportunities that may be "just around the corner" is defined as an entrepreneur. But merely the possession of information is not enough to define entrepreneurship—it is the knowledge of how to obtain information and how to use it to improve one's future situation that defines the entrepreneur. Thus, this approach to studying the entrepreneur suggests that we can consider all of our knowledgeable movers to be acting in an entrepreneurial fashion.

2. Schneider (1989) explores other problems with applying a model of the private market to the local market for public goods.

3. The Tiebout model and its extensions have also been criticized on equity grounds. For example, Hill (1974) described the polycentric system of metropolitan government as "separate and unequal." This contention has been hotly debated in the literature. In this chapter, we are concerned only with the efficiency aspect of the model.

4. In addition to our central concern in this text, the Lowery and Lyons approach can be criticized on several other grounds. For example, on simple methodological grounds, if respondents who live in an area served by a single metropolitan government that provides most services are asked who delivers the service, we would expect higher accuracy rates than in a system with a larger set of providers. But simply because the citizens in the single provider environment make more correct choices does not tell us that they had more effective information—that is, Lowery and Lyons never determine whether or not there were

systematic differences in the quality of the information or in the ability of citizens in different environments to use that information to improve the quality of the services they were receiving. Moreover, Percy and Hawkins (1992) note that counties, not local government, are often perceived as the most important services deliverers in the south, where Lowery and Lyons did their analysis, but not in the rest of the nation. Percy and Hawkins (1992) and Sharp (1986) find that citizens in the Milwaukee and Kansas City metropolitan areas, respectively, are affected by service/tax packages and both argue that they find evidence of Tiebout market mechanisms. Furthermore, users of economic models prefer to focus on revealed preferences as demonstrated by actual individual choices, not on survey responses that have no action component. For example, while surveys of New York City residents routinely find that more than half of them say they are planning to move from the city soon, half the population does not leave. Thus, it is actual, not potential movement that seems more relevant, and Lowery and Lyons do not measure actual exit. Finally, schools are the most important and expensive local public good provided in most jurisdictions and Lowery and Lyons's analysis excluded schools because both of their metropolitan areas have consolidated school districts.

5. For example only 30 percent of buyers of nondurable products shop at more than one store before making their purchases (Katona and Meuller 1955); for larger items, Claxton, Fry, and Portis (1974) found that only 5 percent of furniture buyers and 8 percent of appliance buyers gathered extensive information.

6. This may reflect the influence on political science of Hirschman's (1970) seminal work *Exit, Voice, and Loyalty*. The course of the debate might have been different, if Hirschman had included "Entry" in his title.

7. In this chapter, we use the term "municipalities" broadly. The delivery of local services is accomplished by a variety of government agencies. However, we believe that in the Tiebout model, any agency that delivers services and levies taxes to pay for those services will be subject to Tiebout-like pressure. This includes general-purpose municipalities, but it also includes special districts, including the "municipal" agency (school districts) that is in charge of the most costly local service delivered—public education.

8. While economists do not usually try to isolate particular individuals at a precise point on a market demand curve, following Hirschman (1970), we do this to highlight the difference between the average and the marginal consumer. We also recognize that for private goods, market demand is a horizontal summation of individual demands, while for pure public goods it is a vertical summation. This distinction does not affect the overall thrust of our illustration.

9. Note that this analysis unrealistically assumes that exit and entry behavior are the only factors that shape the service/tax packages of communities. Political voice, as exercised through elections and other activity, will obviously also affect the service/tax prices and may force even monopolistic systems to provide services below the monopoly price.

10. We focus on schools because almost two-thirds of local property taxes in Suffolk County are collected by school districts. Moreover, there is substantial variation in the taxes and expenditures across the seventy-one school districts

that make up the market for education. This variation is much greater than the variance across the ten towns that provide parks and roads, services that we also studied but which we do not combine with schools because of the extreme differences in variances across the services. The results for parks and roads are similar to the general pattern reported for schools. See appendix 10.1 for information about Long Island.

11. To test the accuracy of information, we asked our respondents a series of questions about the taxes and expenditures of their local school district—the most important and most expensive local service. Respondents were asked the following question: "Compared to all school districts in Suffolk County, would you say that the amount spent on each student in your school district is: above average, below average, or about average." Respondents could also offer "Don't know" as a response. A similar question was asked for taxes. Respondents who said they didn't know their expenditures or taxes were automatically classified as holding wrong information. To be judged as having correct information, a respondent had to choose the branch that correctly characterized his or her school district. Thus, a respondent who said local school expenditures (taxes) were above (below) average had to live in a school district whose expenditures were actually above (below) average. Those who responded "average" were considered accurate if they were in one of the 50 percent of districts surrounding the mean. Thus, by chance a respondent had a 25 percent chance of taking any of the four paths and a 50 percent chance of being correct, if they gave any response other than "don't know." By chance we therefore expect a respondent to get the expenditure or tax question correct 37.5 percent of the time and to get both right .375* .375 = .14 by chance.

12. Respondents were read a series of categories of increasing income levels and asked to stop the interviewer when the category was reached that encompassed the respondent's household income. The "average" category for respondents was $40,000–$50,000. We therefore define upper income individuals as those respondents with incomes above $50,000. For movers, we duplicated every analysis presented using house price. Given that local taxes are overwhelmingly based on property values, house values may be a more accurate reflection of the resources municipalities really care about. We report the results for income rather than house price, because accurate house price information was not available for nonmovers. Moreover, there is a high correlation between income and house price and the results reported based on house price are virtually identical to the results reported.

13. This difference between income groups is significant at $p < .0001$. Furthermore, 28 percent is significantly better than the 14 percent accuracy expected by chance, while 12 percent is not significantly different than chance. For comparative purposes note that among established residents, income has a similar effect, increasing the accuracy rate from 22 percent for low-income residents to 28 percent for high-income residents.

14. The trend line in figure 10.2 is the regression line plotting accuracy against the square root of the length of time a respondent has lived in a community. We used the square root because the distribution of the variable is highly skewed, with a handful of respondents having lived in the same community for over fifty years.

15. In a series of questions, respondents were asked if they had ever: attended a meeting called to discuss problems in their neighborhood or local community? Joined an organization attempting to solve these problems? Signed a petition regarding any particular local problem? Telephoned or written to an elected official regarding local problems? Joined a group for parents of school students like the PTA [Parent-Teacher Organization]? Voted on a school budget? We summed responses to create a political activity scale running from 0 to 6. High-income mover reported a mean of 1.7 political activities, significantly higher than the 1.2 average for low-income movers ($p = .04$). Movers who volunteered that local services were important in their choice of community engaged in an average of 1.8 activities, significantly higher than the 1.28 activities engaged in by movers who did not say that local services affected their choice of community ($p = .02$).

16. See appendix 10.2 for a discussion of how small numbers of informed individuals can "make" a market.

Bibliography

Aberbach, Joel, Robert Putnam, and Bert Rockman. 1981. *Bureaucrats and Politicians in Western Democracies.* Cambridge, Mass.: Harvard University Press.

Advisory Commission on Intergovernmental Relations. 1981a. *Regional Growth: Interstate Competition.* Washington, D.C.: Government Printing Office.

―――. 1981b. *Significant Features of Fiscal Federalism, 1981.* Washington, D.C.: Government Printing Office.

―――. 1985. *Significant Features of Fiscal Federalism, 1984.* Washington, D.C.: Government Printing Office.

Akerlof, George. 1970. "The Market for Lemons: Quality Uncertainty and the Market Mechanism." *Quarterly Journal of Economics* 84: 488–500.

Albrecht, Donald, Gene Bultena, and Ed Hoiberg. 1986. "Constituency of the Anti-growth Movement: A Comparison of the Growth Orientation of Urban Status Groups." *Urban Affairs Quarterly* 21: 607–616.

Alchian, Armen, and Harold Demsetz. 1972. "Production, Information Costs, and Economic Organizations." *American Economics Review* 62: 777–95.

Alchian, Armen, and Susan Woodward. 1987. "Reflections on the Theory of the Firm." *Journal of Institutional and Theoretical Economics* 143: 110–136.

Alderson, William. 1965. *Dynamic Marketing Behavior.* Chicago, Ill.: Irwin.

Aldrich, Howard, and Catherine Zimmer. 1986. "Entrepreneurship Through Social Networks." In *The Art and Science of Entrepreneurship*, edited by D. L. Sexton and R. W. Smilor. Cambridge, Mass.: Ballinger.

Aldrich, John, and Forrest Nelson. 1984. *Linear Probability, Logit, and Probit Models.* Newbury Park, Calif.,: Sage.

Alford, Robert, and Eugene Lee. 1968. "Voter Turnout in American Cities." *American Political Science Review* 62: 796–813.

Allison, Graham. 1982. "Public and Private Management: Are They Fundamentally Alike in All Unimportant Respects?" In *Current Issues in Public Administration*, 2d ed., edited by Frederick Lane. New York, N.Y.: St. Martin's Press.

Almond, Gabriel. 1988. "The Return to the State." *American Political Science Review* 82: 853–901.

―――. 1990. *A Discipline Divided: Schools and Sects in Political Science.* Newbury Park, Calif.: Sage.

Altshuler, Alan, and Marc Zegans. 1990. "Innovation and Creativity: Comparisons between Public Management and Private Enterprise." *Cities* (February): 16–24.

Ammons, David, and Charldean Newell. 1989. *City Executives: Leadership Roles, Work Characteristics, and Time Management.* Albany: State University of New York Press.

Arnold, R. Douglas. 1990. *The Logic of Congressional Action.* New Haven, Conn.: Yale University Press.

Austen-Smith, David, and William Riker. 1987. "Asymmetric Information and the Coherence of Legislation." *American Political Science Review* 81: 897–918.

Axelrod, Robert. 1981. "The Emergence of Cooperation Among Egoists." *American Political Science Review* 75:306–18.

————. 1984. *The Evolution of Cooperation.* New York, N.Y.: Basic Books.

Baldassare, Mark, and William Protash. 1982. "Growth Controls, Population Growth and Community Satisfaction." *American Sociological Review* 47: 339–346.

Barber, Daniel. 1988. "Newly Promoted City Managers." *Public Administration Review* 48: 694–699.

Barnard, Chester. 1938. *The Functions of the Executive.* Cambridge, Mass.: Harvard University Press.

Barnekov, Timothy, and Daniel Rich. 1989. "Privatism and the Limits of Local Economic Development Policy." *Urban Affairs Quarterly* 25: 212–238.

Barzel, Yoram. 1982. "Measurement Cost and the Organization of Markets." *Journal of Law and Economics* 25: 27–48.

————. 1987. "The Entrepreneur's Reward for Self-Policing." *Economic Inquiry* 25:103–116.

————. 1989. *Economic Analysis of Property Rights.* New York, N.Y.: Cambridge University Press.

Baumgartner, Frank. 1989. " Strategies of Political Leadership." In *Leadership and Politics,* edited by B. Jones, 114–139. Lawrence: University of Kansas Press.

Baumgartner, Frank, and Bryan Jones. 1993. *Agendas and Instability in American Politics.* Chicago, Ill.: University of Chicago Press.

Baumol, William. 1968. "Entrepreneurship in Economic Theory." *American Economic Review* 58: 64–71.

Baumol, William, John Panzar, and Robert Willig. 1982. *Contestability Markets and the Theory of Industrial Structure.* New York, N.Y.: Harcourt Brace Jovanovich.

Beatty, Sharon, and Scott Smith. 1987. "External Search Effort: An Investigation Across Several Product Categories." *Journal of Consumer Research* 14: 83–95.

Becker, Howard. 1970. *Sociological Work: Method and Substance.* Chicago, Ill.: Aldine.

Bendor, Jonathan, and Dilip Mookherjee. 1987. "Institutional Structure and the Logic of Ongoing Collective Action." *American Political Science Review* 81: 129–154.

Berger, Brigette. 1991. "The Culture of Modern Entrepreneurship." In *The Culture of the Entrepreneur,* edited by Brigitte Berger. San Francisco, Calif.: Institute for Contemporary Studies.

Berry, Frances, and William Berry. 1990. "State Lottery Adoptions as Policy Innovations: An Event History Analysis. *American Political Science Review* 84: 395–415.

————. 1992. "Tax Innovation in the States: Capitalizing on Political Opportunity." *American Journal of Political Science* 36: 715–742.

Bianco, William, and Robert Bates. 1990. "Cooperation by Design: Leadership, Structure, and Collective Dilemmas." *American Political Science Review* 84: 133–147.

Birch, David. 1987. *Job Creation in America.* New York, N.Y.: Free Press.

Birley, Sue. 1985. "The Role of Networks in the Entrepreneurial Process." *Journal of Business Venturing* 1: 107–117.

Blair, John, Rudy Fichtenbaum, and James Swaney. 1984. "The Market for Jobs: Locational Decisions and the Competition for Economic Development." *Urban Affairs Quarterly* 20: 64–77.

Blank, Rebecca. 1985. "The Impact of State Economic Differentials on Household Welfare and Labor Force Behavior." *Journal of Public Economics* 28: 25–58.

Bledsoe, Timothy, and Gerry Stoker. 1992. "Citizen's Knowledge of Local Government Structures and Representatives in the United States." Prepared for the Midwest Political Science Association Annual Meeting, Chicago, Ill.

Blinder, Alan. 1989. *Macroeconomics Under Debate.* Ann Arbor: University of Michigan Press.

Bollens, John, and Harry Schmandt. 1970. *The Metropolis: Its People, Politics, and Economics.* New York, N.Y.: Harper and Row.

Bollens, Scott. 1990. "Constituencies for Limitation and Regionalism." *Urban Affairs Quarterly* 26: 46–67.

Bower, Joseph. 1983. *The Two Faces of Management: An American Approach to Leadership in Business and Politics.* Boston, Mass.: Houghton Mifflin.

Boynton, Robert, and Deil Wright. 1971. "Mayor-Manager Relationships in Large Council-Manager Cities: A Reinterpretation." *Public Administration Review* 31: 28–36.

Brehm, John, and Scott Gates. 1993. "Speed Traps and Donuts Shops." *American Journal of Political Science* 37: 555–581.

Brockhaus, Robert, and Pamela Horwitz. 1986. "The Psychology of the Entrepreneur." In *The Art and Science of Entrepreneurship,* edited by D. L. Sexton and R. W. Smilor. Cambridge, Mass.: Ballinger.

Brockhaus, Robert, and William Nord. 1979. "An Exploration of Factors Affecting the Entrepreneurial Decision: Personal Characteristics vs. Environmental Conditions." Proceedings of the National Academy of Management, Washington, D.C.

Browne, William. 1985. "Municipal Managers and Policy: A Partial Test of the Svara Dichotomy-Duality Model." *Public Administration Review* 45: 620–622.

Buchanan, James. 1981. "Principles of Urban Fiscal Strategy." *Public Choice* 36: 1–14.

Buchanan, James, Robert Tollison, and Gordon Tullock. 1980. *Toward a Theory of the Rent-Seeking Society.* College Station: Texas A&M University Press.

Bucklin, Louis. 1966. "Testing Propensities to Shop." *Journal of Marketing* 30: 22–27.

——. 1969. "Consumer Search, Role Enactment, and Market Efficiency." *Journal of Business* 42: 416–438.

Bull, Clive. 1983. "The Existence of Self-Enforcing Implicit Contracts." *Quarterly Journal of Economics* 97: 147–159.

Burns, Nancy. 1991. "Making Politics Permanent: The Formation of American Local Governments, 1950–1987." Paper presented at the Midwest Political Science Association meetings. Chicago, Ill., April 19, 1991.

Cain, Bruce, John Ferejohn, and Morris Fiorina. 1987. *The Personal Vote.* Cambridge, Mass.: Harvard University Press.

Calabresi, Guido, and D. Melamed. 1972. "Property Rules, Liability Rules, and Inalienability: One View of the Cathedral." *Harvard Law Review* 85.

Carlson, Robert. 1961. "Succession and Performance Among School Superintendents," *Administrative Sciences Quarterly* 6: 210–227.

Caro, Robert. 1974. *The Power Broker: Robert Moses and the Fall of New York.* New York, N.Y.: Random House.

Casson, Mark. 1982. *The Entrepreneur: An Economic Theory.* Totowa, N.J.: Barnes and Noble Books.

Cave, Michael. 1985. "Market Models and Consumer Protection." *Journal of Consumer Policy* 12: 335–351.

Cheung, Steven. 1983. "The Contractual Nature of the Firm." *Journal of Law and Economics* 26: 1–21.

Clark, Jill. 1985. "Policy Diffusion and Program Scope: Research Directions." *Publius: The Journal of Federalism.* 15: 61–70.

Clark, Peter, and James Q. Wilson. 1961. "Incentive Systems: A Theory of Organizations." *Administrative Science Quarterly* 6: 129–166.

Clark, Terry, and Lorna Ferguson. 1983. *City Money.* New York, N.Y.: Columbia University Press.

Clarke, Susan. 1990. "Local Autonomy in the Post-Reagan Period." Paper presented at the Annual Meetings of the American Political Science Association. San Francisco, Calif.

Clavel, Pierre. 1986. *The Progressive City.* New Brunswick, NJ: Rutgers University Press.

Claxton, John, Joseph Fry, and Bernard Portis. 1974. "A Taxonomy of Prepurchase Information Gathering Patterns. *Journal of Consumer Research* 1: 35–42.

Coase, Ronald. 1937. "The Nature of the Firm." *Economica* 4: 386–405.

———. 1960. "The Problem of Social Cost." *Journal of Law and Economics* 3: 1–44.

Cobb, Roger, and Charles Elder. 1983 [1972]. *Participation in American Politics: The Dynamics of Agenda-Building.* 2d. Boston, Mass.: Allyn and Bacon.

Cobb, Roger, Jennie Keith-Ross, and Marc Howard Ross. 1976. "Agenda-Building as a Comparative Political Process." *American Political Science Review* 70: 126–138.

Cohen, Michael, James March, and Johan Olsen. 1972. "A Garbage Can Model of Organizational Choice." *Administrative Science Quarterly* 17: 1–15.

Cox, Kevin. 1982. "Housing Tenure and Neighborhood Activism." *Urban Affairs Quarterly* 18: 107–129.

Cyert, Richard, and James March. 1963. *A Behavioral Theory of the Firm.* Englewood Cliffs, N.J.: Prentice Hall.

Daft, Richard, and Selwyn Becker. 1978. *The Innovative Organization.* New York: Elsevier.

Dagger, Richard. 1981. "Metropolis, Memory, and Citizenship." *American Journal of Political Science* 25: 715–737.

Dawes, Robyn, John Orbell, Randy Simmons, and Alphons Van De Kragt. 1986. "Organizing Groups for Collective Action." *American Political Science Review* 80: 1171–1185.

Demsetz, Harold. 1983. "The Structure of Ownership and the Theory of the Firm." *Journal of Law and Economics* 26: 375–393.

———. 1988. "The Theory of the Firm Revisited." *Journal of Law, Economics, and Organization* 4: 141–161.

Derthick, Martha, and Paul Quirk. 1985. *The Politics of Deregulation.* Washington, D.C.: The Brookings Institution.

DeSantis, Victor, James Glass, and Charldean Newell. 1992. "City Managers, Job Satisfaction, and Community Problem Perceptions." *Public Administration Review* 52: 447–453.

DiLorenzo, Thomas. 1983. "Economic Competition and Political Competition: An Empirical Note." *Public Choice* 40: 203–209.

Doig, Jameson, and Erwin Hargrove, eds. 1987. *Leadership and Innovation: A Biographic Perspective on Entrepreneurs in Government*. Baltimore, Md.: Johns Hopkins University Press.

Donovan, Todd, and Max Neiman. 1992. "Community Social Status, Suburban Growth, and Local Government Restrictions on Residential Development." *Urban Affairs Quarterly* 28: 322–336.

Downs, Anthony. 1957. *An Economic Theory of Democracy*. New York, N.Y.: Harper and Row.

———. 1967. *Inside Bureaucracy*. Boston, Mass.: Little, Brown.

Downs, George, and Patrick Larkey. 1986. *The Search for Government Efficiency: From Hubris to Helplessness*. Philadelphia, Pa.: Temple University Press.

Dunleavy, Patrick. 1991. *Democracy, Bureaucracy and Public Choice*. Englewood Cliffs, N.J.: Prentice Hall.

Dye, Thomas, and John Garcia. 1978. "Structure, Function and Policy in American Cities." *Urban Affairs Quarterly* 14: 103–122.

Eisinger, Peter. 1988. *The Rise of the Entrepreneurial State*. Madison: University of Wisconsin Press.

Elkin, Stephen. 1985. "Twentieth Century Regimes." *Journal of Urban Affairs* 7: 11–28.

———. 1987. *City and Regime in the American Public*. Chicago, Ill.: University of Chicago Press.

Fainstein, Norman, and Susan Fainstein. 1983. "Regime Strategies, Communal Resistance, and Economic forces." In *Restructuring the City*, edited by Susan Fainstein, Norman Fainstein, Richard Hill, Dennis Judd, and Michael Smith. New York, N.Y.: Longman.

Feagin, Joseph. 1988. "Tallying the Social Costs of Urban Growth under Capitalism: The Case of Houston." In *Business Elites and Urban Development*, edited by Scott Cummings, 205–234. Albany: State University of New York Press.

Feick, Lawrence, and Linda Price. 1987. "The Market Maven: A Diffuser of Marketplace Information," *Journal of Marketing* 51: 83–97.

Feller, Irwin. 1992. "American State Governments as Models for National Science Policy." *Journal of Policy Analysis and Management* 11: 288–309.

Fenno, Richard. 1978. *Home Style*. Boston, Mass.: Little Brown.

Fields, Gary. 1979. "Place-to-Place Migration: Some New Evidence." *Review of Economics and Statistics* 61: 21–32.

Fiorina, Morris. 1977. *Congress: Keystone of the Washington Establishment*. New Haven, Conn.: Yale University Press.

———. 1993. "Divided Government in the American States: An Unintended Consequence of Legislative Professionalism?" Harvard University Occasional Paper 93–95.

Fischel, William. 1985. *The Economics of Zoning Laws*. Baltimore, Md.: Johns Hopkins University Press.

Friedman, James. 1986. *Game Theory with Applications to Economics.* New York, N.Y.: Oxford University Press.

Friedman, Milton. 1953. *Essays in Positive Economics.* Chicago, Ill.: University of Chicago Press.

———. 1962. *Capitalism and Freedom.* Chicago, Ill.: University of Chicago Press.

Frohlich, Norman, and Joe Oppenheimer. 1990. "Testing Leadership Solutions to Collective Action Problems." Paper presented to the American Political Science Association annual meetings, San Francisco, Calif.

Frohlich, Norman, Joe Oppenheimer, and Oran Young. 1971. *Political Leadership and Collective Goods.* Princeton, N.J.: Princeton University Press.

Fudenberg, Drew, and David Levine. 1990. "Reputation and Equilibrium Selection in Games with a Patient Player." *Econometrica* 57: 759–778.

Fudenberg, Drew, and Jean Tirole. 1991. *Game Theory.* Cambridge, Mass.: MIT Press.

Garfinkel, Howard. 1967. *Studies in Ethnmetholodogy.* Englewood Cliffs, N.J.: Prentice Hall.

Garreau, Joel. 1991. *Edge City: Life on the New Frontier.* New York, N.Y.: Doubleday.

Gasse, Yvon and d'Amboise, Gary. 1981. "Managerial Problems of Entrepreneurs." In *Frontiers of Entrepreneurship Research,* edited by K. Vesper, 56–64. Wellesley, Mass.: Babson College.

Gatswirth, Charles. 1976. "On Probabilistic Models of Consumer Search for Information." *Quarterly Journal of Economics* 86: 90–108.

Gilligan, Thomas, and Keith Krehbiel. 1990. "Organization of Informative Communities by a Rational Legislature." *American Journal of Political Science* 34: 531–564.

Glick, Henry, and Scott Hays. 1991. "Innovation and Reinvention in State Policymaking: Theory and the Evolution of Living Will Laws," *Journal of Politics* 53: 835–850.

Goetz, Edward. 1990. "Type II Policy and Mandated Benefits in Economic Development." *Urban Affairs Quarterly* 26: 170–190.

Golden, Olivia. 1990. "Innovation in Public Sector Human Services Programs: The Implications of Innovation by 'Groping Along.'" *Journal of Policy Analysis and Management* 9: 219–248.

Gormley, William. 1989. *Taming the Bureaucracy: Muscles, Prayers and other Strategies.* Princeton, N.J.: Princeton University Press.

Gottdeiner, Mark, and Max Neiman. 1981. "Characteristics of Support for Local Growth Control." *Urban Affairs Quarterly* 17: 55–73.

Gramlich, Edward, and Deborah Laren. 1984. "Migration and Income Redistribution Responsibilities." *Journal of Human Resources* 9: 489–511.

Granovetter, Mark. 1985. "Economic Action and Social Structure: The Problem of Embeddedness." *American Journal of Sociology* 91: 481–510.

Gray, Virginia. 1973. "Innovation in the States: A Diffusion Study." *American Political Science Review* 67: 1174–1185.

Green, Ed, and Robert Porter. 1984. "Non-cooperative Collusion under Imperfect Price Information." *Econometrica* 52: 87–100.

Hammond, Thomas. 1986. "Agenda Control, Organizational Structure, and Bureaucratic Politics." *American Journal of Political Science* 30: 379–420.

Hammond, Thomas, Jeffrey Hill, and Gary Miller. 1986. "Presidential Appointment of Bureau Chiefs and the 'Congressional Control of Administration' Hypothesis." Presented at the annual meeting of the American Political Science Association, Washington, D.C.

Hansen, John Mark. 1985. "The Political Economy of Group Membership." *American Political Science Review* 79: 79–96.

Hardin, Russell. 1982. *Collective Action.* Baltimore, Md.: Johns Hopkins University Press.

Hargrove, Erwin, and John Glidewell. 1990. *Impossible Jobs in Public Management.* Lawrence: University Press of Kansas.

Hayek, Frederick August von. 1976. *Denationalisation of Money.* London: Institute of Economic Affairs.

Heclo, Hugh. 1978. "Issue Networks and the Executive Establishment." In *The New American Political System,* edited by Anthony King, 82–124. Washington, D.C.: American Enterprise Institute.

Hilgartner, Stephen, and Charles Bosk. 1988. "The Rise and Fall of Social Problems: A Public Arenas Model." *American Journal of Sociology* 94: 53–78.

Hill, Richard. 1974. "Separate and Unequal: Government Inequality in the Metropolis." *American Political Science Review* 68: 1557–1568.

Hirschman, Albert. 1967. "The Hiding Hand Principle." *Public Interest* 3: 26–53.

———. 1970. *Exit, Voice, and Loyalty.* Cambridge, Mass.: Harvard University Press.

Hofstadter, Richard. 1955. *The Age of Reform: From Bryan to F.D.R.* New York, N.Y.: A. A. Knopf.

Hughes, James. 1986. *The Vital Few: The Entrepreneur and American Economic Progress.* New York, N.Y.: Oxford University Press.

Hyman, David. 1989. *Modern Microeconomics: Analysis and Applications.* Boston, Mass.: Little, Brown.

———. 1979. "The Fiscal Performance of Local Governments: An Interpretative Review." In *Current Issues in Urban Economics,* edited by Peter Mieszkowski and Mahlon Straszheim, 270–321. Baltimore, Md.: Johns Hopkins University Press.

Inman, Robert. 1978. "Testing Political Economy's 'As If' Proposition: Is the Median Income Voter Really Decisive?" *Public Choice* 33: 45–65.

Iyengar, Shanto, and Donald Kinder. 1987. *News that Matters.* Chicago, Ill.: University of Chicago Press.

Jensen, Michael, and William Meckling. 1976. "Theory of the Firm: Managerial Behavior, Agency Costs, and Capital Structure." *Journal of Financial Economics* 3: 305–360.

Jones, Bryan, ed. 1989. *Leadership and Politics: New Perspectives in Political Science.* Lawrence: University of Kansas Press.

Kahneman, Daniel, and Amos Tversky. 1979. "Prospect Theory: An Analysis of Decision Under Risk. *Econometrica* 47: 263–291.

Kammerer, Gladys. 1964. "Role Diversity of City Managers." *Administrative Sciences Quarterly* 8: 421–442.

Katona, George, and Eva Mueller. 1955. "A Study of Purchase Decisions in Consumer Behavior." In *Consumer Behavior,* edited by Lincoln Clark. New York, N.Y.: New York University Press.

Kilby, Paul. 1971. *Entrepreneurship and Economic Development.* New York, N.Y.: Free Press.

King, Paula. 1988. *Policy Entrepreneurs: Catalysts in the Policy Innovation Process.* Unpublished Ph.D. dissertation. University of Minnesota.

Kingdon, John. 1984. *Agenda, Alternatives, and Public Policies.* Boston, Mass.: Little Brown.

Kirchheimer, Donna. 1989. "Public Entrepreneurship and Subnational Government." *Polity* 22: 15–44.

Kirzner, Israel. 1973. *Competition and Entrepreneurship.* Chicago, Ill.: University of Chicago Press.

———. 1979. *Perception, Opportunity and Profit.* Chicago, Ill.: University of Chicago Press.

———. 1985. *Discovery and the Capitalist Process.* Chicago, Ill.: University of Chicago Press.

Knott, Jack, and Gary Miller. 1987. *Reforming Bureaucracy: The Politics of Institutional Choice.* Englewood Cliffs, N.J.: Prentice Hall.

Kozol, Jonathan. 1991. *Savage Inequalities: Children in America's Schools.* New York, N.Y.: Crown.

Krasner, Stephen. 1982. "Approaches to the State." *Comparative Politics* 16: 26–55.

Kreps, David. 1990. "Corporate Culture and Economic Theory." In *Perspectives on Positive Political Economy,* edited by James E. Alt and Kenneth A. Shepsle. New York, N.Y.: Cambridge University Press.

Krueger, Anne. 1974. "The Political Economy of the Rent-Seeking Society." *The American Economic Review* 64: 291–303.

Kuhn, Thomas. 1963. *The Structure of Scientific Revolutions.* Chicago, Ill.: University of Chicago Press.

Landa, Janet. 1991. "Culture and Entrepreneurship in Less Developed Countries: Ethnic Trading Networks as Economic Organizations." In *The Culture of the Entrepreneur,* edited by Brigette Berger, 53–72. San Francisco, Calif.: Institute for Contemporary Studies.

Lanzetta, John, and Victor Kanareff. 1962. "Information Cost, Amount of Payoff and Level of Aspiration as Determinants of Information Seeking in Decision Making." *Behavioral Science* 7: 459–473.

Lavrakas, Peter. 1987. *Telephone Survey Methods.* Beverly Hills, Calif.: Sage.

Lavoie, Don. 1991. "The Discovery and Interpretation of Profit Opportunities: Culture and the Kirznerian Entrepreneur." In *The Culture of the Entrepreneur,* edited by Brigitte Berger. San Francisco, Calif.: Institute for Contemporary Studies.

Lehrer, E. 1989. "Lower Equilibrium Payoffs in 2-Player Games with Non-Observable Action." *International Journal of Game Theory* 18: 57–89.

Leibenstein, Harvey. 1968. "Entrepreneurship and Development." *American Economics Review* 58: 72–83.

Lewis, Eugene. 1980. *Public Entrepreneurship: Toward a Theory of Bureaucratic Power.* Bloomington: Indiana University Press.

Libecap, Gary. 1989. *Contracting for Property Rights.* New York, N.Y.: Cambridge University Press.

Lindblom, Charles. 1977. *Politics and Markets.* New York, N.Y.: Basic Books.

Lineberry, Robert, and Edward Fowler. 1967. "Reformism and Public Policies in American Cities." *American Political Science Review* 61: 701–716.

Livesay, Harold. 1982. "Entrepreneurial History." In *The Encyclopedia of Entrepreneurship*, edited by Calvin Kent et al., 7–14. Englewood Cliffs, N.J.: Prentice Hall.

Logan, John, and Harvey Molotch. 1987. *Urban Fortunes*. Berkeley: University of California Press.

Logan, John and Gordana Rabrenovic. 1990. "Neighborhood Associations: Their Issues, Their Allies, and Their Opposition." *Urban Affairs Quarterly* 26: 68–94.

Logan, John, and Min Zhou. 1990. "The Adoption of Growth Controls in Suburban Communities." *Social Science Quarterly* 71: 118–129.

Long, Larry. 1974. "Poverty Status and Receipt of Welfare among Migrants and Nonmigrants in Large Cities." *American Sociological Review* 39: 46–56.

Lovell, Catherine, et al. 1979. *Federal and State Mandating on Local Governments: An Exploration of Issues and Impacts*. Washington, D.C.: National Science Foundation.

Lowery, David, and William Lyons. 1989. "The Impact of Jurisdictional Boundaries: An Individual-Level Test of the Tiebout Model." *Journal of Politics* 51: 73–97.

Lowery, David, William Lyons, and Ruth DeHoog. 1990. "Institutionally Induced Attribution Errors: Their Composition and Impact on Citizen Satisfaction with Local Government." *American Politics Quarterly* 18: 169–197.

Lowi, Theodore. 1992. "The State in Political Science: How We Became What We Study." *American Political Science Review* 86: 1–7.

Lynn, Lawrence. 1990. "Managing the Social Services Net: The Job of Social Welfare Executive." In *Impossible Jobs in Public Management*, edited by Erwin Hargrove and John Glidewell. Lawrence: University Press of Kansas.

Lyons, William, and David Lowery. 1989. "Citizen Responses to Dissatisfaction in Urban Communities: A Test of a General Model." *Journal of Politics* 51: 841–868.

McClelland, David. 1961. *The Achieving Society*. Princeton, N.J.: Van Nostrand.

McClosky, Donald. 1983. "The Rhetoric of Economics." *Journal of Economic Literature* 21: 481–517.

McCraw, Thomas. 1984. *Prophets of Regulation*. Cambridge, Mass.: Harvard University Press.

McCubbins, Matthew, and Thomas Schwartz. 1984. "Congressional Oversight Overlooked: Police Patrols versus Fire Alarms." *American Journal of Political Science* 28: 165–179.

McGuire, Robert, Robert Ohsfeldt, and T. Norman van Cott. 1987. "The Determinants of the Choice between Public and Private Production of a Publicly Funded Service." *Public Choice* 54: 211–230.

McKelvey, Richard. 1976. "Intransitivities in Multidimensional Voting Models and Some Implications for Agenda Control." *Journal of Economic Theory* 7: 472–482.

———. 1979. "General Conditions for Voting Intransitivities in Formal Voting Models." *Econometrica* 47: 1085–1111.

McKelvey, Richard, and Norman Schofield. 1987. "Generalized Symmetry Conditions at a Core Point." *Econometrica* 55: 923–933.

Maddala, G. S. 1983. *Limited Dependent and Qualitative Variables in Econometrics.* New York, N.Y.: Cambridge University Press.

Maillat, Denis, and Bernard Lecoq. 1992. "New Technologies and Transformation of Regional Structures in Europe." *Entrepreneurship and Regional Development* 4: 1–20.

March, James, and Herbert Simon. 1958. *Organization.* New York, N.Y.: Wiley.

Markusen, Anne. 1987. *Regions: The Economics and Politics of Territory.* Totowa, N.J.: Rowman and Littlefield.

Markusen, Anne, Peter Hall, and Amy Glasmeier. 1986. *High Tech America: The What, How, Where, and Why of the Sunrise Industries.* Boston, Mass.: Allen and Unwin.

Mazmanian, Daniel, and Paul Sabatier. 1983. *Implementation and Public Policy.* Glenview, Ill.: Scott, Foresman.

Menzel, Donald, and Irwin Feller. 1977. "Leadership and Interaction Patterns in the Diffusion of Innovation Among the American States." *Western Political Quarterly* 30: 528–536.

Miller, Gary. 1990. "Managerial Dilemmas: Political Leadership in Hierarchies." In *The Limits of Rationality,* edited by Karen Schweers Cook and Margaret Levi. Chicago, Ill.: The University of Chicago Press.

———. 1992. *Managerial Dilemmas: The Political Economy of Hierarchy.* New York, N.Y.: Cambridge University Press.

Miller, Gary, and Terry Moe. 1983. "Bureaucrats, Legislators, and the Size of Government." *American Political Science Review* 77: 297–322.

Miller, Thomas, and Michelle Miller. 1991. "Standards of Excellence: U.S. Resident's Evaluations of Local Government Services." *Public Administration Review* 51: 503–513.

Milward, H. Brinton, and Wendy Laird. 1990. "Where Does Policy Come From?" Paper presented at the Western Political Science Association Meeting, Newport Beach, Calif., March 23–25.

Milward, H. Brinton, and Heidi Hosbach Newman. 1989. "State Incentive Packages and the Industrial Location Decision." *Economic Development Quarterly* 3: 202–222.

Mises, Ludwig von. 1949. *Human Action: A Treatise on Economics.* New Haven, Conn.: Yale University Press.

———. 1962. *Ultimate Foundations of Economic Science.* Princeton, N.J.: Van Nostrand.

Moe, Terry. 1980. *The Organization of Interests.* Chicago, Ill.: University of Chicago Press.

———. 1984. "The New Economics of Organization." *American Journal of Political Science.* 739–777.

———. 1991. "Politics and the Theory of Organization." *Journal of Law, Economics, and Organization* 7: 106–129.

Mohr, Lawrence. 1969. "Determinants of Innovation in Organizations." *American Political Science Review* 63: 111–26.

Mollenkopf, John. 1983. *The Contested City.* Princeton, N.J.: Princeton University Press.

Molotch, Harvey. 1976. "The City as Growth Machine." *American Journal of Sociology* 82: 309–332.

Morgan, David, and John Pelissero. 1981. "Urban Policy: Does Political Structure Matter?" *American Political Science Review* 75: 999–1006.

Morgan, David, and Sheilan Watson. 1992. "Policy Leadership in Council-Manager Cities: Comparing Mayor and Manager." *Public Administration Review* 52: 438–446.

Nalbandian, John. 1989. "The Contemporary Role of City Managers." *American Review of Public Administration* 19: 261–279.

Nelson, Barbara. 1984. *Making an Issue Out of Child Abuse: Political Agenda Setting for Social Problems*. Chicago, Ill.: University of Chicago Press.

Nelson, Phillip. 1970. "Information and Consumer Behavior." *Journal of Political Economy* 78: 311–329.

Nelson, Richard, and Sidney Winter. 1982. *An Evolutionary Theory of Economic Change*. Cambridge, Mass.: Harvard University Press.

Newman, Joseph, and Richard Staelin. 1972. "Prepurchase Information Seeking for New Cars and Major Household Appliances." *Journal of Marketing Research* 9: 249–257.

Niskanen, William. 1971. *Bureaucracy and Representative Government*. Chicago, Ill.: Aldine.

——. 1975. "Bureaucrats and Politicians." *Journal of Law and Economics* 18: 617–643.

Nordlinger, Eric. 1988. "The Return to the State: Critiques." *American Political Science Review* 82: 875–883.

North, Douglass. 1990. *Institutions, Institutional Change, and Economic Performance*. New York, N.Y.: Cambridge University Press.

Oakerson, Ronald, and Roger Parks. 1988. "Citizen Voice and Public Entrepreneurship: The Organizational Dynamic of a Complex Metropolitan County." *Publius: The Journal of Federalism* (Fall): 91–112.

Olson, Mancur. 1965. *The Logic of Collective Action*. Cambridge, Mass.: Harvard University Press.

——. 1982. *The Rise and Decline of Nations*. New Haven, Conn.: Yale University Press.

Orbell, John, and Toru Uno. 1972. "A Theory of Neighborhood Problem Solving: Political Action vs. Residential Mobility." *American Political Science Review* 66: 471–486.

Osborne, David, and Ted Gaebler. 1992. *Reinventing Government: How the Entrepreneurial Spirit Is Transforming the Public Sector*. Reading, Mass.: Addison-Wesley.

Ostrom, Elinor. 1972. "Metropolitan Reform: Propositions Derived From Two Traditions." *Social Science Quarterly* 53: 474–493.

——. 1990. *Governing the Commons*. New York, N.Y.: Cambridge University Press.

Ostrom, Vincent, Charles Tiebout, and Robert Warren. 1961. "The Organization of Government in Metropolitan Areas." *American Political Science Review* 55: 835–842.

Ouchi, William. 1980. "Markets, Bureaucracies and Clans." *Administrative Sciences Quarterly* 25:129–141.

Parker, Glenn. 1986. *Homeward Bound: Explaining Changes in Congressional Behavior*. Pittsburgh, Pa.: University of Pittsburgh Press.

———. 1991. "Congressmen as Discretion-Maximizers." Paper presented at the Workshop in Political Theory and Policy Analysis, Indiana University, Bloomington, April 15, 1991.

Parks, Roger, and Elinor Ostrom. 1981. "Complex Models of Urban Service Delivery Systems." In *Urban Policy Analysis*, vol. 21, edited by Terry Clark, 171–200. *Urban Affairs Annual Review*. Beverly Hills, Calif.: Sage.

Pasour, Edward. 1989. "The Efficient Market Hypothesis and Entrepreneurship." In *The Review of Austrian Economics*, edited by Murray N. Rothbard and Walter Block, 95–106. Lexington, Mass.: Lexington Books.

Percy, Stephen, and Brett Hawkins. 1992. "Further Tests of Individual-Level Propositions From the Tiebout Model." *Journal of Politics* 54: 1149–1157.

Peterson, Paul. 1981. *City Limits*. Chicago, Ill.: University of Chicago Press.

Peterson, Paul, and Mark Rom. 1989. "American Federalism, Welfare Policy, and Residential Choices." *American Political Science Review* 88: 711–728.

Plott, Charles. 1967. "A Notion of Equilibrium and Its Possibility Under Majority Rule." *American Economic Review* 57: 787–806.

Polsby, Nelson. 1984. *Political Innovation in America: The Politics of Policy Initiation*. New Haven, Conn.: Yale University Press.

Porter, Michael. 1980. *Competitive Strategy*. New York, N.Y.: Free Press.

Powell, Walter. 1991. "Neither Market nor Hierarchy: Network Forms of Organization." In *Markets, Hierarchies and Networks: The Coordination of Social Life*, edited by Grahame Thompson et al. Newbury Park, Calif.: Sage.

Pratt, John, and Richard Zeckhauser. 1985. *Principals and Agents: The Structure of Business*. Boston, Mass.: Harvard Business School Press.

Protasel, Gary. 1988. "Abandonments of the Council-Manager Plan: A New Institutionalist Perspective." *Public Administration Review* 48: 807–812.

Protash, William, and Mark Baldassare. 1983. "Growth Policies and Community Status." *Urban Affairs Quarterly* 19: 397–412.

Punj, Girish, and Richard Staelin. 1983. "A Model of Consumer Information Search Behavior for New Automobiles." *Journal of Consumer Research* 9: 366–380.

Quattrone, George, and Amos Tversky. 1988. "Contrasting Rational and Psychological Analyses of Political Choice." *American Political Science Review* 82: 719–736.

Radner, Roy. 1986. "The Internal Economy of Large Firms." *Economic Journal* 96: 1–22.

Reekie, W. Duncan. 1984. *Markets, Entrepreneurs, and Liberty: An Austrian View of Capitalism*. New York, N.Y.: St. Martins.

Reich, Robert. 1991. *The Work of Nations: Preparing Ourselves for 21st Century Capitalism*. New York, N.Y.: A. A. Knopf.

Rhoads, Steven. 1985. *The Economist's View of the World: Government, Markets, and Public Policy*. New York, N.Y.: Cambridge University Press.

Ricketts, Martin. 1987. *The New Industrial Economics*. New York, N.Y.: St. Martins.

Riker, William. 1980. "Implications from the Disequilibrium of Majority Rule for the Study of Institutions." *American Political Science Review* 74: 432–446.

———. 1982. *Liberalism against Populism: A Confrontation between the Theory of Democracy and the Theory of Social Choice.* New York, N.Y.: Freeman.

———. 1986. *The Art of Political Manipulation.* New Haven, Conn.: Yale University Press.

———. 1990. "Heresthetic and Rhetoric in the Spatial Model." In *Advances in the Spatial Theory of Voting,* edited by Jim Enelow and Mel Hinich. Cambridge: Cambridge University Press.

Riker, William H., and Itai Sened. 1991. "A Theory of the Origin of Property Rights: Airport Slots." *American Journal of Political Science* 35: 951–969.

Roberts, Nancy. 1991. "Public Entrepreneurship and Innovation." Typescript. Monterey, Calif.: Naval Postgraduate School.

Romo, Frank, and Michael Schwartz. N.d. "The Structural Embeddedness of Business Decisions: A Sociological Assessment of the Migration Behavior of Manufacturing Plants in New York State Between 1960 and 1985." Manuscript.

Ronen, Joshua. 1983. "Introduction." In *Entrepreneurship,* edited by Joshua Ronen, 1–12. Lexington, Mass.: Lexington Books.

Rosenthal, Donald, and Robert Crain. 1968. "Structure and Values in Local Political Systems: The Case of Fluoridation Decisions." In *City Politics and Public Policy,* edited by James Q. Wilson. New York, N.Y.: Wiley.

Rossi, Peter. 1955. *Why Families Move.* New York, N.Y.: Free Press.

Rothenberg, Lawrence S. 1988. "Organizational Maintenance and the Retention Decision in Groups." *American Political Science Review* 82: 1129–1152.

Rothschild, Michael. 1973. "Models of Market Organization with Imperfect Information: A Survey." *Journal of Political Economy* 81: 1283–1308.

Rotter, James. 1966. "Generalized Expectations for Internal versus External Control of Reinforcement." *Psychological Monographs* 80: 609–623.

Salisbury, Robert. 1969. "An Exchange Theory of Interest Groups." *American Journal of Political Science* 13: 1–32.

Sandler, Todd. 1992. *Collective Action: Theory and Applications.* Ann Arbor: University of Michigan Press.

Sanger, Mary Bryna, and Martin Levin. 1992. "Using Old Stuff in New Ways: Innovation as a Case of Evolutionary Tinkering." *Journal of Policy Analysis and Management* 11: 88–115.

Sayre, Wallace. 1958. "The Unhappy Bureaucrats: Views Ironic, Helpful, Indignant." *Public Administration Review* 18: 240–256.

Schneider, Mark. 1986a. "The Market for Local Economic Development: The Growth of Suburban Retail Trade, 1972–1982." *Urban Affairs Quarterly* 21: 24–41.

———. 1986b. "Fragmentation and the Growth of Local Government." *Public Choice* 48: 255–264.

———. 1989. *The Competitive City: The Political Economy of Suburbia.* Pittsburgh, Pa.: University of Pittsburgh Press.

———. 1992. "Undermining the Growth Machine: The Missing Link Between Local Economic Development and Fiscal Payoffs." *Journal of Politics* 54: 214–230.

Schneider, Mark, and John Logan. 1982. "The Effects of Local Government Finances on Community Growth Rates: A Test of the Tiebout Model." *Urban Affairs Quarterly* 18: 91–106.

Schneider, Mark, and Paul Teske. 1992. "Toward a Theory of the Political Entrepreneur." *American Political Science Review* 86: 737–747.

———. 1993. "The Antigrowth Entrepreneur: Challenging the 'Equilibrium' of the Growth Machine." *Journal of Politics* 55: 720–736.

Schneider, William. 1992. "The Suburban Century Begins: The Real Meaning of the 1992 Election." *The Atlantic Monthly*. July: 33–44.

Schofield, Norman. 1978. "Instability of Simple Dynamic Games." *Review of Economic Studies* 45: 575–594.

———. 1983. "Generic Instability of Majority Rule." *Review of Economic Studies* 50: 695–705.

———. 1984. *Mathematical Methods in Economics*. New York, N.Y.: New York University Press.

Schon, Donald. 1971. *Beyond the Stable State*. New York, N.Y.: Norton.

Schumpeter, Joseph. 1939. *Business Cycles*. 2 vols. New York, N.Y.: McGraw-Hill.

———. 1942. *Capitalism, Socialism, and Democracy*. New York, N.Y.: Harper and Row.

———. 1961. *A Theory of Economic Development*. Oxford, U.K.: Oxford University Press.

Schwartz, Alan, and Louis Wilde. 1979. "Intervening in Markets on the Basis of Imperfect Information: A Legal and Economic Analysis." *University of Pennsylvania Law Review* 127: 630–682.

Scott, Allen, and Michael Storper. 1987. "Industries de haute technologie et developement regional." *Revue Internationale des Sciences Sociales* 112: 237–256.

Selznick, Philip. 1957. *Leadership in Administration: A Sociological Interpretation*. New York, N.Y.: Harper and Row.

Shackle, G.L.S. 1972. *Epistemics and Economics*. Cambridge: Cambridge University Press.

Shapero, Albert, and Lisa Sokol. 1982. "The Social Dimensions of Entrepreneurship." In *The Encyclopedia of Entrepreneurship*, edited by Calvin Kent, Donald Sexton, and Karl Vesper. Englewood Cliffs, N.J.: Prentice Hall.

Shapiro, Carl. 1983. "Premiums for High Quality Products as Returns to Reputations." *Quarterly Journal of Economics* 97: 659–679.

Sharp, Elaine. 1984. "Exit, Voice and Loyalty in the Context of Local Government." *Western Politics Quarterly* 37: 67–83.

———. 1986. "The Politics and Economics of the New City Debt." *American Political Science Review* 80: 1271–1288.

Shepsle, Kenneth. 1979. "Institutional Arrangements and Equilibrium in Multidimensional Voting Models." *American Journal of Political Science* 23: 27–59.

———. 1986. "Institutional Equilibrium and Equilibrium Institutions." In *Political Science: The Science of Politics*, edited by Herbert F. Weisberg. New York, N.Y.: Agathon Press.

Shepsle, Kenneth, and Barry Weingast. 1981. "Structure-Induced Equilibrium and Legislative Choice." *Public Choice* 37: 503–519.

Simon, Herbert. 1969. *The Sciences of the Artificial*. Cambridge, Mass.: MIT Press.

———. 1976. *Administrative Behavior*. New York, N.Y.: Free Press.

———. 1977. *Models of Discovery*. Boston, Mass.: Reidel.

Simon, Herbert and James March. 1958. *Organizations*. New York, N.Y.: Wiley.

Sjoquist, David. 1982. "The Effect of the Number of Local Governments on Central City Expenditures." *National Tax Journal* 35: 79–88.

Slama, Mark, and Armen Tashchian. 1985. "Selected Socioeconomic and Demographic Characteristics Associated with Purchasing Involvement." *Journal of Marketing* 49: 72–82.

Slama, Mark, and Terrell Williams. 1990. "Generalizations of the Market Maven's Information Provision Tendency Across Product Categories." *Advances in Consumer Research* 17: 48–53.

Smith, James. 1991. *The Idea Brokers: Think Tanks and the Rise of the New Policy Elite*. New York, N.Y.: Free Press.

Stanback, Thomas. 1991. *The New Suburbanization: Challenge to the Central City*. Boulder, Colo.: Westview Press.

Stein, Robert. 1990. *Urban Alternatives*. Pittsburgh, Pa.: University of Pittsburgh Press.

Stigler, George. 1961. "The Economics of Information." *Journal of Political Economy* 69: 213–225.

———. 1971. "The Theory of Economic Regulation." *Bell Journal of Economics and Management Science* 2: 3–21.

Stillman, Richard. 1977. "The City Manager: Professional Helping Hand, or Political Hired Hand?" *Public Administration Review* 37: 659–670.

Stimson, James. 1991. *Public Opinion in America: Moods, Cycles, and Swings*. Boulder, Colo.: Westview Press.

Stone, Clarence. 1989. *Regime Politics*. Lawrence: University of Kansas Press.

Stone, Clarence, and Heywood Sanders. 1987. "Reexamining a Classic Case of Development Politics: New Haven, Connecticut." In *The Politics of Urban Development*, edited by Clarence N. Stone and Heywood T. Sanders. Lawrence: University of Kansas Press.

Svara, James. 1990. *Official Leadership in the City: Patterns of Conflict and Cooperation*. New York, N.Y.: Oxford University Press.

Swanstrom, Todd. 1985. *The Crisis of Growth Politics: Cleveland, Kucinich, and the Challenge of Urban Populism*. Philadelphia, Pa.: Temple University Press.

Taylor, Michael. 1982. *Community, Anarchy, and Liberty*. New York, N.Y.: Cambridge University Press.

———. 1987. *The Possibility of Cooperation*. New York, N.Y.: Cambridge University Press.

Thorelli, Hans, and Jack Engledow. 1980. "Information Seekers and Information Systems: A Policy Perspective." *Journal of Marketing* 44: 9–27.

Tiebout, Charles. 1956. "A Pure Theory of Local Expenditures." *Journal of Political Economy* 64: 416–424.

———. 1961. "Economic Theory of Fiscal Decentralization." Pp. 79–96 In *Public Finances: Needs, Sources, Utilization*, National Bureau of Economic Research. Princeton, N.J.: Princeton University Press.

Tirole, Jean. 1988. *The Theory of Industrial Organization*. Cambridge, Mass.: MIT Press.

———. 1989. *The Theory of Industrial Organization*. Cambridge, Mass.: MIT Press.

Tullock, Gordon. 1965. "Entry Barriers in Politics." *American Economic Review*, Papers and Proceedings: 458–466.

———. 1967. "The General Irrelevance of the General Impossibility Theorem." *Quarterly Journal of Economics* 81: 256–270.

Tversky, Amos, and Daniel Kahneman. 1981. "The Framing of Decisions and the Psychology of Choice." *Science* 211: 453–458.

Udell, John. 1966. "Prepurchase Behavior of Buyers of Small Electrical Appliances." *Journal of Marketing*: 50–52.

Van de Ven, Andrew. 1986. "Central Problems in the Management of Innovation." *Management Science* 32: 592–603.

Vernon, Raymond. 1966. "International Investment and International Trade in the Product Cycle." *Quarterly Journal of Economics* 80: 190–207.

Walker, Jack. 1969. "The Diffusion of Innovations Among the American States." *American Political Science Review* 63: 880–899.

———. 1973. "Comment: Problems in Research on the Diffusion of Policy Innovations." *American Political Science Review* 67: 1186–1191.

———. 1981. "The Diffusion of Knowledge, Policy Communities and Agenda Setting." In *New Strategic Perspectives on Social Policy*, edited by John Tropman, 75–96. London: Pergamon.

———. 1991. *Mobilizing Interest Groups in America: Patrons, Professions, and Social Movements*. Ann Arbor: University of Michigan Press.

Weimer, David, and Aidan Vining. 1992. *Policy Analysis: Concepts and Practice*. Englewood Cliffs, N.J.: Prentice Hall.

Weissert, Carol. 1991. "Policy Entrepreneurs, Policy Opportunities and Legislative Effectiveness." *American Politics Quarterly* 19: 262–274.

Welsh, James, and John White. 1981. "Converging of Characteristics of Entrepreneurs." In *Frontiers of Entrepreneurship Research*, edited by Kenneth Vesper. Wellesley, Mass.: Babson College.

Welsh, Susan, and Timothy Bledsoe. 1988. *Urban Reform and Its Consequences: A Study in Representation*. Chicago, Ill.: University of Chicago Press.

Whitaker, Gordon, and Ruth Hoogland DeHoog. 1991. "City Managers Under Fire: How Conflict Leads to Turnover." *Public Administration Review* 51: 156–165.

Wikstrom, Nelson. 1979. "The Mayor as a Policy Leader in the Council-Manager Form of Government: A View from the Field." *Public Administration Review* 39: 270–276.

Wilde, Louis. 1981. "Information Costs, Duration of Search, and Turnover: Theory and Applications." *Journal of Political Economy* 89: 1122–1141.

Wilde, Louis, and Alan Schwartz. 1979. "Equilibrium Comparison Shopping." *Review of Economic Studies* 64: 543–553.

Williamson, Oliver. 1975. *Markets and Hierarchies: Analysis and Antitrust Implications*. New York, N.Y.: Free Press.

———. 1985. *The Economic Institutions of Capitalism*. New York, N.Y.: Free Press.

Wilson, James Q. 1973. *Political Organizations*. New York, N.Y.: Basic Books.

———. 1980. "The Politics of Regulation." In *The Politics of Regulation*, 357–394. New York, N.Y.: Basic Books.

————. 1989. *Bureaucracy.* New York, N.Y.: Basic Books.

Young, R. C., and Frances, J. D. 1991. "Entrepreneurship and Innovation in Small Manufacturing Firms." *Social Science Quarterly* 72: 149–162.

Zax, Jeffrey. 1989. "Is There a Leviathan in Your Neighborhood?" *American Economic Review* 79: 568–577.